Rumors from the Cauldron

Rumors from the Cauldron

Selected Essays, Reviews, and Reportage

VALERIE MINER

Ann Arbor

THE UNIVERSITY OF MICHIGAN PRESS

Copyright © by the University of Michigan 1992
All rights reserved
Published in the United States of America by
The University of Michigan Press
Manufactured in the United States of America

1995 1994 1993 1992 4 3 2 1

Library of Congress Cataloging-in-Publication Data

Miner, Valerie.
    Rumors from the Cauldron : selected essays, reviews, and reportage
/ Valerie Miner.
        p.   cm.
    Includes bibliographical references.
    ISBN 0-472-09472-6 (cloth : alk.). — ISBN 0-472-06472-X (paper :
alk.)
    I. Title.
PS3563.I4647R8 1991
814'.54—dc20   91-31422
                                                                CIP

For Susan Schweik and Madelon Sprengnether

Acknowledgments

Rumors from the Cauldron is dedicated to Susan Schweik and Madelon Sprengnether, with whom I worked in a writing group for five years. Sue and Mimi were unfailingly acute and sensitive in their responses to my fiction and my nonfiction. I benefited significantly from the stimulus of their own projects. The writing group was an oasis for all of us during a period of geographical transitions, serious illnesses, and family crises. I am grateful for their support, their criticism, and their friendship.

Many thanks, too, to others who have read parts of the manuscript, including Sandy Boucher, Julia Douthwaite, Zoë Fairbairns, Elizabeth Horan, Myrna Kostash, Melinda McCracken, Joan MacGregor, Mary Mackey, Toni McNaron, Erna Paris, Eve Pell, Kalima Rose, and Peggy Webb. I am very grateful to the women whose work is reviewed and whose lives are discussed in this volume.

Most of these essays and articles would not have survived if it had not been for excellent journal and book editors. First, I would like to honor Robert Fulford, who as editor of *Saturday Night* in Toronto in the early 1970s had faith in a young American journalist. Bob often disagreed with me, but never censored my work. He and the muckraker Paul Jacobs provided the most important early support I received. I also especially thank Laura Doan, Tom D'Evelyn, Jeff Escoffier, Linda Gardiner, Doug Gibson, Joanne Glasgow, and Karla Jay for their wise editing. I owe a special debt to LeAnn Fields at the University of Michigan Press for her fine work on and commitment to this volume.

Rumors from the Cauldron would not have been completed without the gracious, intelligent contributions of Nancy Hellner, a graduate research assistant at Arizona State University. I am obliged to her for editorial comments, library and phone research, indexing, photocopying, and aid in gathering permissions.

Finally, I thank Helen Longino for her keen eye, sharp wit, heroic patience, and abiding spirit during the last decade.

Books by Valerie Miner

All Good Women

Winter's Edge

Murder in the English Department

Movement

Blood Sisters

Trespassing and Other Stories

Co-authored books:

More Tales

Tales I Tell My Mother

Her Own Woman

Co-edited:

Competition: A Feminist Taboo?

Contents

Memory and Vision:
Roads to and from Eressos

You may forget but
let me tell you
this: someone in
some future time
will think of us.

                     —Sappho, fragment 60

The true woman is as yet a dream of the future.
      —Elizabeth Cady Stanton, *The History of Woman Suffrage*

Lately I find myself contemplating links between recollection and premonition, between lessons from history and dreams of a future. Perhaps this meditation is natural for someone entering her middle years, conscious how historical distortion in her own lifetime has promoted calamity (as the misrepresentation of American aggression in Southeast Asia fosters our current wrongheaded interventions in Central America and the Middle East). I come from a generation who thought we were both history and future. Now humility settles on my shoulders as I find body parts growing creaky and as I observe a whole new generation joining us on the streets.

    I studied history at college as well as literature, but that didn't do me much good in terms of understanding women's lives or letters. I never heard of Sappho or Elizabeth Cady Stanton or Sojourner Truth or Mary Wollstonecraft or Ding Ling until *after* I received my university degrees. Thus it is with amazement and then great distress that I hear people volleying the word *postfeminist*. With this term, journalists and academics imply that feminist activism, analysis, and art have peaked, that we are now in a new stage where issues of sexual equality, identity, and reproductive rights are no longer central or crucial. Wait, hold on, I want to say, it's not over, we haven't really started. What are you talking about? This term is a silencing device. Women's stories have been ignored, rewritten, disrupted, coopted, destroyed since—indeed before—the tablets of Sappho's poetry from Eressos were shattered.

The essays in *Rumors from the Cauldron* were formed from the membrane between memory and vision. Publishing them as a collection is my own small resistance to our cultural amnesia. We can continue to imagine as feminists only if we remember. The title, *Rumors from the Cauldron,* is a theme and metaphor for the nonfiction I wrote between 1972 and 1991 while living in Britain, Australia, Canada, and the United States and traveling extensively elsewhere. *Rumors* is organized into three sections. "Becoming a Writer" includes essays about writing as well as some early feminist reportage. "Reading Lives" is a series of interviews with and portraits of contemporary writers. The "Reviews" section traces responses to a number of texts during the last two decades. The work comes from mainstream media as well as from feminist and radical journals. The subjects in this volume range from Canadian poet and novelist Margaret Atwood to Japanese-American storyteller Hisaye Yamamoto; from life inside the beauty contest biz to Indian women's land rights; from Iris Murdoch's esoteric philosophers to Audre Lorde's dykes; from Chinese literature to British book fairs. *Rumors from the Cauldron* is not a scholarly volume, but rather a collection of one writer's responses to reading and writing. Women are the subject matter. The perspectives here are different shades of feminist. In some senses, this is a personal chronicle of aesthetic growth and political awakening.

I may be a tired feminist, but I am not a postfeminist. It is hard enough to continue as the outside world vanishes us. In one recent year, I lost three friends to breast cancer. Just last year, three more friends found malignant lumps. During this time I have watched my mother's brain being eaten away by Alzheimer's Disease. All around us we see access to abortion subverted by the "Their rights to our lives" squads. Yes, it is hard to keep the bloom of sisterhood alive amid the ashes of our friends. It is easier to say feminism is over. But only temporarily easier because soon our gains will be lost and we will have to start all over again.

The current postfeminist fashion show flourishes with the collusion of women. So far, I have met very few people willing to call themselves postfeminist, but it is a label some social critics readily apply to others. As a writer who has earned a living teaching for twenty years I *know* how the academy forces us to invent new codes to demonstrate our originality and win job security. But too often these codes are regressive rather than progressive, naming a past when there are only incipient beginnings or simply destroying those beginnings. Likewise in the political and arts worlds, people create new agendas to appear revolutionary or avant garde. So we have the postfeminist literary critic; the post-lesbian social scientist; the shock schlock novelist. Scratch each one of them and you will find a vulnerable writer who is kind to her mother and her cat and who simply wants/needs to make her mark. What has happened to the notion of making *our* mark, to the idea of collective change?

Once on a rainy fall day in Central Tasmania, the women in my writing workshop took all the pictures off the wall; the next session of the class was more lively, freer somehow. At U.C. Berkeley, I regularly taught in a small seminar room where we sat in an oval around moveable tables. One class lined the tables vertically; the next group formed a T. No matter how much self-determination one builds into the syllabus, people need to reconstruct. Perhaps we should fiddle with the furniture before leaving the women's room altogether.

The supporters of postfeminist ideologies suggest it is easier to leave the room than to change it. Certainly, the women's room isn't as cozy as we thought it could be during the early moments of sisterly solidarity twenty years ago. In those heady days of them (men) and us (women) the answers seemed easier, the direction clearer. A number of these shifts are recorded in "Competition among Feminist Writers" and "Indian Women and the Indian Act." Subsequently, the "we" has emerged as polymorphous and polyphonic. And the different "we's" now confront tensions and biases across lines of race, class, ethnicity, sexuality, language, nationality. Those who do leave the room may feel feminism has failed them or they have failed feminism, not realizing that we simply haven't given it enough time. They may shake their heads at their losses, interpreting their pasts as naive, running from the guilt or transmuting it into anger at being misunderstood, retreating to more "personal spaces."

All of us can hear the Furies echoing, "The personal is political." Those who have worked in the room know that feminism is a political movement. *Political*—implying a force of people, not a stroke of individuality—and *movement*—forecasting a gradual, ongoing change. Grace Paley, Shen Rong, Mary Daly, Leah Englander Erna, and other women discussed here understand, indeed embody, these personal-political connections. What historian Nancy Cott says of the 1920s in *The Grounding of Modern Feminism* has resonance for the 1990s:

> The modern Feminist agenda—to enable female individuals with several loyalties to say *we* and to achieve sexual equality while making room for sexual differences between women and men—was shaped then. What historians have seen as the demise of feminism in the early 1920's was, more accurately, the end of the suffrage movement and the early struggle of modern feminism. The struggle was, and is, to find language, organization and goals adequate to the *paradoxical* situation of modern women, diverse individuals and subgroups. (P. 10)

Most readers can recount our losses. We know about the devastation of matriarchal cultures, the rewriting of myths, the execution of witches, and the thousand traditions and laws men have invented to restrain women, to disappear us. I believe one task of the feminist novelist is to *reappear* us. Journalism taught me to be conscious of history in my fiction, and I have worked to represent less visible lives and modes of existence—whether it is a portrait of World War II through the friendship of four typists in *All Good Women,* a record of 1970s feminism in *Movement,* a story about old working women in San Francisco's Tenderloin in *Winter's Edge,* or a novel about three generations of Irish women in *Blood Sisters.* As Michelle Cliff writes in *Chrysalis 8,* "We exist separate from each other—past and present—and we are deprived of the knowledge of our common past and present" (p. 37).

If any woman has resisted erasure, it is the writer Ding Ling, whose life spanned much of twentieth-century China. I was honored to meet Ding in Beijing in 1983, two years before she died. Known as the author of the "feminist" *Miss Sophie's Diary* and as a Communist, she was kidnapped by the Kuomintang in 1933. Soon after she was reported dead and her fame expanded through "posthumous" publication. Eventually she escaped and was welcomed as a hero by the Communists. During the years at Yanan, Ding fought with Mao about literary and gender issues. In 1951, her only novel, *The Sun Shines on the Sanggan River,* won the Stalin Prize. In 1958, she was exiled to the Great Northern Wilderness for twelve years. Her troubles escalated along with the power of reactionary forces in 1966. Then, after the Cultural Revolution, Ding Ling emerged again as a major literary figure. Always resilient, she was continuing to write at age seventy-nine. The work of Ding and her compatriots provokes us to consider the value of making literature in the face of crisis. This collection contains three pieces about Chinese women's writing.

> If you are squeamish
>
> don't prod the
> beach rubble.
>
> —Sappho, fragment 84

The vanishing of women in this country is fostered by rumors—rumors we tell ourselves, rumors we tell our male friends at parties or at work, rumors in the media. These rumors fester in a culture of the quick fix, the can-do aesthetic, the everything-is-simpler-than-you-think mentality, the buy-your-way-free economy.

Rumor #1: Feminist Literature Monopolizes Publishing

I am taking a walk with a former student, the son of wealthy white parents, who has just completed a graduate degree at a prestigious private university. He is worried about getting his first book published. "I'm not lucky like you," he says, "after all, women's literature is in."

I am at a party having a good time seeing old friends. One of them, a former fellow organizer in the writers' union, tells me he has just received a $40,000 advance to write a book about men. He is expansive. "It's so easy to get a book published now," he says. I shake my head. "OK, it's hard to get books distributed—but surely not published," he says. I shake my head again and tell him that my most recent novel was submitted to thirty-six mainstream publishers before I went to an independent press. Once published, it got excellent reviews and sold very well. But it was hard to get a large house to take a risk with this feminist novel. He discreetly changes the topic.

As I am writing this essay, I spend several days enjoying back issues of *Chrysalis*, wondering why this innovative "magazine of women's culture" went out of business. I also return to a book I coedited in 1976, *Tales I Tell My Mother*. The pages are yellowing and it is out of print. I browse my shelves, grateful for the women's work that has been published, but conscious that many of the challenging books have come from radical presses and that without the support of readers, they are going out of print.

Rumor #2: We No Longer Need Women-Only Spaces

I am reading an issue of one of my favorite feminist journals, a paper I would like better if it published more fiction reviews, but still a wonderful alternative to male-monopolized magazines. It makes me think back to those days when we created women-only consciousness-raising groups and readings and concerts to claim space in a world where it was often hard for women to breathe or speak. There is more room for women's voices now, but we are still almost mute in such mainstream review media as the *New York Review of Books*.

As I read the feminist journal, I come across an acclamatory review of a novel by a famous male writer. I wonder why they have given space to this book when they have room for so few women's novels. I am going to write a letter to the journal asking this question and saying that I found the women characters in this man's book victims at best and that the portrayal of working-class people offended me. But I do not write the letter. I am too busy, too shy, too intimidated. What if my letter appears self-serving? Months have passed since the review. It is too late to write my letter but I am still burning. I think how in 1990 all the National Book Critic Circle Awards went to men. All the Pulitzer Literary Awards went to men. These concerns are explored in my essay "The Feminist Reviewer." In 1978, Tillie Olsen observed in *Silences* that 88–90 percent of canonical literature is male. Not much has changed since *Silences*. Ursula Le Guin wrote in 1986, "No matter how successful, beloved, influential her work was, when a woman author dies, nine times out of ten she gets dropped from the lists, the courses, the anthologies while the men get kept" (*Dancing at the Edge of the World*, pp. 176–77). If anything, the record of American feminist publishing will get worse in the 1990s as the United States paddles frantically to maintain economic and military power.

Rumor #3: Women's Studies Is Taking Over the Academy

Pardon me, run those employment statistics by me one more time. Why do men still hold 92 percent of the full professorships in the United States? Explain why the University of Southern California doesn't have a women's studies program but rather a Program for the Study of Women and Men in Society. Explain why women's research institutes are changing their focus from "women" to "gender." Explain why female faculty and students are complaining about being dismissed, ridiculed, physically threatened, and assaulted for their *ideas*. The Commission on the Status of Women in the Profession of the Modern Language Association has been documenting intellectual harassment of feminists on campus. The committee has received voluminous testimony about jeering by colleagues, discrimination on dissertations, defacement of women's posters, and physical threats to visible feminists in the liberal academy. This rumor has been around for a long time and its implications are confronted in the interview with Adrienne Rich and Mary Daly.

Rumor #4: Feminism Is a Middle-aged Movement

Have you been to pro-choice demonstrations lately? They are filled with women of all ages. The presence of old women in our movement is well-documented in Barbara MacDonald's *Look Me in the Eye* and Baba Cooper's *Over the Hill*, in the critical writing of Tillie Olsen and Elizabeth Janeway, in the fiction of Grace Paley and May Sarton.

Recent feminist protests by students at Wellesley College on the East Coast and Mills College on the West Coast have helped combat this particular ageist rumor. The Wellesley women's success lay in their very public protest against the choice of Barbara Bush as a commencement speaker because she was invited for her husband's status rather than her own social contributions. The Mills students won their right to attend a women's college (at least for the next five years). They had the support of the majority of faculty and even more of the staff; however it was really the work of *students,* striking, contacting alumnae, promising to recruit future students, that forced the school trustees to return the college to women.

> We shall enjoy it.
>
> As for him who finds
> fault, may silliness
> and sorrow take him.
>
> —Sappho, fragment 2

Amid all the postfeminist gloom-peddling, the expanding bookshelves form a literary barricade against despair by marking the essential link between memory and vision. In its most immediate sense this link provokes us, as Adrienne Rich says, to *ask women's questions.*

What Is the Future of Feminist Literature and How Do We Get There?

First, let's amend the query to "What is the future of feminist literatures?" Then, let's ask the most *basic* of questions: *How do we save our own lives?* Throughout the world we are threatened by lack of reproductive rights. By lesbian bashing. By myths about homelessness and about AIDS. By environmental pollution that is causing the rates of breast cancer, skin cancer, and lung cancer to escalate. In the United States, we are threatened by poor living conditions and an inadequate health care system that result yearly in the deaths of 40,000 infants under the age of one. In postcolonial nations, wars (often fueled by privileged countries) threaten women's lives every day. *All* of us are at risk from the nuclear weapon arsenals untouched, unnoticed in the START talks.

What does this have to do with literature? After emphasizing the sometimes forgotten fact that literature depends on *living* writers and readers, I want to say that authors are more vital when they open their minds, walk past the security guard and on to the street. Writers *need* the stimulus of history and the provocation of future visions.

So we writers must pay attention. We need to continue working as activists— marching, picketing, caucusing, feeding, sheltering. The good old letter of protest is a classic form of feminist literature. The future of feminist literatures is *in* reproductive options, pay equity, daycare provision, lesbian rights, labor unions, peace treaties, independence movements, expanded literacy, environmental protection.

People hear the familiar cadence and feel the fatigue of years ago. We say, "Spare me. I've done my stint. I have career demands and family pressures—what do you want me to do—everything?"

The simple and frustrating answer is yes.

If we do not work for social change we will have no careers, no families. And perhaps—although this is heretical in our self-actualizing era—we need to account for these responsibilities before we take on our careers and create our families. It is easier to deconstruct into one's subjective consciousness than to reconstruct with other people. Sometimes I believe that because we humans are the only animals conscious of our mortality, we prefer death by our own agency rather than that of fate. Therefore we bring about our own ends more than other creatures do, through such suicidal tendencies as war and social apathy.

But this bleak thought fades somewhat in the face of the next good book. What characterizes serious literature is the courage to continue, such as the courage manifest in Nadine Gordimer's *The Essential Gesture,* Marge Piercy's *Fly Away Home,* Shen Rong's *At Middle Age,* and Audre Lorde's *Zami.*

What Is the Future of Feminist Literatures and How Do We Get There?

We confront censorship. In this country radical feminist material is vulnerable to external censorship by editors, reviewers, and booksellers and to self-censorship by those of us sensitive to family or cultural taboos or charges of political correctness in the feminist arena.

We might begin by trying to demystify the production of artistic merit. "The Media Monopoly," as Ben H. Bagdikian calls it, creates a covert form of de facto censorship. Merit in the United States is created by selective visibility: What we read is determined by market strategies. Ads in the right places beget reviews which beget awards and fellowships which in turn beget literary reputations that preserve books and publishing houses. At this critical time in American letters—when the National Endowment for the Arts (never a very risk-taking or representative body) is caving in to right-wing pressure for censorship; when chain stores monopolize trade book sales, squeezing out independent booksellers who represent a plurality of voices; when gadfly publishers like Pantheon are being compromised by corporate bottom lines—it is crucial to maintain perspective on how taste, quality, and reputation are manufactured. Partly in response to this corporate hegemony, the "Reviews" section here highlights a number of books from independent publishers.

We are *also* silenced by self-censorship. Public censorship encourages us to doubt our rights and/or abilities to portray the worlds in which we grow up and work and make love. The essays "Writing with Class," "Reading along the Dyke," and "An Imaginative Collectivity of Writers and Readers" discuss this reflex particularly in relation to working-class and lesbian material.

What Is the Future of Feminist Literatures and How Do We Get There?

The most interesting work will surface from an international and multicultural consciousness. It will be enriched by environmental awareness. It will be alert to the various classes and castes and divisions among women as well as the bridges to be built and crossed. And hopefully we will have more literature about old women and young girls. The reviews here reveal contributions in these areas by Wang Anyi, Jane Smiley, Thea Astley, Sherley Anne Williams, Fay Weldon, Suniti Namjoshi and others.

Global sensibility depends on access to each other's work. It's thrilling to watch the growth of feminist presses in different parts of the world: Stramullion in Scotland, Kali in India, Attic in Ireland, Press Gang in Canada, Tantrum in Australia, and others described in "Going to the Fair." As an American, it's exciting to see a number of our publishers—especially the Feminist Press, Seal, and the University of Nebraska Press—producing international material. But one day I hope we don't have to rely so much on translations and that we will be a more truly multilingual country.

International conferences, courses, archives are crucial to the futures of feminist literatures. Beyond this, we need to foster a deeper labor identity among writers to promote better wages, working conditions, and publishing contracts. I dream of the day when authors have collective bargaining and believe that this must be accomplished on an international scale if it is to be equitable and effective.

What Is the Future of Feminist Literatures and How Do We Get There?

The future of feminist fiction is not in realist narrative. It is not in the postmodern story. It is not in magical realism. It is in all these and more. It is in the work of Hisaye Yamamoto, Tess Gallagher, Jackie Kay, Toni Morrison. It is in the writing of my MFA students. It is in the work of their daughters. And perhaps the words of their sons.

What Is the Future of Feminist Literatures and How Do We Get There?

As Adrienne Rich says in the foreword to *On Lies, Secrets and Silence,*

> It is crucial that we understand lesbian/feminism in the deepest, most radical sense: as that love for ourselves and other women, that commitment to the freedom of all of us, which transcends the category of "sexual preference" and the issue of civil rights to become a politics of *asking women's questions,* demanding a world in which the integrity of all women—not a chosen few—shall be honored and validated in every aspect of culture. (P. 17)

> Tell everyone
>
> now, today, I shall
> sing beautifully for
> my friends' pleasure.
>
> —Sappho, fragment 1

The definition of genre has always made me uneasy. Therefore I'd like to conclude with some comments on connections and distinctions between fiction and nonfiction. When I was a child attending parochial school, we learned that the fundamental division in the world was between Catholics and non-Catholics. We Catholics—who were on the path to Heaven—were the new Chosen People and, as such, felt sorry for and wary of non-Catholics. The nuns and priests instructed us to be careful as we went downtown in our school uniforms because we were junior representatives of God. Years later at university I learned that prose was divided between fiction and nonfiction. Only those practicing fiction had a chance at achieving Art.

Many of my fellow fiction writers have the same wariness of nonfiction writers that Sacred Heart students had of non-Catholics. In the 1990s, fiction writers are warned not to contaminate their art with social context. The fiction writers who prefer High Mass are even suspicious of the vernacular and of realism. Clarity and usefulness are "near occasions of sin." Like the non-Catholics in my provincial town, nonfiction writers tend to be wealthier and represent a larger section of the world. Once a Catholic, always a Catholic, of course. But I confess to being a hybrid—the daughter of a Scots Presbyterian mother and an Irish Catholic father. Consequently, as a mutt, I've always had mixed allegiances and tastes. It's hard to believe the doors to Heaven or Art are as narrow as is rumored.

Some novelists and poets dismiss nonfiction as their stepchildren, as the paid labor that supports their higher art. Such short-sightedness entails a loss both to the reader of the essay and to the writer, who may find, as I do, that the different forms nurture each other. I began my writing life as a free-lance journalist in Canada. Then I moved to London for several years where I wrote for British journals. I turned my focus to fiction in the mid-seventies because I thought that my own talents could strike deeper with the story than with the article. However, I still enjoy writing nonfiction and find that it provokes my work as a novelist. Through journalism, I learn about discipline, persistence, succinctness, and imagination and am required to enter new worlds. Writing reviews keeps me engaged with contemporary fiction. Writing essays allows me to weigh theoretical guidelines about art and politics.

Editing this collection has been a much more vulnerable experience than writing any of my novels or stories. My fiction is less overtly autobiographical than that of many of my contemporaries. And I have never considered writing a long personal memoir. But I have come to realize that a collection such as this *is* a literary/ intellectual autobiography. *I* am the protagonist here, not Beth or Susan or Nan or Margaret or Wanda or Josie. I am the one with the foibles (why didn't I understand *that* in 1975 or 1986 or 1991?), and the limited vision (why did it take me so long to write about class?) and the hubris (how could I be so didactic in places?) and the infelicitous phrasing (where is a good editor when you need her?). *Rumors from the Cauldron* reveals an aesthetic and political journey. Of course all art is political and of course nonmainstream art is the only work likely to be acknowledged as political. I don't mind when people disagree with my ideas; I do object when they veil their ideological disagreement. My fiction and nonfiction are conscious of social context. I find that consciousness a source of vitality and a provocation to artistic complexity. This is not a scholarly collection in intent, approach, or tone. It represents a kind of crossover writing. As might be expected in an autobiography, the essays here expose a compass of voices—academic, colloquial, conversational, mournful, celebratory, meditative.

The hardest part of editing this book was deciding what to cut. While *Rumors* traces my feminist development in the 1970s, 1980s, and early 1990s, it leaves out much of my philosophical journey. For the sake of thematic consistency, I have had to shelve much writing on international issues, civil rights, and antiwar movements. (Occasionally, I have abridged material included here to avoid repetition and stylistic awkwardness.) The second hardest aspect of the editing process was deciding to send the final manuscript to the editor, for these pieces reveal all the flaws, inconsistencies, and contradictions of one woman's twenty years. There are many things I would have done differently, many essays I would have written differently. But truth—insofar as we can know it—is the most useful location for memory.

The road from Eressos leads back to Eressos just as surely as writing leads to reading and memory leads to vision. Sappho was a woman of the upper classes. Can we imagine her as a Chinese peasant, a Zambian laborer, an orphaned Scottish girl working the night shift in an Edinburgh café? Yes, we can imagine. If we remember, we will imagine.

I. Becoming a Writer

This section opens with recent essays about the relationship between writers and readers, about the reception of contemporary working-class literature, and about competition among women writers. The next two articles explore literary reviews, readings, exhibits, and other ways of making books visible.

Then we swing back to the early 1970s and reporting from the four years I lived in Canada—reporting that drew me deeper and deeper into feminism as a writer and as a woman. These stories about peace marches, beauty pageants, middle-class housewives, and native wives' land rights show how various people were approaching women's questions. While I am abashed by the naïveté in this early work, I am nevertheless pleased by the idealism and urgency. As I reread these essays, I think about subsequent discourse regarding the personal relationship between author and biographical subject. Bell Gale Chevigny writes, "Women's biography is simply a special case of our current study of women in which we work to recover our history and ourselves, each at least partly in terms of the other" ("Daughters Writing," p. 99). And Elizabeth Minnich notes, "The relation of author to subject, informing the work, may then become part of a new relation, that of woman to woman across time and cultures, helping to create the public space so long denied us" ("Friendship between Women," p. 288).

This section ends with two pieces considering other bridges and borders within feminism: one essay about how lesbian poetry addresses social marginalities and the other observing problems and rewards of writing fiction across generations.

An Imaginative Collectivity
of Writers and Readers

Recently I dreamt that my two lesbian neighbors had been raped and beaten. In my dream I was wakened by the ambulance. I ran out to the driveway but it was too late to be of use. Each woman lay on a stretcher with wounds on her face and terror in her eyes. I felt this had been my fault. If only I hadn't been sleeping when the man broke in. If only I had heard the noises in time. Then I woke to what we sometimes call reality. All day I fought the impulse to tell the neighbors my story, their story, to warn them to watch out. Instead I went to my desk and finished the first draft of this essay.

Perhaps the dream is a transparent metaphor for my work as a lesbian novelist. Every day I sit at a desk sifting through experience, drawing from common memory and imagination, sometimes issuing warnings. Just as readers may enter my novels through dreams, I hope to enter readers' dreams occasionally through my books.

The nightmare about my neighbors also represents the fears I have writing this essay. Although I have "come out" many times in print and in person, it still feels dangerous. At first I try to dismiss my writer's block as personal homophobia, and perhaps that is part of the cause. But while we confront the shadow of our own internalized biases, we need to keep our eyes open for very real outside threats. Our books get censored by publishing houses, review journals, bookshops, libraries, schools. Even in liberal environments where people support one's right to perversion, our lesbianism—which for some of us is a political choice—is still only temporarily tolerated. It *is not safe* to be a lesbian writer or reader today; we need our collective wits to survive.

I write as a lesbian. I write as someone who grew up in an immigrant, working-class household. I write as a feminist who found my voice—as well as my mind—in the women's movement. I write as a reluctant American who has lived

This essay is reprinted by permission of New York University Press from *Lesbian Texts and Contexts*, edited by Karla Jay and Joanne Glasgow. Copyright © 1990 by Karla Jay and Joanne Glasgow. Parts of the essay were delivered at the forum "Living Afresh: Women as Authors and Scholars Reflect on Writing and Research" at the 1989 Conference of the Modern Language Association. The forum was sponsored by the MLA's Division of Women's Studies in Language and Literature.

abroad for many years. These various identities all enrich my work, yet sometimes they seem to contradict each other and readers who align with separate camps. Not all lesbians are feminists and not all feminists are lesbians, but for me the two identities are inextricable because I became a lesbian through the feminist worldview I developed in the women's movement. Thus while I present my ideas here about the relationship between *lesbian writers and readers,* my voice emerges in different registers, drawing on class background, cultural identity, international experience, and, particularly, feminist politics, highlighting the multidimensionality of lesbian fiction.

To claim a strong bond between writer and reader is to transgress much that is sacred in Western criticism. Scholars charge that only those scribblers afflicted with commercial motives or exhortatory messages have a direct, conscious relationship with readers. This artificial isolation of storyteller from audience is characterized by most Americans' distinction between art (which is rewarded) and work (which is paid). Writing brings "royalties" or awards or prizes, but *never wages.* The perception of writers as supernatural beings who create through singular genesis and the segregation between artist and audience is at the core of a crisis facing American fiction. So many contemporary novels lack imagination, depth, conscience, and vitality because they are dissociated from society. I notice myself continually turning back to feminist writing for aesthetic pleasure and intellectual provocation.

Like many feminist writers, I cannot insulate my art from my politics. My feminism is nurtured by other women on the streets where we all work and live. Many stories would not be written without such inspiration. They would not be published without feminist editors. They would not be visible without feminist reviewers, booksellers, librarians, and teachers. They would not endure without word-of-mouth campaigns among feminist readers. I call this vital web an "imaginative collectibity of writers and readers." Feminists have made profound contributions to my novels as well as to my life. Conversely, I try to engage audience actively in the *process* of my fiction.

Genre

To begin at the beginning, audience provokes the work itself. Feminists have influenced my very choice of genre.

I started writing as a journalist. During my twenties, I worked as a reporter in Great Britain, Canada, Tanzania, and other countries. In those days, my primary impulse was "to help other people communicate with each other." The motivations were varied. As a woman I was drawn to the traditional role as cipher (for the opinions of my mainly male interview subjects). As a young radical, I was eager to leave this country, to go out and find other people's answers. Essentially my movement was outward, toward more information, toward patriarchal wisdom, toward external union and reunion.

Yet the articles I wrote about *women* always made me pause and reflect inward. Consistently I was forced back to my personal experience as I reported about Native Canadian wives fighting for land rights, sexual stereotyping in high schools, beauty pageants, suburban housewives, women farming in Ujamaa villages. Likewise, I was encouraged to examine my own life in consciousness-raising groups and in organizations affected by feminist process. Gradually, I found the nerve to speak and write in a different way.

First, I was given voice to ask questions about my own life, my mother's life, my grandmother's life. My grandmother, Mae Campbell, died from an abortion on the kitchen table in an Edinburgh tenement during World War I. My mother, Mary McKenzie, orphaned at age twelve, quit school and began to work at a coffee shop. She immigrated to the United States at the age of twenty, and last year, at seventy-seven, she was laid off her job at a San Francisco coffee shop. Feminism helped me see the lives of these women as more than individual cases of suffering and courage, but as part of a daily, international history. Moreover, feminism provided survival strategies for my own life. When I was vomiting every morning and convinced I was pregnant although my doctor kept denying this, it was through the women's movement that I found someone who told me the truth and was willing to perform an illegal abortion. It was feminist friends who listened to my quandaries about a marriage which was keeping me mute. And it was in the women's movement that I learned to speak a new language as a lesbian.

I began to read more women novelists in the early 1970s. Doris Lessing and Toni Morrison and Jane Rule and Margaret Atwood inspired me to write my own words. I wanted to move from journalism to the deeper communication—emotionally, psychologically, sensually, intellectually—that I personally found in fiction. I wanted a more substantial relationship with readers. In an article, one is lucky if readers spend an hour with one's work. In a novel, readers are involved for days or weeks at a time. The book becomes a companion in all sorts of unlikely places. Consequently, the characters and issues remain alive between readings and have a longer afterlife.

Thus, from the beginning, I was conscious of my art emerging from a world of women. I have received considerable flack from mainstream critics for this self-identification, as well as stimulating support from readers. In recent years I have been disturbed by the growth of "postfeminist discourse"—not only because I disagree with much of it, but because just as the women's movement gave me and others permission to write, this line of criticism silences us by denying our continuing existence. Sometimes when I hear people discussing "postfeminist" literature, I am amused, imagining telephone poles along the highway, each with a dead book nailed to it. But more often I am terrified by the censorship that can result when such codes are absorbed into the cultural psyche. Before we say that the second wave of feminist writing is over, let us distinguish between the writing and the publishing. Let us look at the marketplace. Literary fashion is not designed by fate but by a homogeneous, incestuous network of editors, reviewers, academics, and foundation people. Many books are written; comparitively few are published—particularly those which don't have the proper credentials for the primarily white, male, middle-class, Eastern seaboard publishers. For instance, Doubleday receives 10,000 unsolicited manuscripts a year, of which they publish three or four (Coser, Kadushin, and Powell, *Books,* p. 130).

Inevitably at this stage in the argument someone points to a few books by Black women or Indian lesbians or impoverished Appalachian mothers, asking, "What do you mean, censorship?" I call these the "despite" books. They get published *despite* their demographical demerits, *despite* the conventional judgments of editors, and they are published in small enough quantities to be unthreatening. They are also the "because" books. They surface and thrive *because* they have something to say, *because* they shake things up. However, the American publishing industry, monopolized by media conglomerates, is not in the business of triggering earthquakes. God knows what would happen to those profitable canonical backlists so assiduously organized along the faultlines of capitalist taste and value if we had more aesthetic temblors.

Feminist books *are* being written. A few are getting published by mainstream houses. A few, particularly the more radical and lesbian books, are produced by independents such as Kitchen Table/Women of Color Press, Alyson, Spinsters/Aunt Lute, and Crossing. But what chance do these books have if they are shunned even in our most liberal of environments? At the University of California, 36 percent of faculty surveyed on the nine campuses said they refrained from doing research on lesbian and gay topics for fear of negative response from colleagues. As many as 41 percent decided against including such material in their courses (University of California Lesbian and Gay Intercampus Network, "Report to the Regents," app. A). Yes, a few lesbian novels are being published and taught. A lot are stuffed into drawers and sometimes closets and sometimes graves.

It is hard to keep publishing—indeed, writing—while the contemporary women's movement is being eroded from without and within. How do we write in a world where vocabulary has been transformed—where "solidarity" has dissolved into "community"; "comrades" have metamorphosed into "colleagues"; women's studies has lost momentum and funding as it is subsumed into "gender studies";

"right" has been transformed into "choice"; and "choice" is now read as "preference"? Some of us feel great pressure to cash in social goals to mortgage our houses. Others have discovered spirituality as a substitute for (rather than a supplement to) political action. All around us the culture invites women to trade sisterhood for motherhood. Too often these former sisters wind up battling each other for their children's places in exclusive schools. Rhetoric of the family has become the reflexive language. Dreams of mass movement are lost in cloistered, privatized routines. Yet it is not only dangerous but inaccurate to brand this time as an era of postfeminist literature, for many women do continue to imagine and fight and create and march and organize as feminists; many do continue to write with the old words and the spirit of change.

Form and Style

Feminist discourse has encouraged me to view the "canon" from different perspectives and to play with new approaches to fictional form. The conventional novel has become an endurance test in which the writer and reader begin at the beginning and pursue the end relentlessly without pause, in form, for reflection, consideration, question, or argument. The writer's role is paternalistic as he provides a catharsis—raising a dilemma, presenting a set of variables, stringing the reader along a line of tension and insinuating a resolution.

My vision of feminist fiction is storytelling which so deeply involves the reader in feelings, issues, and ideas that she asks, "How does this apply to my own life?" Good feminist fiction is not policy statement, although some women's writing, in an urgency to be politically correct, tries to protect the audience from contradictions. I think stories are most effective not when they are didactic, but quite the opposite, when they empower readers by raising a range of possibilities and the momentum to deal with them. And, partially because of my working-class family, I try for a clarity of language which makes my fiction accessible to a broad audience. Perhaps the best way to explain this philosophy is to articulate some of the strategies behind my different books.

Blood Sisters, my first novel, is about three generations of women in an Irish-American family, how they relate to each other, and how questions of sexuality, nationalism, and feminism affect them. I want readers to stand in the middle of arguments between Liz, a lesbian feminist, and Beth, a member of the Provisional Wing of the IRA. I hope they will hear the voices of the mothers as well as the daughters. I present various images of Ireland—as a romantic state of mind, a war-wrenched country, a metaphor for international politics. The book is a feminist reinterpretation of *Hamlet* and, as such, ends more in provocation than in cataclysm. Survival, not sacrifice, is the act of courage in all its continuing complexity.

My second book, *Movement,* is both a novel and a collection of stories, a book which explores the territory between as well as beyond these forms. Readers accompany the protagonist, Susan, through ten years of spiritual, political, emotional, and geographical movement. In contrast with linear novels which can distance the reader through a forced march forward, *Movement* can be read in any order. Life, or "movement," is experienced as fantasy, memory, premonition, and this fiction is layered to express the intricacies. Most chapters follow one another in a chronological sequence, yet they are also self-contained stories. Susan's chapters are introduced by short-short pieces about women from different races, classes, ages, and cultures who are experiencing similar kinds of movement. I write these short-shorts to break through the isolationism and individualism of the *Bildungsroman.* Susan does not know, and may never meet, any of these women. Their stories are told as shadows and illuminations of our mutual momentum. The book begins and ends in the same restaurant, completing a circle, surrounding readers with questions about Susan's unsettled choices regarding sexuality, motherhood, and political allegiance.

Next, I wrote *Murder in the English Department,* a novel of ideas suspended against an untraditional mystery. In this alternative to the genre detective story, readers are told "who done it" and who was "done" near the beginning of the book. They, like the protagonist Nan, are peripheral to the death, yet intensely caught up in subsequent moral issues. When Nan, a middle-aged college professor, risks her life in defense of a student, they are embroiled together in quandaries about innocence, loyalty, and love. The quicksand between private feeling and public action is the setting of this book as well as of *Winter's Edge,* which depicts the friendship between two old women who live and work in San Francisco's Tenderloin district. Their relationship is sparked by the differences between Chrissie's radical causes and Margaret's more discreet kind of social responsibility. The violence of a local political campaign gets turned on them, threatening their neighborhood, their friendship, and their lives. I leave it to readers to consider who is right or whether they are both right.

All Good Women, the most recent novel, examines the friendship among four young working-class women during World War II, tracing the impact on women's feeling of possibility. Many war women, like the suffragists and more recent feminists, were pioneers. For many, war was a time without men. What did this do to their sense of self and community?

My new book of stories is called *Trespassing.* I feel as if I am always trespassing—as a working-class woman in a middle-class world; as a frequently expatriate American; as an artist who doesn't quite fit into the university where I earn my living; as a political person indulging in art; as a novelist who writes about social issues; as a formerly obedient Catholic girl who grew up to pierce my ears, have an abortion, get divorced, and become a lesbian.

Some people complain about the questions and contradictions in my books. Some demand answers. Who speaks the truth, Beth or Liz? Will Nan continue teaching? Has Chrissie convinced Margaret or has Margaret convinced Chrissie? A couple of reviewers have complained about my "neglect" of resolution, while others have insisted that I speak for various (mutually exclusive) sides of a point. Still, I persist with my open endings because we live in a world where literary answers are cheap and eminently forgettable in the face of real life. Concluding fiction with stimulating contradictions pays more respect to the text and to the reader. The contradictions serve as lumpy bookmarks which make the novel, and hopefully the reader's mind, harder to close, thus leaving the questions reverberating in "real life."

For the lesbian writer, questions and contradictions about sexuality are especially problematic. When she chooses a heterosexual protagonist, she is often charged with being "inauthentic" or "selling out." This is a problem not just in the gay press. When May Sarton published *Anger*, a heterosexual reviewer criticized her for not making the main character a lesbian. Likewise, I have had people ask why Chrissie and Margaret in *Winter's Edge* are not lesbians and why Nan in *Murder in the English Department* is still making up her mind about sexuality. One answer is that I am particularly engaged by relationships among women which cross cultures, classes, and sexual choices. It's far more interesting to make connections between lesbians and heterosexual women than simply to write about a particular group all the time. One of my strategies is to incite readers' consciousness about choice. What decision will Susan make in *Movement*? The cathartic solution might inhibit the reader from considering what choice she, herself, is making.

This raises the touchy question: What is a lesbian novel? I think that the definition proceeds from the term *woman-identified*. For example, I'd say what makes *All Good Women* a lesbian novel is as much the deep bonds among the four protagonists as the explicit lesbianism of one of them. Moreover, I wonder why critics refuse to recognize a lesbian unless she is wearing a lavender T-shirt. Why do some people presume Chrissie MacInnes is heterosexual?

Occasionally lesbian readers warn writers not to "betray the community." Because homophobic harassment is so pervasive, some say that we shouldn't portray lesbians in a negative light—that we shouldn't show women battering, or drinking to excess, or being exploitative—lest we feed harmful stereotypes. Others say not to share lesbian secrets with the general public because that information can be used against us. Still others protest that lesbian erotica can be abused by men. All these concerns are real, yet as a writer I think the dangers of silence are always greater than the dangers of exposure. As Nadine Gordimer declares in *The Essential Gesture,* "Censorship may have to do with literature; but literature has nothing whatever to do with censorship" (p. 260).

Reaching Out

The imaginative collectivity of writers and readers is not always in agreement. I picture a quilting bee where women are arguing, gossiping, challenging, recollecting, and envisioning. The "women's writing group" is a good metaphor and model. Writing has long been glorified as virtuoso performance; therefore working together provides significant feminist testimony. These writing groups can create environments where our voices will be heard and our languages understood. They provide forums for analytical argument and artistic support where the writer is reader.

During the early 1970s in Toronto, I met regularly with a group of women journalists. Eventually we published a joint collection of essays, *Her Own Woman.* Later, in London, I worked with four women to create a fictional documentary of the British women's movement. For five months in a row, *Spare Rib* published a story by each of us. In 1978, Journeyman Press published *Tales I Tell My Mother.* Back in this country, I have participated in several groups in which women concentrated on their own books. From these very direct reader reactions I have learned to weather editors' rejections and reviewers' biases and impossibly low wages, which, too often, lead me to the edge of despair. These writing groups have given me the spirit to continue writing.

On a large scale, the writing circle includes other women writers and readers. When I read *Zami: A New Spelling of My Name,* Audre Lorde provokes me toward new possibilities for the lesbian novel. When I read Sandy Boucher's *The Notebooks of Leni Clare* or Tess Gallagher's *Instructions to the Double,* my awareness of working-class feminists is deepened. "For books continue each other in spite of our habit of judging them separately," as Virginia Woolf observed. Later Sylvia Plath was to say of Woolf, "Her novels make mine possible."[1] Gertrude Stein, Mary Daly, and Kathleen Fraser have all taught me to be more playful with words. Adrienne Rich gives me hope for communication with her *Dream of a Common Language.* Paula Gunn Allen teaches me about fiction as ritual in *The Woman Who Owned the Shadows.* Again, the writer is reader.

Everyone asks, "Whom do you write for?" Ursula Le Guin explained in a letter in a recent issue of the *Women's Review of Books* that we create our own audience. I imagine different readers at each stage in a novel. In the beginning, I write to myself. I follow a story, hoping to make a discovery. During the first draft I am "reading" the text in my brain as I transfer it to paper—the mirror image of my audience's ultimate experience. During the many subsequent drafts, I am more conscious of "communicating" than of "expressing" and I think of members of that imaginative collectivity—hoping to recycle the inspiration they have given me.

As my books have become more widely available, I've had many different kinds of feedback from my own readers. The encounters are often provocative in surprising ways. Let me offer four examples.

In 1987, a woman told me that after hearing me read an erotic lesbian scene from *All Good Women* at the convention of the Modern Language Association, she and her partner went back to their hotel room and made love, forgetting the conference for the rest of the day.

A few years ago I was standing in Giovanni's Room Bookstore in Philadelphia when a young woman entered and asked the manager, "Do you have any good new lesbian trash?" "No," the clerk said, then nodded to me by way of introduction, "but you might want to read Valerie Miner's new book. It's a very good lesbian novel." The young dyke eyed me suspiciously, nodded semipolitely, and disappeared toward the back of the bookshop.

One summer evening, after a panel in Bristol, a woman spoke to me in the bathroom. With tears in her eyes, she told me how much she appreciated my coming out as a lesbian and how she hoped to come out one day herself.

Last spring I received a letter from a woman in Tasmania who had admired my work until she reached a certain point. She wrote, "Let me remind you of the fate of homosexuals in Sodom and Gommorah. Genesis 18, 19. I appreciate your struggle in life and your upward mobility but I hope and pray you'll find your way out of the course of Lesbianism before you delay too long and are beyond redemption." The only thing that puzzled me about the letter was what she meant by upward mobility.

Public presentations are direct, dynamic ways to widen the circle. Audre Lorde noted in a recent issue of *Coda*, "A poem is not finished until I feel the flavor of the audience reaction rising to me. Reading is part of the creative process." These presentations also alert audiences to forthcoming books and give writers sustenance (sometimes financial) to complete a work. I have read to gatherings ranging from four women in the back of a Brooklyn bookstore, to hundreds of academics at a California conference, to loudly cheerful patrons at a Sydney pub. Sometimes the individual feedback is quite helpful. Sometimes readings have more of a symbolic value, reminding us of the continuing trial of making female voices heard. I'll never forget the afternoon Marge Piercy read at an ourdoor café in San Francisco. She had to stand on top of a chair which was on top of a table, shouting her poetry against the fierce Bay winds.

The Moving Movement

Movements, of course, move. Varying readerships develop according to race, culture, sexuality, and language, creating a vigorous exchange about the definition of feminism and lesbianism. Authors tend to have distinct relationships with their constituencies, with the larger feminist audience, and with readers in general.

At a recent literary conference, I heard a lesbian critic disparage gay novels which cross class or cultural lines and "get overinvolved in external issues." And this year at a progressive bookstore, I heard critics on the Left advising writers not to complicate their writing with marginal sexual identities to which working people "can't relate." Meanwhile, astute publishers explain they may be able to market one of the above, but combination plates (books about working-class, lesbian feminists, for example) do not sell.

On the contrary, I think sexual marginality offers a valuable lens through which to appreciate other marginalities—national, ethnic, linguistic, economic—and to learn about uniqueness and commonality. We can't create solidarity by denying difference. We can relish individual identity and cultural distinctiveness while observing the similarities within the differences.

Can we write about cultures other than our own? (Is it permissible to? Are we able to?) My life has been immeasurably enriched by the powerful fiction and poetry of contemporary women of color. My own writing has been invigorated by Barbara Burford, Linda Hogan, Joy Kogawa, and a number of authors already mentioned. Thanks to their voices as well as to the consciousness of race in the fiction of white women like Grace Paley, feminist literature is becoming increasingly multicultural. In my early books, I was tentative about describing nonwhite characters, always placing them in minor parts. My reluctance was based in timidity as well as in politics. I didn't want to "get a character wrong"—to slip on a reference or a dialect or to expose my racism inadvertently. For years I also felt it was impertinent for me to portray Asians or Blacks or Latinas or Native Americans. As a white person who already took up a lot of space in the world, I wanted to leave room for them to write about themselves. Now more and more fiction by women of color is published, indeed heralded. They have hardly needed me to make room for them. And I have recovered somewhat from my timidity. In *Winter's Edge,* a Black and a Chicano play pivotal roles. In *All Good Women,* one of the four protagonists is Nisei. No doubt each characterization has its faults, but over the years I've developed several practices to mitigate against inauthenticity and stereotype. I write many drafts of each book and after each draft, several people read the manuscript. I make sure to invite readers from my characters' cultural backgrounds to help me catch errors. I have learned that the scrupulous omission of nonwhite characters perpetuates invisibility as well as seriously limits the heart of the fiction itself. I believe we must integrate our art if we hope to integrate our imaginations and the societies our imaginations create.

In 1983 I attended a party in Beijing where Chinese and American women writers stood in a circle holding hands while Alice Walker led us singing a song Ding Ling had requested, "We Shall Overcome." This scene illustrates for me the rich spirit of international feminism. Simply living abroad for seven years allowed me to look past the blinders of American provincialism. (Perhaps this has worked too well in some regard because I find it harder to publish my books in this country. American editors have an allergy to social or political literature. Five of my six books of fiction and two other collaborative collections of stories were published in Great Britain before they appeared in the United States.) It's easy in this country to be persuaded that feminism and even lesbianism are American phenomena. I try to keep perspective through international journals and translated books. Of course, U.S. presses have a long way to go in publishing foreign literature, particularly from Third World countries. When our small writers' delegation returned from China, we were loaded with books. But one does not have to get on a plane to take the journey.

Writer as Worker

Tensions arise between audience and author when we confuse the writing with the writer herself. Most Americans romanticize art as magic. We perceive literature as the result of "creativity" rather than "creative labor," forgetting that writers are workers.[2] We invest the writer with special powers, in part because we want to experience the romance vicariously. And lesbians, perhaps because we often identify with a subculture, expect women writers to perform miracles at public events or to solve readers' romantic problems (since "it was just like you wrote in the book"). Sometimes a sadomasochistic struggle develops in which readers want the author to be addicted or psychotic or impoverished or dead as proof of or penance for her art. When we confuse the writing with the writer, we often expect her to be a stronger or more sensitive or more developed human being. Denise Levertov insists on a different perspective in *Light Up the Cave*: "My own belief . . . is that a poet is only a poet when engaged in making poems, and has no rightful claim to *feeling* more than others, but only to being able to *articulate* feeling through the medium of language" ("On the Edge of Darkness," p. 117).

Writers like myself from working-class families find the act of writing a complicated form of disenfranchisement. For whom are we writing when over sixty million adult Americans are illiterate or functionally illiterate? Certain cultures emphasize reading more than others, but for many working-class people, becoming a writer is an irrevocable immigration to a country beyond the family's imagination. For years I've kept a comment from Simone Weil over my desk, "This domination of those who know how to handle words over those who know how to handle things is rediscovered at every stage of human history. It is necessary to add that, as a group, these manipulators of words, whether priests or intellectuals, have always been on the side of the ruling class, on the side of the exploiters against the producers" (Petrement, *Simone Weil*, p. 207).

Acknowledging writing as work might have pervasive consequences. It might result in a less neurotic relationship between writers and readers. It might encourage better wages and working conditions for artists. It might inspire a clearer portrayal of working-class people in our books. It might open a light on how art can emerge from and contribute to an impulse for social change.

The—Open—End

My fiction has developed through the women's movement. I am conscious, while writing, of involving readers in the process of a story. Meanwhile, readers have influenced my themes, styles, and forms and have provided me with courage to continue. As Gertrude Stein declared in *The Making of Americans:*

> It is a very strange feeling when . . . you write a book and while you write it you are ashamed for every one must think you are a silly or a crazy one and yet you write it and you are ashamed, you know you will be laughed at or pitied by everyone and you have a queer feeling and you are not very certain and you go on writing. Then someone says yes to it, to something you are liking or doing or making and then never again can you have completely such a feeling of being afraid and ashamed that you had then when you were writing or liking the thing and not anyone had said yes about the thing. (P. 304)

I cannot predict the ways feminist readers will continue to affect me. Yet I do know that because of this imaginative collectivity, I am not alone.

NOTES

1. Virginia Woolf, *A Room of One's Own* (1929; rpt. New York: Harcourt, 1957), p. 84. Sylvia Plath, *The Journals of Sylvia Plath,* ed. Ted Hughes and Frances McCullough (New York: Dial, 1982), p. 168. I am grateful to Sandra M. Gilbert for directing me to the quotes from Plath and Woolf in her essay, "In Yeats's House: The Death and Resurrection of Sylvia Plath." The essay is published in *Coming to Light,* ed. Diane Wood Middlebrook and Marilyn Yalom, pp. 145–66 (Ann Arbor: University of Michigan Press, 1985).

2. For a fuller discussion of these issues, see *Competition: A Feminist Taboo?* ed. Valerie Miner and Helen E. Longino (New York: Feminist, 1987).

Writing with Class

When working-class people aren't ignored in current literature, they are portrayed as Other—either characters who "used to be" or caricatures fundamentally alienated from the New World promise. As the author of five novels about working-class lives, I grow cranky over what gets published and angry about what doesn't. For writers from working-class families, the making of art is cultural disenfranchisement, for we do not belong in literary circles and our writing rarely makes it back home. Those of us who write about our class heritage experience a variety of censorship and self-censorship.

Every day I wonder whether writing is a form of lunacy or of betrayal. One of my parents didn't go past grade eight and the other didn't finish high school. My mother works in an all-night coffee shop, and her goal for me has always been "to get a good job at the telephone company." She still doesn't understand my work and worries—justifiably—how I make a living from writing. There were few books in our house, no symphonies on the Victrola, no high drama except at the Sunday dinner table. One of my brothers grew up to be a carpenter. The other works for a maritime union. I've always carried that Miner suspicion that laboring with words is not real work. I ask myself: Does writing mean anything? Do I have a right to feel tired at week's end? Shouldn't I be doing something useful?

I talked with poets and novelists whose parents were waitresses, builders, typists, migrant farmers, and mechanics, and who chose to write about working-class subjects. I chose writers from "the first generation" Tillie Olsen discusses in *Silences,* people who emigrated from working-class backgrounds into the professions. Many, like me, were the first to go through college, surprising everyone by becoming something as exotic and impractical as a writer. Many no longer call themselves working-class, given their current possibilities and privileges. Yet their work remains influenced by childhood experience. They were all adamantly grateful to their families for a certain kind of vigor and common sense. Our conversations turned on the

This essay originally appeared under the title "Labor Pains" in the *Village Voice,* 5 January 1988. Reprinted by permission of the author and the *Village Voice.* The essay emerged gradually from presentations I gave at various conferences (and from the subsequent audience feedback), including the National Women's Studies Association Conference, 1985; the International Feminist Bookfair, 1986; the Marxist Scholars Conference, 1987; and the Modern Language Association Conference, 1987. After the article came out in the *Voice,* I received more letters about it than about any other piece I have written.

treatment of our books in the American literary scene as well as on our experiences of cross-class immigration.

Stan Weir is a writer and publisher of Singlejack Books in San Pedro, California, which specializes in prose about manual labor. He told me, "I think the rejection of working-class material by publishers is political because it's almost impossible to write about work without putting the employer in a negative position. I once read a piece about a Spanish prisoner who said that one of the worst tortures was not having a mirror. After a while she began to think she had become deformed. That's what happens to labor. There is no mirror in the media about what we do."

Americans pretend we are a classless society. Everyone is potentially middle class. Like Original Sin, working-class origin is a state from which we are saved— by working hard and being good Americans. We acknowledge our working-class past only when we want to demonstrate how far we have progressed. American fiction seems to be turning more and more solipsistic. As a reviewer, I read endless odysseys of lawyers and doctors and teachers paddling through psychotherapy, divorce, bankruptcy, and religious crisis. Diane Johnson has named such work "fiction of the self." Indeed, it is a fiction of the middle-class self.

As Joyce Carol Thomas says, "It's easier to find material from middle-class life in contemporary American literature—perhaps because publishers are from that world. We're all more comfortable with what we know." Thomas's *Marked by Fire* is a dramatic novel about a Black girl in Oklahoma. She considers it serious adult fiction, but when it failed to sell to that market, she was forced to publish it as a "young adult novel." It later won an American Book Award.

In contrast to more voguish literature, working-class novels rarely situate their characters in isolation. They are often portrayed in the workplace, in union meetings, in neighborhoods. Robert Ward says, "All my books are about friendship. I came from a tightly knit neighborhood in Baltimore."

Ward begins his novel *Red Baker* with a forty-year-old man being laid off his steel-plant job.

> I waited there for my friend Dog Donahue to get his jacket and stared at the tilting tables on the blooming mill, where I had spent the last twelve years of my life turning the huge bars of steel over with my tongs. So many days of dreaming of getting the hell out of here. But now that they were shutting the place down—rumor had it that it might be for good—I would have given about anything to climb back up there, put on protective goggles, and get back to work. Already I missed the clack of the tongs as Dog and I guided the molten steel through the pass to shape it down.

The often unconscious dismissal of working-class writing in publishing houses and review media is a pernicious sort of censorship because it is subtle and often hard to document. But we can piece together the personal stories. Robert Ward had twenty-one rejections for *Red Baker*. "One publisher said that it wouldn't have any real commercial sales. Another publisher said that if it had been about upper-middle-class people he would have bought it." After a substantial track record, William Kennedy submitted his novel *Ironweed*, about an ex-ballplayer and part-time grave digger, for a year and a half before it was accepted by Viking. Later, *Ironweed* won a Pulitzer Prize, and now it has been made into a big-budget film.

Of course, writers from all backgrounds complain of rejection. What unifies the responses to these writers is that they were informed the *subjects* of their work were boring or inappropriate literary material. Kennedy explains, "When I submitted *Ironweed*, it wasn't being judged the way I thought literature should be judged. There was an intense prejudice against a man who was at the bottom of the world. When *Ironweed* was accepted, it was treated as an anomaly."

When such books do traverse the publishing hurdles, few win the Pulitzer Prize. More likely, they encounter ignorant or hostile critics. Many of the writers I interviewed referred to "better days" in the 1930s and 1940s. Before the Cold War, radical artistic solidarity flourished; that fellowship of hope is taken less seriously now, and contemporary literature is marinated in cynicism.

Studs Terkel told me,

> The problem is the whole climate of the country. Never before has labor been held in such ill repute. You have young kids today who are critical of the labor movement, yet they don't know that it was because of labor organizing that we got a minimum wage. They don't know about Haymarket. They don't know about the Memorial Day Massacre of 1937. Look at the daily newspapers. None have labor sections. Which have labor pages or even a labor journalist?

Perhaps a deeper problem is self-censorship by writers who never imagine the possibility of publishing or of others who omit material to accommodate editors. At best, the class bias makes authors from working-class families angry and provides a momentum to "catch up." At worst, it paralyzes writers with doubt. You think you are a poor writer. You think you are crazy for wanting to describe such people, your people. At first you are not sure why your people are different, for the American denial of class is seamed into our culture.

The very content—descriptions of waitresses and secretaries and construction workers—is passing family codes to middle-class outsiders. Of course, anyone who writes faces issues of confidentiality. But class compounds the dilemma because of the power inequity between the working-class characters and the often middle-class audience. For some working-class people, the secrets are almost all they have. Writing about them feels like betrayal.

Or desertion. Moving from this background into the professions is an immigration. Writing is particularly alien because it embraces literacy, sometimes the major obstacle to parents' success. Some cultures emphasize reading more than others, but for many working-class people, becoming a writer is like moving to a country where a different language is spoken. Your family cannot reach you. Gradually you lose touch with them. Soon you become a stranger. Writers from middle-class or upper-class families also protest, "My parents don't understand me." But the rift between writer and working-class parent is more profound than the friction between an artist and the parent who wanted to pass on the family law shingle. In becoming a writer, the working-class person makes an irrevocable shift, moving beyond the family's imagination.

Novelist and poet Maureen Duffy discusses this in the introduction to the new edition of *That's How It Was,* her passionate novel about a working-class childhood in London during World War II:

> As I had gone along with the educational process my goal had receded toward the glorious heights of ambition to go to university and be a writer. This last I hadn't really confessed to anyone. I disguised it under the professed intention of becoming a teacher. It was asking a lot to be the first of the family to go to university. Then to propose to throw away everything that had been struggled for in the vain hope of being that most despised thing, a poet, was unmentionable.

Ishmael Reed adds, "My parents thought my work wasn't serious, that the stuff I was doing was jive. They worked with their hands."

Tess Gallagher, whose fiction and poetry often draw on the lives of her farmer mother and longshoreman father, has written a poem called "3 A.M. Kitchen: My Father Talking":

> I quit the woods. One day just
> walked out, took off my corks, said that's
> it. I went to the docks.
> I was driving winch. You had to watch
> to see nothing fell out of the sling. If
> you killed somebody you'd
> never forget it. All
> those years I was just working
> I was on the edge, every day. Just working.

Gallagher comments: "My father shook his head when I said I wanted to be a writer. My mother told me I was just nervous and she taught me to knit. They took it seriously when I earned some money. I made $350 for a poem in the *New Yorker*. I got a steady job teaching. They knew I wasn't going to be destitute."

My own experience is similar. My mother still wants me to get a real job. My father, who is retired after forty-four years in the merchant marine, has never read my work. When I visited recently, the only book in his house was the telephone book. He asked a neighbor to read my new novel and tell him about it. My brother the carpenter thinks I'm crazy to work without a contract. How can I put four or five years into a novel when I don't know if anyone is going to publish it? He wouldn't install a kitchen without a contract.

Chances are, by the time you are a published writer in this country, you have moved into the middle class. Because you have gone through college—and even if you're not making a grand salary, you have certain middle-class choices not available to your parents. This process can leave you wrenched by guilt, angry and ashamed at the limitations of your youth yet still disoriented in the middle-class America where you supposedly belong. Your family dismisses the irrevocable changes (after all, they were on their way there, too), and the journey is discredited. To the outside world you may look middle-class, but you know your birthmarks.

In Marge Piercy's *Braided Lives*, Jill distills her identity during the fourth week of college: "We are poor; we are on scholarships; we are ill dressed; we take the hard courses and come from the wrong cities and addresses; we will not be rushed by sororities." The tangible differences between Jill and her college roommates is measured in her sorties to the dorm laundry to steal lingerie, her strategy of eating ravenously on dates to ward off next week's hunger, the brutal abortion she inflicts on herself because she cannot afford safe medical care, the fact that the word *camp* conjures up her brother's basic training rather than summer expeditions or idiosyncratic humor. Throughout college, Jill and her cousin Donna reassure each other that they are not crazy, that they just came from a "different" background.

Those who cross classes often remain dissociated for life. Long after they become writers, their nerves pinch—a dialect slips, a social cue is missed. They are gripped by cultural agoraphobia, paralyzed in "normal" society yet unable to return to the working class.

Most of the writers I talked with cite vast legacies of insight and strength from their working-class parents. Many also mention a tolerance for hard work and a consciousness about limited time. Philip Levine says, "I was disciplined already when I started writing. I wasn't a wastrel. I've never had trouble writing and teaching. This teaching is nothing compared to the work I did before."

Tess Gallagher: "I learned that the world doesn't give you what you ask for.

You had to struggle to insure fairness. There were always unions in the house. I grew up learning about the world of the boss. I decided I didn't want a boss. As a writer, you are the boss."

Ishmael Reed: "I admire my mother and stepfather. They integrated a neighborhood in Buffalo and they went in there armed. With guns. I came from a working-class background where people didn't mince words. People say I'm outspoken. They compare me to Muhammad Ali. But I prefer to think of Joe Frazier."

Despite their very different books, these writers had common concerns about content, language, audience, and censorship. I am grateful to them for reminding me about the gifts of a working-class heritage—including skepticism about American-dream politics, a low tolerance for verbosity, and a talent for common sense. Of course the conflicts haven't disappeared. But such writers give me hope that we may yet temper what Simone Weil called "the domination of those who know how to handle things."

As Jill says in *Braided Lives*, "I feel as if I have come through rough terrain and across the wasteland around factories and down unmarked streets without a map and I both know and do not know where I have been. I want to explain to somebody. . . . I want to revisit that burned-over district where I learned to love—in friendship and in passion—and to work."

Competition among Feminist Writers

Why do I sometimes feel a twinge when another woman succeeds? Why do I occasionally become livid? Shouldn't I feel gratified when any of my sisters does well? Isn't feminism anithetical to competition?

The impetus for this essay and, indeed, for this book came from the 1980 National Women's Studies Conference in Bloomington, Indiana. The variety of panels about crucial issues, presented with feminist perspective as a given, filled me with exhilaration. Since I am a novelist and not a scholar, I've always experienced more pleasure than anxiety at academic conferences. Since this one was about women's issues, I knew I had landed in particularly exciting territory. The euphoria dissipated when I visited the book display. There I was gripped by an old, humiliating jealousy of other writers. I tried to be grateful that women's voices were available. Still, I wondered, why has *she* been published more? I tried to revel in the emergence of a new feminist literary tradition. Yet, I wondered, why did that editor like *her* work better than mine? Because I write about lesbian and other "marginal" characters? Because I come from a working-class family and thus don't have the proper demeanor or degrees or contacts? Because I'm a Westerner, living too far from the center of U.S. literary power? Because I have brown hair? With the same intensity that I experienced excitement at the panels, I now felt competitive with other feminist writers. Then I was drenched in guilt. How could I begrudge a sister her success? Instead, shouldn't I be raging at the men who manipulated the gentlemanly hypocrisy of publishing? Somehow I found myself more and more aggravated with other women.

I wrote to a friend about these feelings. Oh, yes, she commiserated, she felt the same way. Then I talked with women from other fields. Oh, yes, it was horrible; they had never admitted it before, but they, too, felt especially competitive with women. Soon I began to wonder whether it was harder to talk about competition in the women's movement than about sexuality. Competition is a moral problem and an emotional tangle and a political conundrum. In this essay I am

---

This essay is reprinted from the anthology *Competition: A Feminist Taboo?*, which I coedited with Helen E. Longino for the Feminist Press in 1987. I am particularly grateful to Helen Longino for her advice on this essay. An abridged version of this essay appeared under the title "Rumours from the Cauldron" in *Women's Studies International Forum* 8, no. 1 (1985). Reprinted by permission of Pergamon Press PLC.

more interested in opening a forum for discussion than in posing specific remedies. I resist the kind of holy authorship through which the author becomes a rigid authority, so identified with her ideas that when someone disagrees, she uses all her spirit to defend (rather than confer about) the right answer. I am conscious of asking many questions here. I look forward to a variety of answers in the future—in conversation, on panels, in other essays and books.

I must begin by acknowledging all the momentum and support I've received from the women's movement.[1] I do not think that competition is the final step in an inevitable downward spiral of sisterhood. I do think we have to face the existence of competition if we are to preserve feminism and our sanity.

During the last few years, I have learned how we often confuse competitive feelings with competition, suffering with virtue, and criticism with conflict. I have found a need to distinguish between competition for ego gratification within the androcentric system—that is, for fame and status—and competition in meeting our own standards of aesthetic excellence. Ultimately, I want to consider the possibilities of a cooperative framework in which we "compete" with one another's ideas and with our own ideas toward collective wisdom. Is it possible to return to the Latin root of the word *compete* ("to meet," "to be fitting," " to strive together toward") and develop a "feminist competition" which allows for both individual and collective progress?

First, some stories I've gathered from a variety of women. We've all told such tales—on the telephone, over supper; we've told them with anger and confusion and a sense of betrayal.

I had a mentor. Well, we didn't call it that then. But she read everything I wrote. Gave me criticism. Advice. And when my book was honored, she turned away. It was almost as if she were jealous.

I had a student. I gave her all I had. Time, concern, contacts. But always she seemed to be measuring herself against me, needing to prove her worth by diminishing me.

I had a friend. We worked in a writing group together. Without her, I would have stopped writing poetry. But when my work was published, she ignored it. Didn't come to the book party. Wouldn't talk to me.

I had a play produced in New York and another in California. My New York friends said, "Oh, it must be easier to produce in California, with all those funky artistic people." And my California friends said, "Oh, New York, of course there are so many theaters there. Of course it must be easier in New York.

Competition among women, especially among women writers, is a highly charged topic. Literature is a peculiarly public product of a particularly private endeavor. Writing is dismally paid labor, putting extra pressure on us to make our work visible because only the most renowned writers even earn a living by it. The average American author makes $4,775 a year from writing, and of course the story is sadder in many other countries.[2] Our avenues to achievement are frighteningly ephemeral and therefore escalate the anxiety over success. What *is* achievement in feminist literature? Writing well? Finishing a good book? Recognition from whom? Readers? Feminist critics? The *New York Review of Books?* Too many writers are caught in the contradiction that it is a privilege to publish and a personal failure not to be published.

The dilemma descends in part from a broad social denial of the labor involved in the making of art. Contradictions compound each other. While society celebrates some artistic competition with televised award ceremonies, critics demand that "serious" writers eschew any notion of contest. Readers often require a special purity of motive from authors who they expect will place personal vision above base material considerations. The pressures are exacerbated for many women authors, who have more ambivalence than men authors about conflict, achievement, and success. Feminist writers bear additional, valid qualms about hierarchy.

Street sense says that decisions about who gets published, granted money, well reviewed, and honored with awards have as much to do with connections as with merit. Even when outsiders are acknowledged it can be a political maneuver. Black critic Barbara Christian tells me: "The establishment seems to have room for one of us a year. It's easier to accept a Black novel if you perceive it as *one* point of view, as the culture of an isolated individual." So what should feminist writers do? Some women prescribe ignoring the patriarchal literary scene altogether. Yet if one tried to be completely separatist, could one create a feminist publishing world sanitized of petty politics? Perhaps I've skipped a step. It's worth considering how we already *do* behave before speculating about how we *might* behave.[3]

In studying the market, it becomes clear that this is a men's emporium. It's useful to distinguish between short-term friction generated by limited resources and the long-term development of feminist literature. Immediately, we do seem to compete for advances, publication, review space, and acknowledgement. Everyone knows of cases where *her* poem was published instead of ours, where *she* got a grant and we didn't. Arts money is tight and there are still unofficial quotas working against women. While admitting the constraints of the current market, I believe that most competitive behavior among women is pointless shadowboxing. In the long run, reading one feminist novel leads to reading another feminist novel. Publishing one feminist journal leads to publishing another feminist journal. While we may compete today, what we do with our competitive feelings can shape our mutual creativity in the future. We need to make more room for ourselves.

For a clearer view of competition, we have to find our way through a cave hung with veils. The webs of envy, jealousy, and resentment. The net of manipulative criticism that keeps us from taking each other's work seriously. The mystique of creative magic that hides the fact that art is work. Finally, beyond these veils, we may escape androcentric competition and even discover ways for competition to serve feminism.

Only by acknowledging competition, then reclaiming and redefining it, can we endure in and surface beyond the misogynist literary establishment. To most of us *competition* is a hot word, associated with rabid capitalism and the self-serving impulse to elevate oneself while diminishing others. So I am tempted to replace the word *competition* with *cooperation* or *collaboration* or another currently politically correct term. But I'd like to entertain the possibility of a *feminist competition* because I think it may afford us a special edge from which we can stretch for personal and collective excellence. The Latin root for compete does not pose an exclusive winner. It suggests that we "meet, be fitting, be capable, strive together." In this sense feminist writers may *need* competition for survival. Our work depends on and flourishes within an "imaginative collectivity of writers and readers."[4]

The Stepsisters: Envy, Jealousy, and Resentment

One reason this topic causes so much emotional distress and political wariness is that often it is easy to confuse the *feelings* of envy, jealousy, and resentment with the *process* of competition.

The "competitive syndrome" for women writers proceeds something like this: First a woman internalizes her fears about writing and her frustrations about getting published. Then she sees that another woman has been published or honored. She feels jealous. She may begin with self-denigration: "I'm not good enough." Often she swivels to resentment: "But is *she* good enough? Why her?" Then she feels remorse. She talks with someone else, someone equally marginal, about their relative lack of success. She scapegoats the "successful" woman writer. She trashes. She allows her impotence in male literary terms to paralyze her power to communicate with other women.

Personally, I also feel envy of male writers, but never with the same intensity I feel of women writers. One reason is that I know that in the current system, women have a smaller portion of the publishing pie. Beyond this, I am more likely to compare myself with other women writers, particularly other white, U.S. women from the working-class homes.[5] This is, I believe, a natural searching for context. It is when the context becomes confinement, when we assume the unfairness of family patterns, that sibling rivalry ensues and becomes destructive.

Envy, jealousy, and resentment are emotions. Competition is a behavior, about which we might feel many different ways. Given the current squeeze on publishing, many of us are bound to lose and consequently to feel badly. Because the modes of judgment seem arbitrary at best, and usually quite biased, it seems naive to ask advice about how to improve our lot. Because those in power are often invisible or inaccessible, we often direct our fury and bitterness at sister writers. Some people get ruthless, undermining the work of others to serve their own careers. After someone wins an award, her next book may be reviewed with special harshness. The anger about our "failure" is misdirected at her "success." In this sense, perhaps, envy, jealousy, and resentment become blocks to a feminist competition. The problem arises when we take the male literary arena too seriously, when we buy the rules of their fixed game, when we look outward for our core of artistic validation.

If one woman writes a good story, does that mean I can't? Of course not. If she publishes, does that mean I can't? Of course not, in the long run. One journalist I know suggests that "if we worked together, we could change the blockbuster system of conglomerate publishing. But jealousy doesn't wait for collective action, except where we turn and scapegoat other writers."

The Shroud of Ambition

Discussing competition also induces anxiety because many women are squeamish about owning their ambitions, and because ambition itself is difficult to contain or to quantify. Earlier I asked what achievement is. Novelist Betty Roszak says, "What is success anyway? Once you have one thing, you want another." Women are conditioned to avoid external conflict. We perceive a contradiction between personal achievement and collective success. Critic and novelist Diane Johnson tells me, "There is a taboo on success. People move away from you when you're successful."

Personally, I have always been more afraid of succeeding than of failing. The latter would be expected, comfortable. We are so thoroughly trained that we often can't even recognize our own accomplishments. If we sat back and absorbed our own success, enjoyed it for a moment, we might feel less contentious about other writers.

Women's psychological resistances to success are legend. Some women identify public awards with their fathers and think them unnatural for themselves. Others associate power with evil. Some fear they must choose between love and work. As Phyllis Chesler observed fifteen years ago in *Women and Madness:*

> Women mistrust and men destroy those women who are not interested in sacrificing at least something for someone for some reason. Rather than achieve at least half or all of Caesar's power, many women, including some feminists, would prefer to leave it in Caesar's hands altogether and, in a misguidedly "novel" gesture, sacrifice their individual advancement for the sake of less fortunate women.[6]

It often feels easier to recognize someone else's success than to admit our own. Perhaps because, as Toronto feminist organizer Leah Erna says, "Women have breasts and guilt." *It seems more sisterly to struggle than to be successful.* And "being successful" is different from "succeeding." People may celebrate with you the night your novel turns into a movie, but what happens the morning after? Or the morning after that?

Better to suffer together than to achieve in isolation. Barbara Christian tells me, "Our criteria as feminists seem to be different from the establishment's. They have art and success. We have art and suffering. Then there's the question of what we do to people who are successful in the establishment. Once the establishment acknowledges you, the readers drop you. If you're successful, then you're not suffering and you're not with us."

Who Wins from Our Competition?

Not everyone suffers when feminists evade success or when we fight unnecessarily among ourselves, and it's crucial to consider who benefits from our fuzzy competitiveness. Louise Bernikow observes in *Among Women:* "Tradition tells me that we compete for men, that our conflict takes the form of envy, jealousy and pettiness. We are brought up to think of other women as enemies, to be in a state of conflict with them, but not to express it directly."[7]

Friendships like that between Virginia Woolf and Katherine Mansfield can get so caught up in sisterly rivalry that the women fall mute. They resist each other where they might shout back at the father. Why do we continue to sulk and snipe and spit when we could be confronting patriarchal publishing together?

As Christian points out, we compete for suffering. Perhaps this is because we have become too cynical about the possibility of success for feminists in this world. Perhaps it is also because we confuse suffering with virtue.

A lot of the envy between women that crosses the DMZ of race, class, sexuality, and culture is actually misdirected fury at privileged white men. Clearly feminists need to confront racism, classism, heterosexism, and imperialism inside *and* outside the women's movement. The point of this knowledge is not to create a grading system, but to develop an understanding of the obstacles and a solidarity in overcoming them. It is important, for instance, for white women to acknowledge and to fight against the double jeopardy experienced by women of color. It is important for heterosexual women to understand that lesbians experience both sexism and homophobia from publishers. But why do we waste time bickering about who is more oppressed by conventional publishing? This is a successful divide-and-conquer routine if there ever was one. When we claim "more oppressed than thou," we are often really asking who is more oppressed by men. How is this different from other ways of competing for men? We spend our spirits fighting our sisters rather than helping each other pull away from the roots of our common oppression and moving together to more fertile ground.

Literary standards get lost in all this—whether we compete for suffering or for grudging approbation from the male academy. Wouldn't it be more productive to concentrate on developing our multiethnic, cross-class, international literary criticism?

Criticism Is Not Deadly

Good critics stimulate feminist literature, yet reviewing is an arena in which envy, jealousy, and resentment can fester. The greatest respect we can give each other's work is attentive, constructive criticism. But sometimes criticism is abused as a distorted expression of power. Timid critics are afraid to knock a sister's right to write. Fair feminist criticism is not unqualified applause. It is fully informed, honest response.[8]

Joanna Russ complains in *Sinister Wisdom:*

The Feminine Imperative is forced on all of us. . . . The women's community as a mystically loving band of emotional weaklings who make up to each other by our own kindness and sweetness for the harshness we have to endure in the outside world is a description that exactly characterizes the female middle-class subculture as it's existed in patriarchy for centuries—without changing a thing. . . . So honesty goes by the board, hurt feelings are put at a premium, general fear and paralysis set in, and one by one any woman who oversteps the increasingly circumscribed area of what's permissible is trashed.[9]

While we shouldn't tiptoe as critics, it's also worthwhile to remember not to tromp into a review without trying to enter the writer's vision of her book. I cringe at the memory of the first review I wrote. It was a self-important, overly critical piece about someone's first book. Now I see that I, like a lot of new reviewers, was expressing jealousy that this book—and not mine—was being published. (At the time I hadn't even written a book.) During the next few years I grew more tolerant and generous in my reviewing. But in the period just before my first novel was published, I compared everything that crossed my desk to my own "brilliant" manuscript. I decided to stop reviewing novels for a while, which was good for both me and my potential victims. I was happy reviewing nonfiction. In due time, my first novel did appear. Then, lo and behold, I became a very sympathetic critic of fiction.

Some feminist critics, in their fervor to make a political point, rampage against one author on false assumptions. Being intelligently critical is an intricate balance. Fiction writer Sandy Boucher says, "It's OK to dislike a piece of work, but it's important to distinguish between that work and the person and the person's next piece of work."

Equally, as readers of reviews, if we understand criticism as perspective rather than mandate, we can use reviews as assessment and not censorship. When competitiveness causes us to ignore or to dismiss our sisters' writing, whether from our own envy or from secondhand bias, it is having its most insidious effect.

Work Not Magic

Writers are workers. Books are products; sometimes services. Often we seem to forget this. We romanticize art as solitary genesis. Readers are often envious of the imagined status of writers. They sometimes hold onto conflicting mythologies by venerating an artist's victimhood while investing her with special powers and privileges. Jane Rule argues forcefully against making writers into heroes:

> I am not . . . as a writer, setting myself up as a leader or role model for anyone. If my community, egged on by the media, tries to turn me into one, I will fail just as others have failed before me, not simply because I am a writer but because leaders of that sort are damaging to the sense of self-worth and self-direction all women's consciousness raising is about.[10]

One reason many North Americans don't understand writing as work is that we live in classist societies where we rate professions above trades and art above professions. How can art be labor? In addition to cherishing our status, writers are often reluctant to remember all the time and sweat and retyping that went into a good piece. We would far rather imagine sitting in the morning sunlight, drinking French Roast coffee (or in the moonlight, sipping brandy) and "catharting" onto the page.

If we recognized writing as labor, we would be less hurt by rejections. We might see that what is being rejected is our manuscripts, not our personal characters. As Margarita Donnelly, an editor for *Calyx,* said at the American Writers' Congress in October 1981: "We get so many manuscripts, we can't possibly use them all. So we return some. Don't think of it as being rejected. Think of it as having your manuscript returned." In addition to struggles for recognition and for income, writers have notoriously treacherous working conditions as we battle restrictive libel laws and increasing censorship. In many cases we are no better off than the employees of corporations, like Gulf and Western or ITT, which own our publishing houses.

Too often, however, when we finally *do* budge from our grandiose self-images as singular geniuses, we fall into competitiveness with other writers. We assume we are fighting other geniuses for survival. In the short run, it may be a choice between her work and ours. But literary fashions change over time. And, if we looked more closely, we would notice how everyone slogs and struggles. We might lose glamor, but gain solidarity. If we actually talked about drowning in empty white pages and typing until our fingers grew numb and chasing through book after book for a necessary reference, we would perceive the universal drudge. If we considered another writer on the eighth draft of her novel that is just not working, sitting in a cold flat worried about how to rewrite the first sentence, buy clothes for her daughter, and find enough money to heat the place before winter sets in, I'm confident that we would feel less combative. However, even after years in the field, many writers still believe in the romance, the romance that *other* writers must be experiencing. Most publishers pay so poorly and give us so few design consulting rights because by the time we've won our imaginary battles with other writers, we're so grateful to be printed that we accept their "protective" advice.

Writers have a lot to learn from coal miners and steel workers whose unionism erases any false notion of privilege about the right to be paid or to be treated decently for work done. We might come to realize that the scarcity model of artistic ability is not so different from the conservative faith in the necessity of unemployment to balance the economy. The real "artistic scarcity" is the amount of resources made available by wealthy institutions to hardworking artists. Some progress has been made by writers' unions in various countries. But until we recognize ourselves as part of a larger scheme of workers, we will be organizing in a vacuum. Ultimately, I think, we need to go beyond alliances with other writers to form connections with all book people. Without feminist editors, agents, publishers, printers, reviewers, booksellers, librarians, teachers, students, our words would be invisible.

Conclusion: Competition for Collective Success?

So far I have considered competitiveness within the androcentric system and have asked who is served by it. I have acknowledged how feelings of envy and inadequacy enshroud us. I have shown that writers struggle against each other rather than confront publishers about change. Now, is there any way to get competition to serve us, to work for individual satisfaction and collective progress? What would a feminist competition be? The question is addressed by other writers who will no doubt spark yet more answers from provoked readers. Meanwhile let me offer a few ideas. First, I'd like to return to the Latin root, "to meet, be fitting, be capable, strive together." Paula Gunn Allen tells me, "Traditional Indians—particularly Pueblo Indians—by and large view competition within a group framework, and by and large see it as a socially useful trait."

For me the feminist writing circle has been a microcosm of cooperative competition. What makes such a group feminist is its process as well as its content. Everyone has a chance to speak and to be heard. In Toronto during the early 1970s, I met with other feminists to discuss how our work was being treated by editors and how badly we were getting paid. At first we were very guarded, each of us protective of her reputation as a "successful young writer." We called ourselves feminists although individually we did not believe we had experienced discrimination. (We had yet to learn a whole new way of seeing.) Gradually, we came to trust one another, to share our worries, and to investigate the experiences of other writers. We discovered two things: All writers were being mistreated, and women writers were being especially mistreated. Our collective was one of the seeds of a national writers' union (now called the Periodical Writers' Association of Canada).

We continued to meet for several years to write a book together, *Her Own Woman* (by Myrna Kostash, Melinda McCracken, Valerie Miner, Erna Paris, and Heather Robertson). Several years later in London, I began working with four British women on *Tales I Tell My Mother* (by Zoë Fairbairns, Sara Maitland, Valerie Miner, Michele Roberts, and Michelene Wandor), a fictional documentary of the British women's movement. The *Tales* group was a springboard for all of us in different parts of the world. Six years after the book was published, we presented a panel at the Institute of Contemporary Art in London, discussing the impetus we had received from each other. Between 1978 and 1984, the members of the group published twenty-seven books. In 1986, we published a collection of our new work, *More Tales.* Since I moved back to California, I have written and published five novels—*Blood Sisters, Movement, Murder in the English Department, Winter's Edge,* and *All Good Women*—within the stimulus of writers' groups.[11]

None of these collectives has exhibited flawless sisterhood. In each of them, we have bickered, felt jealous, arrived late, gossiped too much. Yet, because we moved together through some of the same veils, because we discussed the labor of writing, we were better able to surface above petty obstacles and to invigorate each other's work. Here we witnessed other women stretching their imagination and skills and were encouraged to stretch (compete with?) *our own abilities* toward literary excellence.

I am now involved in two writers' groups. Recently one of the groups sat around talking about jealousy. First, of course, we began talking about outside people of whom we were jealous. Then Sandy admitted that she was jealous of Judy's fame, of the fact that she is invited to give so many talks, even though Sandy herself isn't particularly interested in being a public speaker. Paula said she was also jealous of the public appearances—until she started to get invitations and to feel oppressed by them. Judy said that she was jealous of Sandy's royalty advances from a major publisher. I said I was jealous of the grants the other three had received.[12] Sandy said she was jealous of the fact that I had published five novels when she hadn't yet published one. And so on. As we talked, the air got easier to breathe. I found myself stretching comfortably on the floor of Paula's studio. It was a relief, simply, to speak the forbidden. One conclusion was that some of us use jealousy to remind us that we haven't "won" yet or to give us permission to own what we have achieved. We agreed that we rarely felt jealous when we were happy with our work, that often jealousy was a channel for other painful feelings about ourselves. Finally, we articulated areas where we wanted to learn from each other—about structure, about poetic language, and so on—and made plans to discuss these areas at future meetings.

Madelon Sprengnether, a poet and essayist, says her writing group in Minnesota has "provided a stimulus and a permission. The success of others provides an opening for my work. Success seems possible and not too distant. Friends hold you to your best work." I agree. In my other current group, for instance, Mary has a genius for pace in her novels. When I see how well her new book is moving, I think, I can do that too. Sue and I are both working on books about World War II. She knows more about poetry of the period than I. This knowledge not only helps me but spurs me to read more, to broaden my own expertise. Mimi has a gift for physical detail. I read her work and try harder with my descriptions next time. In some sense the writing group is like the family in which I want to be the best child. On a primal level, I want my details to be *sharper* than Mimi's.

Intellectually, I understand that they will only be different. What I hope for is *the best book I can produce*. Their achievement opens the possibility of my own. The group provides the necessary provocation and support for self-competition. Unlike my birth family, I entered this dynamic voluntarily and as an adult. The group provides a measuring stick for the craft of writing and the craftiness of getting published. I "compete" with the others by stretching toward my own literary excellence and professional achievement.

The worldly success of my collective sisters has also spurred me to compete for similar gains. Three of the five *Tales* members published novels before I did. For months I felt jealous and depressed. But I was also stimulated to try harder to get my work published. Later one of the women had her second novel rejected by a press that was publishing two of my books. Now the two of us have published five novels each. The competition between us wasn't always conscious, but the very presence of the other writer made us try harder—gave us both a permission and a further incentive—to get our work published. We gave each other a mutual momentum. In contrast, I personally would find it hard to work in isolation, without news of other writers' successes and failures. Current publishing procedures are so arbitrary that this kind of competitive comparison not only challenges my work; it keeps me sane.

We're not going to end masculinist competition, not for a while. But we do have some choices about how we respond to patriarchal publishing. The real danger is ignoring or censoring a sister's writing because in doing so, we are drawing down a blind on all our work.

In the larger feminist forum, meanwhile, we can stir art in each other. Cooperative competition (I still lean toward reclaiming the old word rather than creating a new one) can provoke us to go deeper emotionally, to play more boldly with form. It can offer comradeship in an all-too-lonely job. It can lend a sense of reality to labor whose ephemeral acknowledgment is crazy-making. It can help us to create new standards of criticism. It can give us the spirit to continue writing.

Cooperative competition creates a better feminist literature. We use each other's work as models for achievement. We see each other's success as a promise of our own. We keep the long-term vision of the enormous bookshelf (with room for everyone's books) while being provoked by daily accomplishments that may preclude our own in the short term. Unlike a race which is won/lost in an instant, a book and a career are built over time. Indeed, they are never finished as long as readers go on reading. Cooperative competitors eschew the veils and acknowledge the vicissitudes of publishing—by fighting for our rights as workers; by challenging the sexism and racism of publishing; by providing a critical forum in which all our work is taken seriously. Now we don't have control over our books, but we do have control over our attitudes about our books and each other's books. And we can "strive together toward" by inciting each other to be better writers and readers.

NOTES

Some of the material in this essay was presented at a panel about competition among women at the National Women's Studies Conference, June 1982, at California State University, Humboldt, California; at the Bay Area Marxist Feminist Group, January 1983, Oakland, California; and at the Society for Women in Philosophy (Eastern Division), April 1986, Hamilton College, Clinton, New York. I am grateful for the feedback I received on each of these occasions.

1. Thanks go to a number of writers who have helped me with the thinking behind this essay during the last few years. Some were formally interviewed. Others talked with me informally. They include Paula Gunn Allen, Sandy Boucher, Maureen Brady, Dorothy Bryant, Charlotte Bunch, Barbara Christian, Renate Duelli-Klein, Erika Duncan, Zoë Fairbairns, Kathleen Fraser, Sally Miller Gearhart, Judy Grahn, Susan Griffin, Jana Harris, Carolyn Heilbrun, Diane Johnson, Ke Yan, Myrna Kostash, Denise Levertov, Helen E. Longino, Mary Mackey, Karen Malpede, Tillie Olsen, Norma Rice, Wendy Rose, Ruth Rosen, Betty Roszak, Susan Schweik, Eleanor Scully, Madelon Sprengnether, Charlene Spretnak, Hannemieke Stamperius, Mary Helen Washington, and Yvonne.

2. Suzanne Gordon, "Too Long at the Mercy of Publishers—Time for a Writers' Union," *Boston Globe,* 28 November 1981.

3. For more information about feminist publishing, readers might consider *Quest* 3, no. 2 (Fall 1976), a theme issue entitled, "Communication and Control."

4. I developed some of these ideas more fully in a previous essay, "Writing Feminist Fiction," *Frontiers* 6, no. 1 (1981). I discuss "the imaginative collectivity of writers and readers" more fully in a previous essay, "Reader Is Writer Is Reader," *Hurricane Alice* (Winter/Spring 1984): 11–12.

5. I also feel twinges when male writers of my background or age or politics win something I don't. But my primary comparison is always with other women writers. Perhaps this is because I see my feminism as the core of my politics. Perhaps it is because I was the only girl in my family, and I learned early it was senseless to waste my time expecting equal treatment with my brothers.

6. Phyllis Chesler, *Women and Madness* (New York: Avon Books, 1972), p. 279.

7. Louise Bernikow, *Among Women* (New York: Harmony Books, 1980), p. 195.

8. Some of these ideas are developed more fully in my previous essay "The Feminist Reviewer," in *Words in Our Pockets,* ed. Celeste West (Paradise, Calif.: Dustbooks/Booklegger, 1985), also reprinted in this volume.

9. Joanna Russ, "Power and Helplessness in the Women's Movement," *Sinister Wisdom* 18 (Fall 1981): 51–52.

10. Jane Rule, "Lesbian Leadership," *Resources for Feminist Research* (Canada), Summer 1983, p. 56.

11. Myrna Kostash, Melinda McCracken, Valerie Miner, Erna Paris, and Heather Rob-

ertson, *Her Own Woman* (Canada: Macmillan, 1975); Zoë Fairbairns, Sara Maitland, Valerie Miner, Michele Roberts, and Michelene Wandor, *Tales I Tell My Mother* (London: Journeyman Press, 1978; Boston: South End Press, 1980); idem, *More Tales* (London: Journeyman Press, 1986); Valerie Miner, *Blood Sisters* (London: Women's Press, 1981; New York: St. Martin's Press, 1982), *Movement* (Trumansburg, N.Y.: Crossing Press; London: Methuen, 1985), *Murder in the English Department* (London: Women's Press, 1982; New York: St. Martin's Press, 1983), *Winter's Edge* (London: Methuen Press, 1984; Trumansburg, N.Y.: Crossing Press, 1985), *All Good Women* (London: Methuen, 1987).

12. As I was writing the final draft of this essay, I received my fifth rejection from the National Endowment for the Arts. This was compounded by recent rejections from the Guggenheim Foundation, the Rockefeller Foundation, the Bunting Institute, and other institutions which help some writers earn a living wage from their work. On the day of the NEA rejection, the only thing that kept me from exploding was going downstairs and doing more thinking and rethinking of this essay.

The Feminist Reviewer

Forty years ago Virginia Woolf, then a popular reviewer herself, advised periodicals to fire their literary critics. She regarded most reviews as superficial, useless or destructive. Her tongue was not fully in her cheek when she suggested, "Let the reviewers then abolish themselves, and resurrect themselves as doctors. The writer would then submit his work to the judge of his choice; an appointment would be made; an interview arranged. In strict privacy, and with some formality—the fee, however, would be enough to ensure that the interview did not degenerate into tea-table gossip—doctor and writer would meet; and for an hour they would consult upon the book in question."

A century before Woolf's epitaph for reviewers, Victorian men like Tennyson, Thackeray, and Dickens were squirming under the critic's eye. Dickens referred to reviewers in the Sunday papers as "rotten creatures with men's forms and devils' hearts [who] discharge their pigmy arrows." He vowed to overcome his rage by "being indifferent and bidding them whistle on."

Despite such wise caveats, I would like to make some arguments for the survival of the feminist reviewer. She is a support to authors and a reference for readers. Most importantly, she is a balance to the seemingly indestructible breed of critics who, although Dickens may have been wrong about the devils' hearts, usually do have men's forms.

Political Identities/Aesthetic Definitions

Literary criticism, whether it is disciplined scholarship or newspaper filler cribbed from the dust jackets, does affect the survival of authors, professionally and psychologically. Getting work published is only half the step. Many women publish books only to see them remaindered in three months due to lack of promotion. Good reviews increase initial sales. Bad reviews can kill a book before it surfaces. We know, for instance, that when *Of Woman Born* received a negative review in the *New York Times,* Adrienne Rich was dropped from a national television program

This essay originally appeared in the *New Women's Times Feminist Review* (now defunct), January 1979. Subsequently it was published in *Words in Her Pockets,* edited by Celeste West (Booklegger Press, 1985). Although aspects of the article are dated, it's worth including here as part of the record.

where she had been invited to discuss and promote the book. Feminist writing is particularly vulnerable in the reviewing mill because even those editors who deign to give the book a second look don't have adequate critical perspective to appreciate it. We can only speculate about the number of women and women's presses who have stopped producing. Certainly we can assume that if there had been a tradition of sensitive feminist reviewing to appreciate Sylvia Plath's poetry, her life might have been more bearable, perhaps even more livable.

The simplest definition of a feminist reviewer is someone who exposes feminist books and other books by women to the public in a serious way. The following pages contain statements about the goals of the feminist reviewer and about the tension of literary standards versus sisterly alliances in the development of feminist literature. These statements are personal, drawn from my extensive experience reviewing books and from having my own five books reviewed.

Feminist criticism requires an informed approach. We have a growing body of theoretical work in psychology, sociology, and politics, as well as creative writing from which we can draw insight and make parallels. A review of *The Mermaid and the Minotaur* is enriched with references to Juliet Mitchell and Phyllis Chesler. Who can imagine evaluating Brecht without a grounding in agitprop theatre? Likewise, an exposure to feminist culture helps us to understand and criticize the new work by women.

The feminist critic, however, need not restrict her consideration to books by women. If we want to understand our printed past and be able to influence our futures, we would do well to reread patriarchal literature from a feminist perspective. Certainly as reviewers we will first want to provide space for women's writing. But given that some male writers like Norman Mailer and Gore Vidal will always be reviewed, it is better that their books be criticized by someone who will discuss their sexism.

The feminist reviewer can function in several camps—writing occasional reviews of feminist books for various audiences; working for the feminist press; or reviewing widely in popular periodicals where she considers a broad range of writing from her special perspective.

The Critics' Critics

Some of the most persistent and vociferous attacks on feminist reviewing come from "objective critics" who demand that writing be judged according to literary standards, regardless of personal allegiance. They seem to forget that involved criticism was the seed of writing communities like Bloomsbury, the Black Mountain School, the Beats, and the salons at Stein's *rue de Fleurus* flat. Standards are not developed in a cultural vacuum; they are created in conversation and argument with peers. The most keen and subtle reviews often come from writers who not only agree on broad social goals like feminism, but who are close colleagues and friends. Their intimacy allows a refinement of understanding inaccessible to more detached readers. I am not advocating doing PR for friends; rather, exposing books which we truly admire. This is a sticky but necessary distinction.

The objective critics call for dispassion, distance, and textual analysis in the same pitch that journalism professors preach "two sides of the story." Those of us who inhabit the real world recognize that the editors' decisions in the selection of books to be reviewed, the hiring of reviewers, the treatment of copy and art work, the placement of pieces on the page are not unbiased decisions. Literary editors observe the same kind of objectivity that the BBC practices in its coverage of the IRA. The discrimination against feminist reviewers would be less outrageous if it were not couched in such hypocritical jargon.

Neither scholarship nor journalism is an antiseptic procedure. If we were to take the feminism from our criticism, we would also be lobotomizing our intelligence and vitality. Sometimes the feminist reviewer is an entrepreneur—part propagandist and part impresario. This does not mean that she is uncritical of women's work, but rather that she acknowledges the impact of her reviews and uses her position to promote a serious consideration of women's work. Certain objective critics value the "aesthetic" quality over social content. They advise us to disregard the sexist or racist material in "masterpieces" like *Light in August* or *In Our Time*. However, extracting the moral scrutiny from literary criticism denies the humanistic duty of the artist. And on the other hand, we can see that conscience is sometimes more perfected than craft. In the developing work of women writers, it is valuable to point up the quality of the theme, in tandem with the difficulties in technique. As artists, academics, and critics, we all write within the limitations of our culture and the momentum of our passions.

Other attacks on feminist critics come from the women's movement itself. How can you knock a sister? they demand. How can you presume to judge a woman's right to write? Isn't it elitist to distinguish between good feminist writers and not-so-good writers who are feminists? The questions are tinged with a certain matronizing protectiveness that implies the little women aren't ready for the big time. *The answers to these questions depend on the audience of the review.*

If we cannot be critical of women's writing within a constructive, supportive framework, then we deny their work respect and credibility. We don't want to burn our cheerleader skirts only to become rah-rah reviewers for the girls. The perfect book has not been written, much less the perfect feminist book. If we do not offer direction to our sisters, where are they going to get it? From William

Buckley or V. S. Pritchett? One model of conscientious feminist reviewing was Mary Daly's piece about *Of Woman Born* in the *Boston Real Paper* where she made considered, specific criticisms. Rich's response was gratitude, "We all have got to feel able to give books that serious kind of reviewing. But at the same time there is that problem of speaking in hostile territory. In territory where you are misquoted, quoted out of context, mangled, that is a very real liability."

Audience, then, is a prime consideration in deciding which books to present and how to present them. We may go into more detailed criticism in *Sinister Wisdom* or *off our backs* than in the *Seattle Times* because these journals give us more space and their readers are more likely to appreciate the constructive spirit (constructive to feminism, if not favorable to the book) and to understand the criticism itself. When I'm reviewing in the popular press, I sometimes decline to review women's books which I view unfavorably. There are too many good books that need the space.

Interpreting Feminist Forms

In conjunction with her work as apologist, impresario, and propagandist, the feminist critic serves as a mediator and interpreter of new forms of feminist writing. A primary task is distinguishing between women's literature and feminist literature. Once the cries of "secretarian" have died down, consider that this is no rhetorical exclusion. It is a serious demarcation, much like the debate about women's studies and feminist studies at our universities. Clearly, we can identify some women's books, like *The Total Woman,* as nonfeminist or even antifeminist. But what do we do about those books which have feminist sympathies, like *Simone Weil, A Life* by Simone Petrement or *Changing* by Liv Ullman? What about those books which are promoted as feminist, like Erica Jong's *How to Save Your Own Life,* but which may be offensive to us? Surely we want to make these distinctions for public clarity, as well as for our own sense of identity and direction. When the Feminist Writers Guild negotiated an end to the feminist boycott of *Mother Jones Magazine* in 1977, it demanded that a quota of *explicitly* feminist articles be run. The critic must be watchful that her editor does not read "feminist" as "female" and deluge her with unwanted galleys.

Feminist interpretation discusses the new form in women's literature. Just as the Marxist critic might be taken with the strains of epic theatre, the feminist critic (or the Black-feminist-Marxist critic) is aware of the female contours. Works like Monique Wittig's *Les Guerillieres,* June Arnold's *The Cook and the Carpenter,* or Alice Walker's *You Can't Keep a Good Woman Down* are impossible to appreciate without some grounding in feminist issues and literary traditions which a good critic can provide her readers. A close review of contemporary literature reveals familiar threads like the hovering metaphor of witches and goddesses, the symbolic use of clothing, and the vision of poetry as a sharing medium rather than a didactic one. We are particularly aware of themes of discovery, celebration, and rebirth. Likewise, the development of the journal as a separate literary genre comes partially from the women's movement's validation of personal experience.

So much of our critical direction has been to reveal how literature fails to portray us—from the suppression of our own work to the stereotyping of female characters and roles. However, there is as much to find out about ourselves in our literature as there is to discard of the old regime.

Strategies

If reviewing is a political activity as well as an aesthetic endeavor, we should descend from the more rarefied considerations to discuss strategy. What are the tactics for getting our books reviewed and our reviews printed?

We might have expected feminist writers to have earned some canniness with their battle scars, but most of us still suffer from the great American romance about writing. We equate being published with being read, and we wait for our audience to respond. The sad truth is that we often have to work as hard to get our books reviewed as we did writing them and getting them published. Even when publishers actually attempt to do promotion, books often wind up in a reviewer's valise on the way to the secondhand bookstore.

First, authors should carefully scrutinize and become as involved as possible in their publishers' promotional campaigns. To whom are they sending review copies? Is there any follow-up? Are they placing ads in appropriate venues? Have they considered the special appeal to the women's movement in our periodicals such as *Feminist Review, Motheroot, Azalea, Onyx,* etc? Have they arranged book parties at local bookstores? What the publishers have not done will be left in our laps, so it's wise to talk to other writers and learn about the possibilities. Local coverage, especially for non–New York writers, may require us to find out who does the reviews, who specializes in women's books. If no one does specialize, we can make suggestions and start submitting feminist reviews ourselves. We should try to do as many readings and/or speaking engagements as we can. We can send out press clippings about ourselves and our books. This is not the time to become shy or coy about selling our wares. In the publishing world, the passive voice is mute.

Despite all these exhortations to go out and be a feminist reviewer, I must admit to the pitfalls, which are financial, emotional, and political. Once the publications for which we write detect the direction of our writing, they may try to stem the feminist flow with contrary books. (One paper recently sent me a hearty memoir of a British soldier of fortune in Patagonia and a maudlin little story about a boy and his grandfather who race pigeons together.) The publications may terminate our nonexistent contracts altogether. In touchy situations, of course, we can't always tell what's going on. They may ask us to review feminist material and then feign surprise or offense at our work. When the literary editor of the *Economist* asked me to review *Housewife* and *The Sociology of Housework* by Ann Oakley, I was delighted. I was less delighted when, upon submitting the piece, I was asked by the editor whether the author was "Miss" or "Mrs." Oakley.

"It's Dr. Oakley," I explained. "She wrote the book as a sociologist."

"Quite so," he said. "But is it 'Miss' or 'Mrs?'"

"I don't think that's relevant."

"The books are about housework."

"You don't have to be married to do housework."

"If you're going to be stubborn about it, my dear."

Eventually, he ran the review with the "Dr." intact. This reviewer had run out of tact. It was the last piece I did for the *Economist*.

Sometimes we are tempted to give up writing for the straight press. We are tempted to write only for women's magazines where our reviews can be both more explicit and more subtle, where they are granted more space and receive more appreciation. The arguments against this temptation are various. First, we limit our audience. The roles of mediator, interpreter, propagandist, and impresario are not as crucial in the feminist press. The development of a women's critical forum is essential, but it serves a different purpose from the exposure of feminist literature in the mass media. Ideally, feminist critics can sharpen their perspectives by moving between camps.

In conjunction with supporting the feminist press, we must not lose sight of our right to be paid by the commercial press for our professional work. Retreating completely into women's periodicals raises economic problems. We cannot subsist on our sisters' approbation. The double jackpot of feminist reviewing is that it can support the work of two women at once—the author and the reviewer—helping them both to survive by their writing.

The Collective Critic

Reviews in the Sunday papers, mass magazines, feminist periodicals, or academic journals are usually addressed to the consumer, not the author. The focus of most reviewing is to make critical points rather than to nurture creativity.

Virginia Woolf's ideal critic would present an impossible expense for most writers. But she approaches a serious suggestion with her attention to the author's need for editing and guidance. One version of the critic as consultant has developed naturally out of feminist collectivity in the form of writing groups.

These groups are perhaps our most vital means of reviewing and being reviewed. From this regular criticism of my writing, I have learned about style, grappled with political issues, and found the courage necessary to continue writing. The work that has been produced by these groups is the unshakable testimony to the life-giving properties of feminist reviewing.

Going to the Fair

It all began last November when I received an enthusiastic letter, my name written in pink ink under a purple letterhead, inviting me to participate in "The First Ever International Feminist Book Fair" in London. I was asked to reply by 28 October. The tardy, enthusiastic letter was in many ways a sign of things to come— the passion, the disorganization, the surprises, the frustrations of reaching across different cultures. I wrote back immediately, excited about the prospects of discussing feminist aesthetics with writers from all over the world and of returning to a city where I used to live.

Now, a month later, I am still stimulated by the event, delighted by what I learned and hopeful that there will be a second fair next year. Nairobi seems an ideal place: the fair might draw more Third World writers and would coincide with the UN Decade for Women Conference. If there were any theme to the London Fair, it would be communication between writers and readers. Unlike such publishing institutions as the American Booksellers Association or the Frankfurt International Book Fair, which discourage participation by "nonindustry" people, the Feminist Book Fair welcomed readers, teachers, students, and reviewers as well as writers, publishers, editors, and printers to consider their mutual pursuits.

The Fair consisted of three phases: a large display of books at Jubilee Hall in Covent Garden; a series of satellite readings and talks about such issues as the reviewing of feminist books and the publishing of Black women's books; and beyond London, an array of local readings, signings, and talks in many British cities. Since this marathon was a personal experience as well as a political and professional enterprise, the clearest way I can describe it all is through the spectrum of my own rich, bewildering ten days "on the road."

Wednesday, 6 June: London

7 P.M.: "Tales I Tell My Publisher" Panel at the Institute for Contemporary Art. I've been invited to speak about feminist writing with the four other authors of *Tales I Tell My Mother.* This is the first time in eight years that we have all been

---

This essay originally appeared in the *Women's Review of Books,* October 1984. Subsequent International Feminist Book Fairs were held in Oslo (1986), Montreal (1988), and Barcelona (1990).

together, so it's wonderful to see Sara Maitland, Michele Roberts, Michelene Wandor, and Zoë Fairbairns.

The five of us are meant to talk about our experiences in feminist publishing since the appearance of our fictional documentary of the women's movement. In the last six years we have collectively published twenty-seven books, most of which are displayed at the table next to the stage. The tone of the evening is self-congratulatory, but in a generally non-offensive way: Michelene asks us which is our favorite book. The question annoys me because I can't answer it. Everyone else is happy to select a special book. I can only stammer that, as my mother says of her children, I like my four novels equally.

Zoë then makes some startling criticisms about the ways women writers are often exploited by feminist presses. She outlines the practice of paying below average royalties while editors make their living from the work. There are noticeable twitches and coughs in the audience. I discuss the relationship between writers and readers. In the middle of my description of a sadomasochistic connection between artist and audience in which readers often expect authors to be alcoholic or insane or suicidal as proof of or penance for their art, Sara pulls a face, dramatically acting the part of the looney novelist and bringing down the house. After we have each nattered on a little, the audience asks questions. A woman in the front row wants to know why we have moved from feminist presses to more mainstream houses. We all answer that we have gone back and forth between straight and political presses, depending on the book. The evening concludes with readings from our new work, revealing the very different directions we have taken since the fiction in *Tales*.

Thursday, 7 June

The exhibit area in Jubilee Hall is chaotic in early afternoon. Someone has lost the floor plan. It must all get settled by 4 P.M., when the press arrives. Meanwhile, my eyes are awash with logos: BattleAxe, Murphy Sisters, Onlywomen, Press Gang, Redress, Sheba, Wild and Woolly, Giovanni's Room, Kitchen Table Women of Color, Zed Press. I see publishers from Zimbabwe and Germany and Ireland and Australia and Spain and make plans to visit each one of them in depth over the next few days. "Hello, Valerie!" A voice from behind. It is Hannemieke, my old friend from Holland. We embrace, have a Coke, make plans to meet the next day at the Methuen booth. I see Zoë across the floor and friends from the Women's Press. "Hello Valerie!" It is Sharon Le Bell, a former student of mine who is now editing at Harper and Row. We make a date to meet the next day at the Journeyman booth. I'm beginning to feel at home.

Friday, 8 June

At 10:30, the stairs are crowded with people waiting to get into the Fair. At the entrance, a woman has set up a table protesting that the Fair is inaccessible to women in wheelchairs. Many women have signed the petition. A number have refused to enter. The organizers say they thought a lift was going to be installed.

The floor is crowded. I make my way to the booth where Methuen has stacked many copies of my new novel, *Winter's Edge*. A few people come by and pick up the book and put it down again. I feel like a painter exhibiting my work along Hyde Park railings. One woman comes by for a long chat about feminist drama. She places her shopping basket on top of my books. After about ten minutes of talking with the editors about various plays, she notices the large picture of me and me sitting next to it. "Oh, you're Valerie Miner," she says. "Yes," I smile cordially. "And where are your books?" she asks. "Underneath your basket," I say. "Oh," she picks up the book. "It looks very interesting." She sets it down and leaves.

Hannemieke comes by. She buys a book. We talk about her work. She sells 50–60,000 copies of her novels in Holland and cannot get them translated into English. In many ways, I realize this is an Anglophone fair. If you don't write in English or if your work isn't translated, you don't exist as a feminist writer. I introduce her to my editor, in hopes of sparking mutual interest.

I wander around the floor. The Zimbabwe Publishing House exhibit is fascinating. They emphasize history, politics, and education. Two Black women and a white woman have come here to lecture about Zimbabwean writers and to peddle books. Since literacy is so restricted, they tend to be fairly utilitarian in what they publish. The Women's List, edited by Kathy Bond-Stewart, is called "Women of Africa" and focuses on three areas: handbooks for practical use in organizing or in learning languages; volumes of creative writing, including Bertha Msora's play, *I Will Wait;* and books of theory which they hope will broaden the now generally white, middle-class world of feminist scholarship. The press, which started in 1981, now has over fifty books on its list.

An announcement sears over the loudspeaker that poet Audre Lorde is signing books. I have wanted to meet her for a long time, so I stand in a queue while eager women tell her their life stories. As I wait, I see she is wearing a close fitting T-shirt, revealing that she has had a breast removed. My admiration for her courage soars. I stand in line a while longer, being pushed and shoved by eager visitors to nearby booths. I decide it will be easier to meet her in New York.

Another press which catches my heart is Stramullion, a Scottish feminist publishing collective founded in 1980. Stramullion is an old Scots word for strong woman. They have published four books: *Moll Cutpurse* by Ellen Galford, a novel about a wild seventeenth-century "Roaring Girl" who laughs down the rich and oppressive, *Incest, Fact and Myth,* by Sarah Nelson, *Hens in the Hay,* poems by Scots women, *The Rime of the Ancient Feminist* by Stephanie Markman, a satire of Coleridge.

The loudspeaker crackles across the room with announcements in English, German, and French about the sale of tickets for tonight's panel. Despite the festive ambience, the Fair doesn't float in unqualified sisterly idealism. Some women complain that there are too many North Americans being published by British houses. The British Black women are delighted to see books by Alice Walker, Toni Cade Bambara, and Maya Angelou, but they want to know where are the books by Black *British* women. Others complain that there are too many Americans of all colors on the panels. In response, the U.S. presses ask why they have been relegated to the last row of the exhibit. They say it's all very well to indicate that there are too many Americans, but why were they invited? And why has the British movement relied so heavily on American ideas and momentum? Meanwhile, people from all countries are irritated that the evening events are almost completely booked before the opening of the fair. London women have monopolized tickets weeks in advance. Black women say too many white women have tickets. Lesbians assert that there are not enough lesbians on the panels.

It is time to quit for the day. I meet Barbara Wilson, a writer and editor at the Seal Press, from Seattle, and we wander off to dinner at an Indian restaurant. It is fun to gossip about more domestic matters—our partners, our writing, our publishers. We get smoked out of the restaurant by an overeager tandoori chef, but the conflagration seems minor compared to the intensity of the book fair. We spend the evening at the lesbian panel, hearing readings by Suniti Namjoshi from India and Canada, Gerd Brantenberg from Norway, Nicole Brossard from Quebec, and Audre Lorde from the United States. And in a touching tribute to American poet Judy Grahn, an actor reads her poetry for half an hour. There is something refreshing about absorbing this "live" literature after running around the floor all day where people are talking about reviewing and printing and subsidiary rights. We need events like this.

Monday, 11 June: Cambridge

My publisher rings to say that a young woman from the Cambridge University student paper wants to interview me about *Winter's Edge.* Is it OK if she comes in half an hour? Sure, I say, that's what I'm here for. I make her tea and set the table with cookies and Sarah Green appears spot on time. She looks tired and cranky and says she has "managed to skim" my book. Not a great start. But she has skimmed it rather closely, has pulled out some good quotes. We have a decent discussion about old age, capitalism, and feminist style until it is time for me to go to the Cambridge Evening News and Radio Cambridge for more interviews where the reporters also haven't had the "opportunity" to read the book. They are more interested in having me define the term "feminist writer."

That evening our reading is at Carpenter Hall. We all help set up chairs for the event. After everything is organized, I go to the back room and sit with the other speakers, British novelist and poet Elaine Feinstein, Italian novelist and screenwriter Dacia Maraini, and American Joy Magezis, who is finishing her first novel. We are all a little nervous, a little leery of each other, but generally good cheer prevails.

The readings are magnificent. I'm very moved by Dacia's *Woman at War,* about a young schoolteacher caught in a claustrophobic affair with a brutal, confused man. This is the fifth of her six novels to be translated into English. Elaine reads from her dramatic book about World War II, *The Border,* a delicate blend of humor and tragedy. Joy reads from her novel about a young American woman surviving the New Left. I read from *Winter's Edge.* The audience is enthusiastic in its response to everyone.

During the discussion I am taken aback by the differences between British and American feminism. Several people in the audience ask why we call ourselves feminist. Why don't we just identify as women writers? Elaine agrees and says that writing is writing. Dacia disagrees, arguing that translating the power of women's experience into words is a feminist act. Joy tries to calm down the audience by declaring that not all feminists are lesbians. I counter that as a lesbian I think it's vital to recognize how many feminists are lesbians. "Why labels?" one woman persists. I suggest that everyone has labels, for instance the woman whose jacket flap says, "She attended Oxford, is married and lives with her husband, two children and dog in Essex" is using a label. People laugh. We all discuss distinctions between didactic writing and political writing. Patriarchy. Form. Traditions of female writing. Elaine asks why we have anthologies of female writers, since there are no anthologies of male writers. She is greeted with laughter and readily admits her error. I find the discussion invigorating, although sometimes I feel I am back in 1975. It is a good-natured row and by the end of the evening, Elaine declares herself a feminist. We could talk on and on. The audience is eager. The speakers are primed. But the hall has to close. Always a good note on which to end. We sell lots of books.

Afterward at Joy's house, Dacia talks about how hard it is to get serious reviews for women's books in Italy. She says she makes her living from her writing, with a combination of scripts and books. Joy and I bemoan the state of American publishing which forces most writers to have a second job. Dacia explains that while feminism is popular in her country now, there are many older women writers in their sixties and seventies who are still overlooked. She explains how she has fought to get her books translated into English.

Tuesday, 12 June: Traveling North

I take the train to Sunderland to visit Zoë Fairbairns, whom I have known since the *Tales* group convened nine years ago. Having just read her new novel, *Here Today,* I am eager to talk with her about it. I am particularly impressed by her descriptions of friendship and class. I wonder about the conclusion, though, where Antonia decides to join the police force. The police force? What is Zoë doing with that? I shall have to ask.

On the train ride, I study the Book Fair catalogue's fascinating collection of articles about publishing in the United Kingdom, India, Zimbabwe, the Nordic countries, and the United States.

The Indian writer, Urvashi Butalia, notes that although India ranks third (after the United States and the United Kingdom) in the number of books published in English each year, the number of women authors is minimal. Aside from male control of the publishing houses, one of the major problems is that most Indian titles come from academia where women are poorly represented. Another obstacle is that, unlike the United Kingdom and the United States where women comprise the majority of readers, the number of literate Indian women is very low. Butalia believes change will come, and she is contributing to that change with her involvement in Kali, a feminist press. Kali, named after the Black goddess who destroys and then creates out of destruction, reminds me of Virago, the English press, Stramullion, the Scottish collective, and Spinster's Ink, the American publisher. In addition to producing more books by women, Kali is training women to print, thereby opening up a traditionally male profession. They will publish books in English and Hindi.

Wednesday, 13 June: Edinburgh and Glasgow

I take an early morning train to Edinburgh for more interviews before this evening's reading. I'm beginning to feel like Jane Fonda, only not as healthy. This ride through the border country, where the land suddenly flows greener and the accents of new passengers are more musical, is a familiar, favorite journey. It is hard to concentrate on these Book Fair articles, but there is so much to learn. Runa Haukaa writes about feminist publishing in the Nordic countries, where readers have to overcome the barriers of seven languages. It is often easier to find books from the United States than from neighboring nations. Haukaa estimates that 30 percent of the published writers in the Nordic countries are women. In 1979 women, protesting the fact that no woman had ever received the Nordic Council's Literary Prize, established an alternative award and honored Marta Tikkanen for her book *Arhundradets Karlekssaga (The Love Legend of the Century)*. The book is now translated into seven languages and has just been published by Capra Press in the United States.

I am to go to Glasgow to do a half-hour appearance on "The Ken Bruce Show," a program listened to by "all of Glasgow." I do not feel like being listened to by all of Glasgow. I feel like lying down and recovering from my bronchitis. When I finally arrive at the radio station, I am told that I have to wait forty minutes and that I will be on the air for ten minutes. So much for Glasgow's adventure in feminist fiction. Finally, I'm led into the studio where a charming man tries to calm me down by telling me that Darth Vader sat in that very chair last week and was petrified. I want to tell him I am not nervous, I am exasperated. However, my Scottish mother supervenes and I am polite.

Ken Bruce organizes the feed-in from Aberdeen, where another writer, Moira Duff, who has just published her first novel with the Women's Press, will be speaking. The interview goes well until he asks what it means to be a feminist. Moira insists she isn't a feminist, that it's embarrassing enough to have a book published by the Women's Press. "It's one thing to call yourself a feminist in London or America, but it's quite another to say it in Aberdeen. People here think feminists are seed-chewing lesbians driving tractors." I answer that it takes nerve to call yourself a feminist wherever you are. Ken Bruce is at first baffled, then delighted by this small frisson. Eventually, he intervenes with some questions about our books—which he clearly has not read—and about the Feminist Book Fair. Then he puts on a snappy piece of muzak, takes off his earphones, and thanks me for a fine interview. I travel back to Edinburgh, wondering what all this has to do with being a writer.

I walk from Waverley Station to the evening reading, thinking how my mother grew up in this neighborhood. They have torn down her street to install a traffic roundabout. I begin to cry. What will the women in the audience think if I arrive in tears?

Tonight Zoë and I are reading together. This is fun because we can talk about our friendship and our mutual influence on each other's work. After the readings, questions. One woman wants to know if there is room for men in feminism. We wind up in a long discussion about the role of men in feminist change. Zoë is more polite than I. On the train back to Sunderland we drink beer and tell ourselves not to run the tape of the evening through our heads. We reassure each other. We wonder at the vehemence of the questions about men in the women's movement. We drink more beer and grow quiet. Arriving at 1:30 A.M., neither of us can sleep. Zoë opens a can of baked beans, makes some toast and we become five-year-old pals.

Thursday, 14 June: Newcastle and Sunderland

I go to Newcastle early in the morning for more interviews. When I arrive at the radio station, I'm told that their other guests are a woman talking about antiques and a man discussing local travel. The disc jockey eagerly greets me as "Val," inquiring after my health. Clearly, he does not see Jane Fonda. Then he confesses that he hasn't read *Winter's Edge,* although he is "quite familiar with it." He begins the interview by getting the title wrong and by mixing up the main characters. I gently correct him and answer his piercing question, "What is a feminist?" I wonder what it's like for Adrienne Rich. Does she subject herself to such horrors? Maybe Jane Austen was right about hiding her fiction under the blotter.

This afternoon Zoë and I walk along the beach and the beautiful, blue day calms me down. I consider how much I value this friendship as we talk about our families and our work again. She is one of my closest friends, although—perhaps because—we live six thousand miles apart. We have some good laughs to ease away the nervousness of tonight's event.

This evening Manny Shirazi and I will be doing a reading at the Sunderland Arts Center, introduced by Zoë. During dinner, Manny talks about the complications of being a "Black" woman in Britain. I am surprised that most women of color, including Middle Eastern women like Manny, refer to themselves as "Black." She is disappointed that there is not more representation by Black British women in the Book Week. Manny also talks about her job as an editor of *Spare Rib* magazine, which has developed a strong editorial commitment against racism. It's interesting to observe how much more race-conscious the British women's movement has become in the last three years. I used to find the white British women supercilious about racism as "an American problem." Manny talks about the positive response her book, *Javady Alley,* has received. It's an autobiographical novel about a seven-year-old girl in Iran in 1953.

The room fills slowly. This is one of those events when you wonder if anyone is going to attend. (I remember a gig in San Francisco where no one showed and the four writers read to each other.) Gradually most of the fifty seats are taken. I read first, then Manny, then we open it up to questions. A man at the back challenges our assertion that writing is work. Both Manny and I say the notion of writing as privilege is antediluvian, class-bound, and dangerous. He is dissatisfied, enlisting Ezra Pound as an example of someone who didn't view art as labor. Other members of the audience make points about race and cooperative forms of publishing and reviewing and the connection between politics and literature. It is a good discussion. Still, I am relieved when Zoë calls an end to it.

People buy books, come up to chat and agree and disagree. Finally it is over. We drive back to Zoë's house to feast on fish and chips and champagne.

The next morning I set off on holiday for the wilds of Skye and the Outer Hebrides where probably no one will ask me to define "feminist." I hug Zoë and tell her I love her. Packing the car, I notice that the largest parcel contains books, papers, leaflets, programs, reviews, and essays I have collected. And I know that the Fair is not really over.

The Last Peace March

They said it would be the last peace march. Peace was at hand. The treaty would be signed that week. I marched because I believed—in my most optimistic soul— that it *was* the last peace march. I marched because I believed—in my most realistic head—that there would never be a last peace march. I don't know why I went.

I didn't want to go. I wanted to stay home that day last January and do all the writing and correcting and reading that had defined my life in the last year. But I couldn't stay home. Perhaps I went out of a faith in ceremonies. Public proclamations of principle. After twenty-five years in the Catholic Church, the march was a profession of faith. Not faith in the imminence of peace, but faith in the justice of peace. In fact, when I didn't go to Mass the next morning, one of the small excuses I offered myself was the march.

I don't know how many antiwar demonstrations I've supported here in Toronto or back in California. My cynical self says "not enough." As an American immigrant in Canada, marches are as much a part of my cultural identity as *festas* are for immigrants from Italy. Anyway, responsibility for the fire in Indochina has spread beyond the American border; the war is a Canadian issue, too. I suppose I really expected marches and chants and speeches and news reports to change the world a few years ago. I expected the November 1969 Moratorium to change things. Thousands of people marching across San Francisco to Golden Gate Park. Crosby, Stills, Nash, and Young telling us we were going to start a revolution. I wonder if they believed it. I did. And in the sense that I don't want to be a liberal cop-out, I still believe it. A little.

So after all those years of working my conscience into a thoroughly muddled state, I should know something about marches. For instance, they never start on time. Yet when I realized I was going to be late, I flew out the door, worried the subway down to my stop, and then raced to the Metropolitan United Church. Inside, four hundred people sat listening to speeches. A warm-up. An examination of conscience. It lasted another forty-five minutes.

This essay first appeared under the title "The Hopelessness of the Long Distance Peace Marcher" in *Saturday Night*, April 1973. This article testifies to the commonalities between fiction and nonfiction. It was republished in 1982, virtually unchanged—as a chapter in my novel *Movement*. As this book goes to press, the U.S. government is giving us yet another chance to participate in the last peace march.

Rhetoric. Did these phrases *ever* mean anything? "Fighting imperialism in the people's struggle" was almost as meaningful as "life, liberty, and the pursuit of happiness." It was a common bond, this rhetoric, perhaps only because we had heard it all before. We knew the platitudes by rote—the middle-aged minister who spoke first and the young socialist bureaucrat who spoke last. Peace and self-determination for all mankind. Amen. Right on. Folded hands. Clenched fists.

But the woman who spoke in the middle, the small gray-haired Montreal nurse who had worked in Vietnam during the Tet Offensive, offered more than rhetoric. She gave figures about Canadian complicity in the war. She tied the Indochinese fighting to other struggles, "I don't know if I'm the first woman to speak from this pulpit, but I know that I won't be the last." From her introduction to her conclusion, she offered informed, intelligent interpretation. She seemed more interested in peace than rubric. An intricate balance when facing hundreds of self-righteous people.

The people didn't look any different. Mostly young, blue-jeaned, like me. Their hair was longer and their clothes thicker; otherwise they looked like the same people with whom I marched in San Francisco three years before. The poor kids—students and at least temporarily committed revolutionaries—wore faded sweaters and rotting shoes. The "weekend working class" insulated themselves in sixty-dollar army-green parkas. The marshals—veterans of other marches—bore red arm-bands. The photographers—everyone is a photographer now—aimed Nikons and Pentaxes at the speakers and listeners. And there was that little man from CKEY who pinned a large red "Press" sign on the lapel of his camel coat to ward off suspicions of his *personal* involvement. Freaks in peacoats and linty mufflers passed the silver collection plates for publicity funds as the radical speakers challenged us from the stained-glass sanctuary. A compromise of images and ideologies.

Out in the vestibule, several leftist groups had set up propoganda tables. The Vanguard Bookstore man peddled inspirations from Marx, Che, Engels, Trotsky. Friends greeted each other after long holiday absences. I recognized several feminists, a *Guerilla* reporter, the lawyer for a political refugee, a friend of a friend who writes Young Socialist articles, a Cabbagetown teacher, the editor of an American exile magazine, and several nameless people I see at every demonstration.

We grouped together outside the church. After sitting inside for forty-five minutes of hot-tempered sermons, walking out into the January winds was a cold shock. I wanted to march with the women's contingent, so I looked around for a few appropriate signs—"In solidarity with our Vietnamese sisters;" "Women against the war"—and a few familiar faces.

"Did you hear the woman's speech? She got the biggest applause," grinned Stephanie.

"Yeah, it was the best one," answered Sandy. "She spoke English instead of rhetoric. She really brought out some useful facts."

We talked about how it was always the same. Not only the same rhetoric and the same people but the same signs: "End Canadian Complicity." The same destination, the U.S. consulate. The same chants, "Stop the bombing; stop the war." Actually, the litany changed somewhat today, abridging recent headlines: "One point peace plan; no Canadian troops." And when one group started, "Ho, Ho, Ho Chi Minh..." several women interrupted with "Madame, Madame, Madame Binh, Madame Binh is going to win."

We crashed the Saturday afternoon shopping scene with our procession of signs and posters. Shoppers rendered different reactions: support, laughter, aversion, anger. More were with than against us. One old drunk who had wandered over from the Fred Victor Mission picked up a placard, "End U.S. aggression," and joined the chanting. By the time we reached Queen and Yonge streets, the contingents had lost their identities. The women's group was jostled into the Evangelicals for Social Action, the NDP, and the Harbord Collegiate Student Council. I recognized one woman and asked her where the rest of the group went. She shrugged her shoulders, "Who knows?"

"Oh, you have an American accent," I said, trying to start a conversation.

"Yes, I'm afraid so. It's not a very pleasant thing to be an American." She was an older woman, forty-five or fifty. Shiny white hair pulled back into a ponytail. A social worker. She brought her teenage kids north last year. Not my stereotype expatriate. "Canada gives you so much more of a chance at life," she said, "You just can't live in the States anymore. I've tried to change things there. Why, I remember marching in the Korean war protest twenty years ago..."

"But don't you regret coming? You must have some friends, relatives left?"

"Yes, but I don't regret coming. Not one bit."

I was explaining that I immigrated two-and-a-half years ago, a veteran of student activism in graduate school and three years teaching in the inner city. Suddenly we were interrupted by the crowd moving into the road, wending their way through stalled traffic, up Yonge Street. "Good, they're taking the streets," she said with a trace of huskiness in her voice. We moved together off the sidewalk, but remained close to the curb. The people in the cars looked startled at first. Then they began to wave.

"It's like a three-dimensional drive-in movie for them," I said, surveying the amused faces behind the windshields.

"But look." She pointed. "They're smiling. If this happened in the States, they'd be scowling and cursing. See, that's a difference between the countries for you right there."

We didn't occupy the street for long before the policemen and their horses ushered us back on the sidewalk. This was different from the States too. No real confrontation. No tear gas or helicopters or bayonets, as in my Berkeley days. These uniformed equestrians weren't hunting foxes, and we knew they could use their horses against us. But they didn't provoke the marchers by their very appearance, the way American police always did.

While we made our way through the shoppers, the older woman and I talked about the defensiveness of Americans in Canada. I suggested that many radical Americans were just as chauvinistic as Republican businessmen. She didn't agree.

"Well, I think you're right," interjected the woman who was holding up one end of the Women's Place banner. "A lot of leftists think they know everything because they're American. They try to take over the Canadian movement. I know. I'm an American, myself."

The older woman and I didn't divulge our identities, leaving the illusion that there were at least *some* Canadians in the procession.

As we walked by the cluster of stereo and camera shops near Dundas Street, a young man shouted, "So what do Canadians have to do with the bloody war?" The woman with the banner explained that over 400 Canadian companies made parts for the U.S. Defense Department. "Well, you gotta have a job somehow." As he argued, his Newfoundland accent grew thicker. I noticed that he was missing five front teeth. "Sure, but there are better ways to make money," I shouted back. Later, I realized how hollow that dogma must have sounded to the Newfoundlander.

"Stop the bombing; stop the war." "Stop the bombing; stop the war." While we marched, a sound truck followed and led our chants. An electronic cheerleader. Somehow, I couldn't get involved. Shouting slogans reminded me of high school basketball games, "We can do it; we can do it if we rea-a-aly try." The effects seemed comparable.

I found an odd sense of loneliness in all this community spirit. Once I lost my friends in the crowd, I walked for blocks "in solidarity" without talking to the person next to me. A congregation of strangers. I suppose that's why I started talking to the older woman. But after a while, after we exchanged enough clichés about the war and expatriation and Americans and Canadians, I wanted to move away from her. I started listening to conversations around me.

A pepper-haired man who looked well-groomed enough to sit at the head of a board table was arguing with a guy who caricatured the classic graduate student with his scraggly beard and bloodshot eyes.

"Don't you think you're a little presumptuous, telling the North Vietnamese how to negotiate—all this one point peace plan stuff?" asked the boardroom liberal. "Why don't you let them decide for themselves?"

"I'm just supporting what I believe," answered the student. "Canadians don't belong in there. A negotiated settlement with peacekeeping forces is just a stall for Thieu. The only way for the country to be run by its citizens is for the U.S. to get the hell out altogether."

"I don't know about that. Or about this business of victory to the NLF. I mean the NLF isn't the only North Vietnamese government. Ah, well, I suppose that we don't have to agree on everything. The main thing is to end this damn war."

The procession continued in a series of vignettes: In front of me a two-year-old cried in her mother's arms. "Why don't you take her for a while, Gerry?" "Okay, sugar, you wanta come to Daddy?" He exchanged his placard for his daughter. A small boy carried a homemade sign, "Victory to the Vietnamese Revolution." He was accompanied by a rather unrevolutionary mother wearing a fur hat and a leather coat. Two freaks were filming the march from a car near Queen's Park. "It looks great," one of them said to nobody in particular. "The march must be a mile long." The older woman had found another companion. "You know, I did a stupid thing today," she said. "I wore tennis shoes and my feet are freezing. You'd think I'd know better after all my experience. I marched against the Korean War." I wondered if she told everyone about her long history of protest. A small red-faced man was talking about Belfast bombings with a young woman. As I moved closer to listen, the woman stared at me suspiciously. She told the man to be quiet and mumbled something about the FBI. So much for my feeling of solidarity.

The procession approached the American consulate. The litany grew louder, "One point peace plan; U.S. out now." The signs rocked above our heads, "End Canadian Complicity"; "Stop Phallic Imperialism." That last one was carried by a radical lesbian.

The big white consulate building was guarded by fifteen or sixteen pale policemen. Four cops in a row wore regulation-small moustaches. They reminded me of my little brother's toy soldiers: slim, handsome, straight, patriotic, inflexible. A small crowd marched in a circle in front of the toy soldiers. One protester raised his fist each time he passed the TV cameras. The rest of us just waited. I think I saw a man watching us through an upstairs consulate window. But perhaps that was another time, another place. My memory for marches wasn't as good as the older woman's. The sound truck arrived with the speakers. The MC explained that the march was a cooperative effort and that representatives of ten different groups were going to speak.

But who needed to hear them? As I headed for the subway, the Evangelical for Social Action was shouting, "Nixon may have postponed the bombing of North Vietnam for a while, but the South is experiencing more bombing than ..." I didn't wait for the rest, to be told that the fires in Cambodia and Laos would rage long after an ineffectual treaty was signed in Vietnam. I knew, everyone knew, that was what it was all about. This march. And the one before that. And the one before that.

A brief walk on a brisk January day. A time to meet friends, to vent anger, to call for peace. A veritable liturgy. "Lamb of God who takest away the sins of the world, grant us peace." Perhaps the marches, like the sacraments, are catharses in themselves. Offering sanctifying grace, moral support. Meanwhile in the faraway land of power, Richard Nixon prepared for his million dollar inaugural ball. And in the faraway land of bombings, Indochinese women watched their children being ripped to shreds. Here, in the land of official observers, we had pretended to serve in the last peace march.

The Rape of Cinderella

Tonight, live from the studios of CFTO-TV in Toronto, it's the twenty-sixth annual Miss Canada Pageant. The big moment is just a heartbeat away . . .

This promises to be a very special night, not only for our twenty-eight beautiful princesses, but we hope for you as well. In less than ninety minutes the new Miss Canada for 1973 will be chosen and this magnificent crown will symbolize the grace, beauty and charm of the girl who. . . .

Miss Canada is a television program. The pageant is owned by Cleo Productions, which is owned by CFTO Television. It earns $216,000 for commercial air time alone. Miss Canada is also a public relations gimmick. In return for her awards, she does publicity stints for Swift's meats, Rexall Drug Company, Exquisite Form underwear. CFTO rakes in the appearance fees. Miss Canada is a commercial grotesquerie. And everyone knows Miss Canada is Camp.

Well, not everyone. Not necessarily the 3.5 million viewers who make the pageant the highest-rated single production in Canadian television. Not the 1,000 women who enter preliminary beauty contests from Newfoundland to British Columbia. Not the twenty-eight princesses who await the judges' decision. For some of them, at least, the Miss Canada Pageant is an important event.

The pageant celebrates the ideal Canadian woman as a chaperoned princess wearing a $10,000 chinchilla coat, using Helena Rubenstein makeup to cover her pimples and clichés to cover her ideas, smiling her way from trade show to convention to trade show.

Perhaps you can dismiss those millions of viewers as children and menopausal parents, but those twenty-eight young women puzzle me. Why would women my age want to be Miss Canada? How do they get people from my freaky, political, ecological, liberated, hip generation to pose in bikinis under banana and avocado facials for press pictures? I tried to find out by following the twenty-eight contestants through their twelve days of pageant rehearsals and receptions. I watched them

---

This essay was written in late 1972 and originally appeared in *Saturday Night,* February 1973. When I reread this article, I think I was too hard on the young women I interviewed. Then I remember that I was equally young at the time—young enough to be mistaken for a "regional princess" at one point in the pageant. Perhaps we should forgive ourselves for being young.

being coiffed, painted, fitted, paraded, posed, and pushed. I think I know how CFTO creates mannequins out of live women, but I'm still wondering why the women volunteer for the ritual.

And here they are, ladies and gentlemen. The twenty-eight contestants . . . tonight is the crowning event in a search that's been going on all across the country during this past year . . . to find the girl with the winning combination of beauty, grace, and charm, qualities needed to wear the crown of Miss Canada.

Pat Mazurick is speeding down Highway 427 in her pink Pinto-for-a-year which, according to the sign on the right door, is "affectionately supplied by Church Motors." The tall, twenty-one-year-old brunette is talking about women "taking care of themselves." As she speaks, her long false eyelashes bob between her blue and white shadowed lids and her rouged cheeks. The words bubble from her glossy lips, "I think girls should look natural. I've taught modeling and"—her tone becomes quieter, more confidential—"some of them didn't know the difference between a mascara brush and a hair brush!"

Pat won the Miss Toronto title on her third try this year. She has also reigned as Miss Wild Wooley, Miss Speed Sport, Miss Union Carbide, Miss A-Go-Go, Miss Jolly Pudding. "But I've always wanted to be Miss Toronto." She smiles and crinkles her nose. "It's great fun and I get to meet all sorts of people in the business."

"The business?"

"The business—you know—show business. I do modeling, commentating, a little dancing, singing—I haven't had time to keep up with the voice lessons yet, but I will when all this is over. I've been in the business for fourteen years." She started taking tap lessons at seven. She won her first modeling job at fifteen—standing next to a Ford Mustang, in a micro-mini skirt.

Pat pulls the pink Pinto into a complex of brick townhouses in Rexdale, suburban Toronto. "This is it," she says, hopping out into the cold night in her yellow knit skidoo thermal mini suit.

Mrs. Mazurick, a heavy woman wearing a multicolored burnoose, greets us at the door. She hurries upstairs for Pat's two scrapbooks, serves us tea and brownies, then discreetly leaves us in her sparkling living room. The large Miss Toronto trophy presides over the just-polished piano.

As I leaf through the first scrapbook, Pat explains why she wants to be Miss Canada. "I'd like to represent my country, to represent Canada's ideals. Canada is a country that pushes peace. We don't have hassles like the States. We don't have a colored racial problem. One of my best friends in modeling is colored. Eddy, her name is. And I would represent nationwide things—like the crippled children's crusade. I did things like that for Miss Toronto—with the Humane Society for a week." She flips to the photograph where she's holding two orphaned puppies on either side of her face.

Pat is perplexed about Miss Canada's role beyond the "charity things." "Morally?" she laughs nervously. "Well, I don't think I'd represent the youth in riots or anything like that and I don't believe in dope. You can become addicted to dope—to marijuana or is it LSD?—well, they're all bad. I don't like to see those girls on Yonge Street—the ones with no makeup and what looks like lice in their hair. I wouldn't go driving around Toronto in jeans and a sweatshirt."

Pat offers me a ride back to my subway shop. She tells me how much she likes driving. She also likes to ski, snowmobile, and swim. "But I don't have much time for anything now that I'm Miss Toronto. Oh, I've wanted it for so long," she smiles brightly, "Now that I've won, it's great. See you at the pageant."

"Yeah, see you at the pageant."

The excitement you can feel tonight is the culmination of what has been a thrilling week for all of us associated with the pageant. These past few days, we've gotten to know the girls a little bit better. We've had a chance to work with them, all in preparation for tonight, the final countdown to the moment when we'll crown Miss Canada 1973. And it's a little overwhelming to meet a group of such lovely ladies all at once. We've had a chance to get to know them and now we'd like you to meet them, individually ... "I'm Brenda Thomson from Sault Ste. Marie, Ontario" ... "Helene Girard, Trois Rivières, Quebec" ... "Hello, I'm Kim Topping from Burlington, Ontario."

Kim's voice is cracking, just as it did twelve days ago when I met her at the Holiday Inn. Miss Burlington is a modest, friendly eighteen-year-old, somewhat overwhelmed by the luxury of her autumn-tone hotel room with color TV, wall radio, and extra long beds. Unlike Pat, she had no idea she would wind up in the Miss Canada Pageant. It all started with winning her high school Snow Queen contest. "Then someone phoned and asked me to enter the Miss Burlington pageant and then"—she tries to stifle her excited giggle—"well, I didn't tell anyone I won. I went to school and my girlfriend met me at my locker. She asked me how it went and I said fine. 'Well, who won?' she said. And I said, 'I did.' And she screamed, 'You won, you won!'" Now when Kim walks down the halls of her school, the ninth graders point and whisper, "There's Miss Burlington."

This first afternoon of the pageant, when the editor of the *Burlington Post* drove Kim to the Holiday Inn, he took her from the cheerleading squad, the gymnast team, and her once-a-weekend boyfriend to sophisticated television land. "I've never been in a television studio before." Her brown eyes light wide. But she didn't leave high school completely behind. She brought along her homework.

Miss Oakville bursts into the room, "Come on down the hall and meet my roommate."

Kim looks at her, then at me, then at Miss Oakville again, "I can't come right now," she answers, flushing. "I'm, uh, being interviewed."

"Oh, I see, an interview? A celebrity! Well, come down afterwards, okay?"

Kim returns to my questions. "Oh, yes, I think Canadian nationalism is a must. I think if Quebec, if it were to leave, it would be a great loss to Canada..." She changes the topic to her charm bracelet, which she dangles in front of me. It has gold tokens from friends and relatives; among them a map of the United States and a replica of Toronto's City Hall. "And this one—my boyfriend gave me this one for the pageant. It's a four-leaf clover for good luck."

Kim doesn't know what she'll do when she graduates from high school this spring. Maybe she'll go to college and study computer science. Maybe she'll become an airline stewardess. Eventually, of course, she wants to get married and raise children in a place like Burlington. "People say there's nothing to do in Burlington, but there are several cinemas and we're ten minutes from the country and close to Toronto and Hamilton." Kim's mother is a housewife; her father is a Ford executive. The family's only other public figure is a cousin, Paul Hellyer.

"I'm really looking forward to the pageant," says Kim, showing me the long skirt she made for her appearance as Miss Burlington. "I can remember when I was little, I used to dream about things like that and I remember my mother letting me stay up and watch Miss America and Miss Canada and all these beauty pageants and here I am and it's still"—she pauses briefly to regain her composure— "still like a dream."

> Before I introduce our five judges, I'd like to explain briefly how the judging of the contestants is done. There are basically four areas of competition and they are evening wear, talent, swimsuit, and finally poise, personality and intellect, which is one category.

As Kim and I enter Miss Oakville's room, we're greeted by open arms. "Welcome, have you finished being a celebrity yet?"

Kim changes the subject to her good luck charm.

Miss Espanola-Sudbury is putting her engagement ring on her charm bracelet. "They told me I'd have to take it off, so I thought I'd take it off before anyone else told me."

"Say," she reaches into her suitcase and pulls out a giant box of Carefree tampons, "Anyone need any? I came prepared for emergencies."

Everyone laughs. There are certain commonalities.

Miss Mississauga, her hair up in curlers for the big welcome dinner tonight, is seated next to me on the bed. She explains that she entered the Miss Toronto pageant three times and lost. After this year's failure, she moved out to Mississauga and won the title there.

Miss Kitchener-Waterloo, a tall, dark-haired model, comes in and perches on the other side of the bed. "And what area are you representing?" No, I explain, I'm not a regional princess, just a reporter. "Oh, that must be interesting..."

The conversation lulls; heads turn to the color tube in the corner. We're all absorbed in an "Addams Family" episode when Miss Oakville asks about everybody's talent.

"Interpretative jazz movement."

"Modern dance."

"A gymnast dance."

"Oh, yeah? I do another uh, interpretative dance. I guess I might as well give up now."

"Oh, no," says Miss Mississauga. "The judging isn't on talent."

"What's it on then?"

"I hear it's on personality."

The others nod approvingly.

The judges are now in the process of choosing the ten semifinalists. We'll be back with their decisions and also our very special guest, Ed Evanko, right after these messages.

Hey, gotta show you this beautiful gift idea—a Lady Schick beauty salon hairdryer, it's the one the women buy for themselves ... and it does great looking hairdos in just about twenty minutes. Now that may not mean much to you, but it does to me and it sure will to her.

The first complete pageant day begins in De Berardini's Hair Salon in the Fairview Mall shopping plaza. The scene at 10 A.M. is chaotic. Small men run around with brushes and mist stylers. "The Official Miss Canada Photographer" is zooming in on Miss Saskatoon's sopping wet hair.

Miss Niagara Peninsula is crying. The hairdresser has chopped seven inches off her hair. "But I had two inches cut off before I came." She tries to restrain her anger. "Do you know how long it took to grow?" The protests are swept away with the long, blonde curls.

Miss Burlington loses two inches, Miss Sarnia loses four, Miss Moncton's new permanent is straightened out. The contestants are frustrated, trying to preserve their locks. The hairdressers are frustrated, trying to preserve their professionalism.

"Some of these girls, I don't know what to do with them!" says a little man, waving his scissors in the air. "Why the one up here, she won't let us touch her hair. I don't think she's ever had a professional stylist work on her. She's trying to tell *me* what to do!"

Miss Toronto walks over to say hello. She looks fashionable even in her hair rollers. "Oh, I'm so tired. We didn't get to sleep until twelve-thirty last night and we had to get up at seven. And you should see what they did to my hair! I just hope people recognize me when they take the rollers down."

She does look different as she walks into Simpson's Arcadian Court for the free lunch sponsored by the Fairview Mall merchants association. Before the contestants are allowed to eat, the hot television lights bear down on their tired, tense heads. Then the bleached blonde Miss Canada official tells us about the lovely mall which has won a beauty award for being such a lovely mall. She introduces us to the mall's lovely fashion director who says a few words to the lovely contestants. "I wish you all 'good luck.' I only wish there could be twenty-eight Miss Canadas." Hands clap. Faces smile. Cameras click.

The contestants have to pass up the wine list because princesses cannot drink in public. "Hey, Calgary," Miss Oakville shouts down the table, "You know we're not supposed to be smoking in public." Miss Calgary responds with a contented puff and a dirty look.

The next stop is the Toronto City Hall reception, for which the party arrives an hour late.

"Okay, girls, we'll stop the bus here for pictures before we go inside. Please put your banners on."

"Inside our coats or outside?"

"Outside for now. We'll change them when we get inside."

The contestants step out into a cold wind which ravages their painfully earned coiffures. They shiver, posing for the cameras. Click. "That's it, smile." Click. "Wave now." Click. "Hold hands." Click.

Inside the mayor's outer office, the contestants repair their hairdos and readjust their banners. The door swings open and they file in to shake the mayor's hand, remembering what the publicist said: "Don't look at the mayor when you're shaking hands with him. Look at the cameras. Otherwise they'll get a nice shot of the back of your head."

"Your worship, I'm happy to present you with these cufflinks and a history of Moncton," says one girl to the mayor.

"Why thank you," he says. "And please thank your mayor for me."

That's the reception: the line-up, the handshake, the individual photo, a few group shots of the mayor and the eager young princesses.

"That's it, the whole group together now." Click. Click.

Out into the wind again for more pictures. "Come on, let's get a shot of you running back to City Hall. That's it, you two hold hands." The TV cameras whir. The Nikons click. The fancy hairdos fly apart.

"Before announcing the names of the other five semi-finalists, we'd like to point out that the judges' decisions are based not only on beauty and talent, but also on poise, personality and on intellect. So we would like to take a moment here to talk with each of the five girls individually.

"Now, Lise LeClerc from Quebec City. Bon Soir. 'Dans la lune' means 'absentminded,' right? And you were once very absentminded, something to do with a refrigerator?"

"Yes, well, I was washing some dishes and instead of putting the dishes in the sink, I just put them in the fridge. So that was really nice and when I came back I opened the fridge and I said who put that in there?"

It's back on the bus to Bobby Blum's Furriers.

"Remember to hurry girls. We're late already."

"Pick something that looks good on you and sign it out before you get back on the bus."

"Hurry girls."

"No, that's much too long for you."

"Did anyone take something off this rack?" says the furrier. "No one is allowed to take anything off this rack."

"Here, try this on." He zips a short blue chinchilla jacket on Miss Saskatoon. She had wanted one of the longer coats but...

"Hurry girls."

Back on the bus, the chaperones run their fingers through the chinchilla and mink. "How much do they cost?"

"Hers is $800. But mine costs $2,000 because it's mink."

The contestants sit back admiring their coats. They don't realize that they're wearing the coats for PR shots and that they have to return them in less than two hours.

The bus rumbles to a start and we jostle the afternoon traffic up to our next appointment—a tea at Casa Loma, the mock-castle in midtown Toronto. The bus driver comes over to the microphone: "Ladies, I see what lovely coats you have on, I thought you might be interested in hearing the story of the girl who told her boss that she'd do anything for a mink coat. By the time she got it, she couldn't fit it around her."

Groans reverberate around the Gray Coach.

"Imagine! Telling us a story like that!" says Miss Toronto.

We pass some police on a street corner and Miss Toronto waves like a starlet to them. "Those are my sponsors," she squeaks. "We have the *best* police in Toronto!" The chaperones nod appreciatively. The other contestants smirk or look confused. Outside, one bewildered cadet waves back.

At Casa Loma, we're greeted by a greying Kiwanian who gasps at the beauty arrayed before him. The contestants disregard his compliment. They're thinking about their coats. It's stifling hot in the castle.

"Can we take them off!"

"Oh, I don't know," says the chaperone, "wait until the pictures are taken."

"Can we go to the washroom?"

"All right," snaps the exasperated pageant official, "Everybody who wants to powder their nose, please follow me."

In the Casa Loma conservatory, waitresses float around with trays of petit fours; the Kiwanis wives serve tea and coffee; the Kiwanians themselves hustle the contestants. One corners Miss Saskatoon. "I told my wife I had to meet Miss Saskatchewan. I used to live there, myself. Do you know a little town called...?" Miss Hull chats with Miss Calgary about her work in a Caisse Populaire. Miss Calgary talks about the friendly stewardesses at Wardair, where she works. The television cameras take it all in, panning, zooming. The Nikons click.

Eventually, a portly Kiwanian interrupts the chitchat to recount the history of the ninety-eight-room castle. He's oblivious to the fatigued, tense, bored faces around him as he describes the $10,000 bronze and glass doors, the 1,568 cavities in the wine cellar. Miss Calgary shifts from one sore foot to the other. And off we go on a guided tour of the building. We wind up in the Great Hall, under 783 glass lights, "Now when you girls go back home, I want you to be sure to invite everyone to see Casa Loma. Tell them what a fine place it is. I must wish everyone of you good luck. It's too bad there couldn't be twenty-eight Miss Canadas."

And now our search for Miss Canada 1973 continues as we invite our judges and you at home to meet our ten semifinalists in just a moment in the next competition, that is, the swimsuit competition.

They have been parading and posing all week, but Friday is their first chance to rehearse in their swimsuits. "That's right. Stand there with the jacket on. Take it off slowly as you approach the judges. Stand there for a moment so they can look at you, then join the girls back in line. No, no. Don't stand like that, and watch your walk." This is a full dress rehearsal in the CFTO studio.

CFTO, in suburban Agincourt, is protected by a high cyclone fence, a security guard who checks your name as you enter the gate, and a receptionist who asks you to "sign in—and note the time of your arrival and departure." It's impossible to escape without signing out, since most of the doors are marked "Emergency Exit. Buzzer will sound."

In Studio Six, Miss Toronto is checking her makeup at a mirror near the door. I wonder why she wears false eyelashes even when her hair is up in curlers. She's been averaging five hours sleep. "I'm so tired," she sighs, "that I'm wide awake." Her enthusiasm for the pageant has dimmed since our talk in the pink Pinto. She bends forward, speaking more confidentially. "What really makes me sort of mad is that some of these girls don't want to be in it; they don't care about winning. I guess you can't blame them. Some of them have never been in a studio before. And you know, some of them have never worn false eyelashes." She seems incredulous. "Of course they have to wear them for the show." She looks around at the other girls being fitted and combed. "Yeah, there are maybe ten percent of us who want to win. And among us the competition is tough." She grits her shiny teeth. "Some of their talent is so good—like Newfoundland, who sings like Julie Andrews! Oh, what am I going to do? I'd give anything to be Miss Canada, anything."

Miss Burlington waves from across the big dressing room. She tells me how she cried when she got the three letters from her boyfriend and the flowers from home and the good-luck telegram from the *Burlington Post*. "The telegram said they thought they had the most attractive girl in the pageant and they thought I was going to win. Some of the girls are here to win and some are here to have a good time. I'd like to do well at both." Last year's Miss Burlington came eighth and she wants to match that. "You know, it's confusing, at first they send you away and say that it doesn't matter how you place just as long as you have a good time. Then they say they think they have a winner in you." She is tired, sore from the penicillin shot she got for her cold, and worried about her talent. "Oh, Oh." She looks at her watch. "I've got to take a Certs before my appointment with the judges."

Miss Burlington's roommate, Miss Saskatoon, had her interview yesterday. She can't figure out how well she did. "Well, they asked some trick questions—like they asked how Premier Thatcher was—and he's dead. No, they didn't ask any philosophical questions and nothing about politics. They asked about my city and about my job. I start with Wardair in the spring and I'm looking forward to it. But you know what else they did that was sorta tricky? When you go in there, you talk to some people before the interview. It's the judges' husbands and wives. Then just before I went in, one of the husbands went in and made a report about me. Now, do you think that's fair?"

The smiles which flashed so often during the first days have receded behind tight lips. Colds flourish in the competitors' fatigue and tension. The smell of Listerine mingles with the odors of perfume and hairspray.

Next to me, Miss Trois Rivières and Miss Sarnia practice "the finalists' walk." Miss Newfoundland practices smiling into the mirror. "No, no," she shakes her head after sixty seconds, "It's still crooked." Miss Saint John rushes backstage in tears about her talent rehearsal. "I just can't do it now. I just can't do it." She grabs a cigarette and sits down. "No, no," shouts the fashion consultant. "You can't sit down in that. You're going to wear it on the program."

"Well, what am I going to do?"

"Stand up until you change."

"But that's going to be a long time."

"Look, you can't crease the things that are going to be on the show."

I go outside to watch the rehearsal. "Well, hello," says the emcee in his rich television voice. "Have you picked your favorite yet?"

"No."

"No? Really? Everybody does. The musicians, of course, pick the ones with the biggest breasts first. Then they get very serious about it. They root for the girls they like. If you haven't picked a winner yet, you must be a very dispassionate journalist."

> *The pageant week really has been an exciting time for all of our girls and I know that each one is going to go home with new friends, a lot of very good memories and I hope some interesting experiences as well.*

While the contestants rehearse, the chaperones sort out the turquoise bathing suits which match the color of the set. The chaperones have picked up the studio jargon—"set" and "promo" and "camera time." Some of them have been around ten years. The real pros do two pageants a year, this one and Miss Teen Canada; both are owned by Cleo and produced by CFTO. The chaperones are not paid for shepherding the girls, mending their costumes, labeling their shoes, pinning their bras. Some call each other "girls" and refer to the contestants as "little girls." They are the sort of gray-haired women who run Brownie packs, scrutineer at elections, type for the school board, and collect for Cancer. They chaperone beauty contestants as another public service. Besides, they say, it's fun. They have twelve days at the Holiday Inn, restaurant food, and a token of CFTO's esteem. Last year it was a silver tray. The year before it was a clock radio.

But not all the chaperones return. One ex-chaperone, Laura Farquhar, told me she refused to let her daughters enter a beauty contest. Mrs. Farquhar chaperoned for the 1972 pageant. "The girls were pushed and shoved and rushed the entire time. The girls were photographed at every meal to advertise what was being eaten or where it was being eaten. One film sequence for Swift's took a whole afternoon of the pageant. Some girls got to eat on time, but the others were kept downstairs. When they finally got to eat, they were starving and the cameras focused on them. The only sight-seeing they had in the twelve days was a trip down to Niagara Falls. But this was used as a commercial endorsement, 'Miss Canada contestants ride Air Canada!'"

Mrs. Farquhar is hardly a radical feminist. She is a housewife in a fashionable north Toronto neighborhood. As she relaxes in her oyster and pink living room, she talks nostalgically about why she went into the pageant—her interest in beauty and fashion. She wouldn't do away with all beauty pageants, but definitely with this one. "The whole thing was a CFTO production. They were there to put on a TV show. The losers didn't get anything for it. Not so much as a 'You're doing great girls.' Oh, there was the odd gift and the odd article of clothing. But that's not much for twelve days of hard work. You sign a contract before you come. You have no rights to yourself. They all belong to Cleo Productions."

And so the judges at this very moment are making their final decisions. And in just a short time we'll know which of our five lovely finalists will be the New Miss Canada. Of course when we make the announcement the reign of Miss Canada 1972 will come to an end. We'd like you to meet her now. Ladies and Gentlemen, I'm very proud to present Miss Canada 1972, Donna Sawicky.

As Miss Canada reads the cue cards about the wonderful time she's had this year, I think back to the time I first met her—at the Snow Show in Toronto. She stood next to a sparkling red snowmobile, handing out brochures for the Scorpion Stinger, 1973. Her hair was plastered in a bouffant ponytail on top of her head. Her eyeshadow, rouge, and makeup base hid any trace of complexion. The white satin "Miss Canada" banner was ragged at the top, where it was pinned to her chic black pant suit. She stood alone, looking perplexed, tired, smiling vacantly. A few children walked up for autographs. She tried to be friendly, to talk to other people. They had nothing to say to her.

Her position was defined for me by Judi Muir, public relations director for the Miss Canada Pageant. "I tell the girls it's a job like any other job. It's a lot of hard work. They receive a salary—no, you better not say that, we call it a cash award—and they work for it. We're very careful about what we let the girls identify with. They can't do promotions for liquor or cigarettes."

Judi Muir proudly indicates the advertising tear sheets on her cork board wall. "Miss Canada says, 'New Awake Protein Hairspray gives back body to hair while holding it in place.'" Exquisite Form products aren't called "underwear," but "inner fashions." Likewise, the Schick merchandise is billed as "personal care products" rather than curlers and razors. Swift's meats is one of the biggest sponsors.

Muir emphasizes that Miss Canada's reign isn't strictly a commercial venture. "She does a lot of goodwill things sponsored by various companies." Last year her "goodwill things" included an interview with a crippled child, a visit to an old age home, an inspirational brotherhood message with Chief Dan George and W. A. C. Bennett. Then there were the "fun things" like the kickoff of the Canadian Football League season and an autograph signing session with . . . Bobby Orr, himself!

Cleo Productions won't release the profit figures from Miss Canada. It isn't anybody's business, they say. Also, they don't know how much they'll make from appearance fees next year. "We have her limoed in when something comes up," explains Muir. "If she has to catch a flight, she'll get a hotel room near the airport with her chaperone. We brief her on the promotion and then she proceeds on the booking."

Miss Canada 1972 has tea with me on one of the last mornings of her reign. Her description of the past year is underlined by tense tact. "Well, there were some things I didn't like about it. I had to work almost every day. I had very little time off. A lot of times it would be like every day a different city and I'd be working from seven A.M. to one A.M. I would get nervous, not shy, but you know, my nerves were getting shot trying to make so many people happy." Her voice is sweet, her words are carefully chosen—so carefully, in fact, that you wonder whether the thoughts behind them have been neutralized completely by the Miss Canada product.

She is a pleasant young woman, materially successful with her Ford Maverick, two snowmobiles, and three year's supply of nylons; socially sophisticated for twelve months of public appearances, interviews, and modeling shows; physically attractive in her personalized makeup and wardrobe. But I wonder what she says when people challenge her about not representing Canadian youth.

"Why," she exclaims as her fashionably thin eyebrows almost disappear into the surprise wrinkles on her forehead, "no one ever suggested that I don't represent Canadian youth."

Ladies and gentlemen, the final decision has been reached. Our auditor has tabulated the results of the voting. And now the moment everybody across Canada has been anxiously awaiting is at hand. May I have the envelope, please . . . Miss Canada 1973 from Victoria, Gillian Regehr.

Attending the formal "pageant night" at the studio is much different from watching it, as I have in the past years, on my eleven-inch black and white television at home.

All around me, parents and adolescent brothers and sponsors have been clutching their blue and silver programs and the Edith Serei makeup samples they received at the door. I learn I am sitting next to an Exquisite Form executive when Miss Toronto comes on stage in a tight, sheer leotard. "Look," he points excitedly, "She's wearing one of my bras!"

The reception after the crowning is even more revealing. Some of the girls kiss and smile and promise to write each other. Other contestants talk quietly, bitterly with friends and relatives.

"And my roommate," whispers the big city contestant, "She never remembers her key. I was asleep last night when she knocked on the door, woke me up, came in and got something, then left again. The night before she woke me up at midnight because she wanted to phone her boyfriend."

"Well, my roommate," complains the suburban contestant, "She thinks *my* side of the room is messy."

And down near the bar table, one of the semifinalists tells her mother, "Actually, I'm glad I didn't win. It's really a rough year. I don't think I could stand having to ask permission every time I wanted to go to the bathroom."

Miss Burlington introduces me to her father. "Oh, yes, we're very proud of her. She did very well."

"I'm glad I made the semifinalists," she adds. "No, I didn't get all my homework done, but the teachers will understand, especially now that I placed so well."

Up by the stage, a hairdresser from De Berardini's Salon is shaking hands with all his friends. "I won, I won," he declares, jumping up and down. Suddenly I realize that his hairdo won. He's right. He won, and so did Exquisite Form and Dominion Textiles and Phantom Panty Hose and Helena Rubenstein Cosmetics.

It's sad to lose dreams, even when the dreams are just naive delusions sustained by fashion model smiles, cheerleader spirit, and bubble bath sociability. The dreams have been popping throughout the pageant. When the contestants had their hair chopped and curled and straightened against their wills. When they had to return their fur coats after two hours. When they had to compromise their talent to television programming. When their expected friends turned into tough competitors. When they got tired of practicing for the cameras, for the audiences, for the ratings, for CFTO's profit margin. When they grew frustrated with the petty tyrannies about smoking and drinking. When they realized that to be Miss Canada they couldn't be themselves.

The reception dwindles as a TV replay of the program ends with the song, "Miss Canada." Over by the TV sets, a photographer snaps a tuxedoed gent in mid-drunk. "What are ya doing? Chronicling a dying culture?" The photographer nods her head, "I hope so." It's too late for philosophical conversation. It's past midnight and Cinderella was raped a long time ago. As the song says, *"We've found her at last, the fairest girl in Canada, the girl who reminds us all what girls should be . . ."*

The Suburban Housewife as Feminist Organizer

—What's she seeing? Housewife, mother of four, this slightly too short and too amply rumped woman with coat of yesteryear, hemlines all the wrong length . . . lipstick wrong color, and crowning comic touch, the hat. Man, how antediluvian can you get? Is that what she's thinking? I don't know. But I still have this sense of some monstrous injustice. I want to explain. *Under this chapeau lurks a mermaid, a whore, a tigress.* She'd call a cop and I'd be put in a mental ward.
          —Margaret Laurence, *The Fire-Dwellers*

At 6:05 on a Tuesday night inside a beige brick house in Willowdale, a suburb of Toronto, the Englander kids are sitting around the colour television watching "Nanny and the Professor." Sharon thumbs through a grade nine textbook. Karen claims the reclining chair because she's the oldest. Sandy sits on the floor eating cream cheese and crackers. Her five-year-old sister, Renée, carefully crayons inside the lines of a coloring book. Alfie the hound munches on Renée's crayons.

From the adjoining dining room their mother Leah announces supper. They pull themselves away from the TV, the cream cheese, and the crayons. Sharon is first at the plastic-clothed table for pork chops, asparagus, and white rice. Alec Englander is on a business trip in New York tonight. Otherwise, it's a typical family dinner with sibling squabbles, consultation on school projects, gossip about friends.

"Will you drive me to the horseback riding lessons?" asks Sandy.

"I told you I'd share the driving if the other parents would."

"But . . . I don't think any of the others are taking the lessons." Sandy's round face is suddenly long. Her mouth purses around her braces in the beginning of a pout.

This essay is reprinted from *Saturday Night,* July 1973. It was one of a number of articles I wrote for the magazine, a national Canadian journal based in Toronto, in the early 1970s. These pieces are written in the very personal "new journalism" of the day. While I imposed my stamp on these stories, they had an enormous effect on me, drawing me further into an understanding of and appreciation for feminism. Leah Englander changed her name to Leah Erna, taking her mother's first name as her surname. She now owns a construction company and is involved in a group called Women in Construction.

"Well, wait till your father comes home," concludes Leah. "If I make a promise he's not in on, he won't feel obligated to follow it and *I'll* get stuck with all the driving."

After gooey chocolate sundaes, the kids adjourn to their bedrooms for homework. Alfie bounds back into the living room to devour the last of the Crayolas. Leah prepares to go out for the evening, but not to a bridge game or a dress sale or a book club. This is where the suburban housewife scene ends. Tonight she is going to present a talk about "Women's Liberation."

The supper is just a brief interlude in Leah's twelve-hour work day at the government-funded Women's Place in Toronto. She distributes information about feminist activities, counsels individual women, speaks to organizations, and initiates consciousness-raising groups. Her most valuable role is in evangelism, testifying to unconverted housewives. Although housewives have symbolized the oppressed in literature from *A Doll's House* to *The Fire-Dwellers,* they are hardly the most visible representatives of women's liberation.

So this small, thirty-six-year-old woman goes out to listen to the myriad of organizations who request "women's lib" speakers. Since Leah's evangelism is not strident, she does more listening than talking at these kaffee klatsches. They schedule her visit somewhere among their Christie's Bakery tour, diet lecture, Christmas ornament demonstration, and local aldermanic debate. She drives through gray snowy winter mornings and slick humid summer evenings, past the shopping malls and liquor stores and beauty salons and golf courses and supermarkets and health clubs. She listens to them talk about the PTA and Take 30 and Corning Ware and Blush On. And afternoon naps. And secret sips of sherry. She listens because she was a housewife for sixteen years.

Leah grew up in Toronto's Forest Hill. She went to the right parties, met the right kids, and tried not to pay too much attention to her good grades. Her Hungarian and Yugoslavian parents owned a factory where she could have worked when she finished high school. Either that or get married. She got married at seventeen and bore her first child at nineteen. A pretty daughter and a responsible husband: what more could a young woman want? She wanted to go back to school, so she started to study accounting part-time. Then she had another baby. Like many women who later became feminists, Leah was always bored with the traditional outlets. She avoided telephone gossip sessions, had her hair done only once a month. She read Freud at night "to be intellectual" and became a serious sculptor. But she was still defined, by herself and others, as a wife and mother.

Meanwhile, her husband worked his way up to a $20,000-a-year job at a toy company which sells baking sets with pictures of little girls on the boxes and tool sets with pictures of little boys on the boxes. She tried to go back to university and study psychology. "But I was getting a lot of flack, that I would want to study on the weekend instead of . . . well, instead of watching my husband watch TV. So then I decided to go to work for him in the office. I did what I thought was manager stuff. I said, 'OK, now, I'd like to learn some of your job.' And he said, 'Oh, no, not on your life.'"

She grew frustrated and angry, and then—next step in the all too classic process—went to see a psychiatrist. Six weeks into Freudian analysis, she somehow found a copy of *Sexual Politics,* the 1969 book by the American feminist Kate Millett. Flash! "Everything I read told me that I was going through this hell because I was a woman, not because I was incompetent or because my family was stubborn. And it just clarified everything for me. I stopped seeing a shrink. And I started feeling firmer and stronger about my role rather than more and more upset about how deviant and fucked up I was."

That was two-and-a-half years ago. Since then she has studied more feminist literature, entered a consciousness-raising (CR) group, joined the women's movement. She no longer worries about what to serve at her husband's dinner parties, because she doesn't give them anymore. She worries about how she should be introduced at speaking engagements. "I don't want to be called a 'housewife,' but 'feminist organizer' sounds heavy."

This week Leah is speaking to YMCA classes on the women's movement. Sometimes these brief encounters develop into CR groups. Sometimes they wind up as dart-throwing sessions with Leah as the dart board. She doesn't know what to expect as she parks her Pontiac Suburban station wagon in front of Knox United Church in Agincourt, another suburb of Toronto. She drags the projector and screen into the modern church hall which also shelters Yoga classes, daycare, Girl Guides, and Explorers. A color picture of Christ hangs on one wall; he and the janitor are the only men in the room. The janitor leaves when Leah tells him thanks, she can run the projector herself. In a few minutes, she has the screen set and the film whirring.

After the Vote: A Report from Down Under, a 1969 film by Bonnie Kreps, opens with a suffrage song. ("Our daughters will adore us and sing a grateful chorus. Well done, sister suffragette.") It chronicles women's nonliberation over the subsequent fifty years. Shots of beauty contestants, housewives, factory workers. Testimony about why women, who make up one-third of Canada's labor force, are relegated to low-paying and low-status jobs. This provokes groans and ironic laughter from the housewife-students who range in age from late twenties to early forties.

After the film Leah suggests that the women move the yellow wooden chairs into a circle. She sits back and listens attentively.

"I've been talking about going back to work," says the blonde woman in the tight beige sweater. "But my husband says I wouldn't make enough money to make it worthwhile. That after taxes and all, it would cut down our income. Also, he doesn't want me to leave the children. He thinks I'm a lousy housekeeper, but a good mother. What should I do?"

"I don't think daycare is such a bad thing," answers the Englishwoman with the streak of gray running through her long black hair. "I know that on the very few occasions I've had a woman take care of the children, I've come home to find her playing with them. Games I play only four times a year."

"Well, I don't know," interrupts another woman. "I grew up in daycare centers and I think that raising a child is important. I think I've done a pretty exceptional job with mine."

Leah suggests that there is good daycare and bad daycare. "Studies show...." She is always quoting recent studies which debunk sexist theories. Now she interrupts herself, "Anyway, why can't *the husband* take the child for part of the day? Now tomorrow, I have to work. My husband is taking the five-year-old to the office."

"But what will she do there?" asks the woman who grew up in daycare.

"Play with the typewriter," answers one woman.

"But," persists the blonde woman, "Don't we all feel guilty when we leave our children?"

"Well," says Leah, chopping the air with her worn, pink hands, "I think it's better for the children to see both parents as functioning rather than have them see one parent as exploited."

The blonde is still looking for her answer, "When I say that I had a terrible day, my husband says, 'Yes, but you don't have the pressures from above that I do.' He forgets, I guess, that we've only been married for two years and that for ten years before that I worked. He buys the latest liberalizing books about child raising and says, 'You read them and tell me what they say.' And the ironic thing is—he *teaches* this—he teaches a family life course."

Several women laugh with her. But the woman in the orange and green hat shakes her head in admonition. "Oh, you just don't have a partnership. You're not playing in the same ball park."

"And we seem to be forgetting one thing," adds the woman who grew up in daycare. "*Somebody* has to take care of the children! If *we* had those children, I say *we* have to take care of them until they go to school."

Leah is frustrated, but she won't interrupt. The men had the children just as much as the women, she thinks. The only reason we say, "until age five" is because the state takes care of them after that. This is one of the most difficult aspects of Leah's work: holding back while other women struggle with stages she has gone through.

Eventually the blonde woman finds an answer for herself, "You know, I guess I'm the best one to take care of the kids because I'm the cheapest and most convenient. That's not a very good reason for not going out to work."

After the meeting the woman in the orange and green hat thanks Leah. "There are a lot of good things about women's lib," she grants, "but you'd have a better chance of changing things if you weren't so *radical*. It takes time to change things. You can't build Rome in a day."

"Yes, yes," nods Leah, somewhere in between fatigue and patience. "I used to think that way once myself."

The next morning Leah prepares for another YMCA class. She jockeys for her shoes in the small foyer with the kids and Alec, who is setting off for work in his electric blue suit. Leah introduces me to Yvonne, their Caribbean housekeeper. A housekeeper? How can a feminist hire a housekeeper?

We talk about Yvonne during the long drive to Markham. "Yes, I know," Leah sighs resignedly, "Some women in the movement tell me I should fire her. They say it doesn't matter that she's out of work. The more people without jobs, the more discontented the lower classes will be and the sooner the revolution will come. I can't disagree with that. But the problem is that I know and like Yvonne. She's a human being. I know if I fire her and she gets any job at all, it will pay much less. She makes $240 a month plus room and board which is about what I make." Leah doesn't apologize for what seems to be a gaping contradiction between her philosophy and her lifestyle. She is bewildered but not paralyzed. For her, feminism is an ongoing process replete with compromises. Leah doesn't pretend to be the ideal feminist. She responds with her gut feelings as well as with the prescribed rhetoric.

St. Andrew's United Church in Markham, Ontario, like Knox Church, is a modern, community-oriented institution. However, Markham is a different community. A one company town. IBM.

The six students range in age from mid-twenties to mid-thirties. Reaction to the film is slow in coming today. Ten seconds pass in heavy silence after the projector sputters to a stop. "Well, what did you think of it?" asks Leah. "Was the film valid?"

"One thing I didn't like about it," returns the woman whose red hair shows the separation marks of all-night rollers, "is that it made being a housewife look so *terrible*. There are some good things about housework. You don't have to have a terrible life if you're *creative*."

"Oh, I don't know about that," says a woman in a brown blouse. "This article in *Time* magazine said that IQ tests on small children show females to be smarter than males and then IQ tests on adults show that males are smarter. The women lose their ability and inclination to think because housework isn't stimulating."

The woman in the multicolored maternity blouse adds, "You know one thing that bothers me about the women's lib is that you say you have to go out to work to be fulfilled."

"No," answers the woman in brown. "I think they're saying you should have a *choice*. And how much of a choice do we have?" Leah is glad when she finds someone who admits and understands her frustrations. Although most housewives have been liberalized since *The Feminine Mystique* was under-the-bedcovers reading, this woman is trying to see her way out of Friedan's "Problem That Has No Name." She adds, "We're socialized to expect to get married and not train for a career."

Breaking the tension, the woman in the maternity blouse declares, "Well, one thing I *agree* with the women's lib about is the housework. I think a man should help. My husband said he would help me when I was working."

"Help *you*," exclaims the woman in brown, "just look at the language you're using. It's *his* work too. At my house, he puts our son in his high chair while I put dinner on the table . . . we share the work."

"Well, that may be fine for you," says the woman chain-smoking filter cigarettes, "but since I don't go out and work, there's no way my husband's going to let me get away with that! I have a friend whose husband writes, 'I love you' in the dust. Mine doesn't go that far, but I know if I asked him to pick up his plate after supper, he'd kick me out the window. Not really. Ha. Ha."

"Yeah," laughs the woman in brown, "my husband used to call me *spunky* before we got married. Now he calls me *wilful*."

After the class, Leah and I drive to a nearby shopping plaza for lunch. Leah is pleased with the meeting—with the "wilfullness" of the woman in brown and the responsiveness of the others. At least this morning no one warned her about building Rome in a day. We also discuss Leah's own "liberation."

"Now Alec allows me to do my thing. No, I should rephrase that—*I'm* doing my thing and *he's* adjusting." He shares care of the children, sews his own buttons, tidies his own room. "We still fuck," she says, her language itself showing the effects of the movement. ("I never used to say words like that in public, but I refuse to censor myself anymore.") Leah keeps a separate bedroom to maintain her independence. I ask her if she, like many feminists, will ultimately liberate herself from marriage by divorce. She seems as confused about this issue as she is about the housekeeper.

Leah worries more about her daughters' response to feminism. She wants them to be proud of her the way suffragettes' children were proud. But she's afraid that the three youngest ones are caught up in the "nice-house-and-family dream." "I tell them that their needs come first and foremost and that if they want to live with a man, do that. Which is fairly radical for Willowdale."

The next week Leah invites me to come along to a CR group she is starting. Before we leave the house, she shows me some of her sculpture. The prefeminist pieces include a handsome bust of her husband in the dining room and a gold composition in the family room depicting a woman kneeling under a man's hand. She's embarrassed by the chauvinism of the latter, so she points out a more recent effort, an illuminated group of red figures, "I wouldn't have attempted to electrify it myself, before the movement." She is also proud of her own room—big, bright, accented with feminist posters, "Sisterhood is blooming; springtime will never be the same." Over her bed hangs a karate diploma.

Driving through the dark, slick night, the image of "Leah the evangelist" recurs. Leah wouldn't appreciate the symbolism, so we talk about the results rather than the imagery of her work. "Housewives are moving more and more into the movement. These groups don't put me down as much now. They ask, 'What do you think about this and that?' You know that pat phrase, 'I'm not a women's libber, but...' Well, that *but* is including more and more things—equal pay for equal work, daycare, legalized abortion."

Leah, herself, finds two groups of housewives hard to reach: women over fifty who see no hope for personal change and young pregnant women who are just starting out on the "nice-house-and-family dream." Otherwise—especially in the twenty-five to thirty-five age group—the middle-class housewife is "coming out," Leah says. Then she applies the power brakes and I look up, surprised that we are already in North York, parked in front of a small one-story house. Through the blanket-draped window, I see several young women sitting in a half-painted room.

Three of the participants have preschool children. The evening is punctuated with cries and gurgles from the hostess's one-year-old. Her décor is post student: bottles of Bacardi and Johnny Walker on the bookcase with *Introduction to Psychology* and *Man Alone*. As she serves tea and oatmeal cookies, a pregnant young woman asks, "Well, what's a consciousness-raising group supposed to do?"

Leah suggests that after a few weeks of getting acquainted they can explore different topics: "What was our earliest childhood awareness of being trained to behave like a girl? What was our reaction to bodily changes in adolescence? What situations make us feel guilty? What are our private terrors? How do we feel about childbirth, aging, menopause? What are our hopes for the future?"

At the classes last week the conversations focused on specific issues—careers and housework. Here, as at most CR groups, the talk is more diffuse. Leah asks why they came. Loneliness. Boredom. Frustration. Isolation. They talk about mothers-in-law, convent schools, sexual stereotyping, health classes. The topics flash by as they release their aggravations one moment and then pull back the next, listening for signs of where and how far they can trust each other.

"My daughter is beautiful," says the hostess in real wonderment, "a free little being."

"And what about you?" asks Leah.

"What?"

"What about *you*?"

"Me?" she laughs dryly. "Well, I'm not a very free being. I'm frustrated." Her voice is tight. "I'm deathly frustrated. I have an honors B.A. in psych. And after all that training, I got pregnant. It was a mechanical failure. And for me an abortion was not a consideration."

Leah can't hold back any longer. "One of the propositions of the women's movement is that legalized abortion gives the woman a right to choose what happens with her body, her life." She is tense, as angry as I have ever known her. "And isn't it interesting, you were programmed to *eliminate choice*."

"I feel it's up to the individual and his conscience," says the pregnant woman. "Or, er, rather *her* conscience."

"Probably *her* conscience," replies Leah sardonically. "I went for an abortion once and my husband paid the doctor not to do it."

"But if you have an abortion," retorts the hostess, "it's ready to bug you at any time of your life."

Leah answers readily. "Women have breasts and guilt. If you're not guilty about an abortion, you're guilty because you went to work when your child was young. Or because you didn't treat your husband right and that's why he has a girlfriend. It's endless. It's all *your* fault—whatever comes your way."

The pregnant woman, who has already gone through a twenty-four-hour labor with her first child, admits she is scared about giving birth again. "Scared?" she repeats. "I'm terrified."

"Well, you know the old saying," adds the hostess, "to be feminine you have to be uncomfortable. For instance, you have to wear a bra even though it can break your tissues." She looks around to see who's braless. Leah is the only one.

"As feminist as I am," adds one young woman, "I still can't get used to my not shaving. Neither can my husband."

"Yes," agrees the woman with a Glasgow accent. "Every winter I go through that—I'm not going to shave my legs. But in the spring," she laughs, "I always notice that I have very dark hair."

Leah pulls up her corduroy pants leg to reveal a jungle of black, curly hair. "So do I, and I haven't shaved for two years. I can't believe they're *my* legs when I look at them. But I'm not going to punish myself anymore."

"I suppose we can be deconditioned," says the pregnant woman. "I mean when I was in high school everyone wore a girdle. We thought we had to. Now most women don't. And lipstick."

The phone interrupts her. The hostess's husband is calling to say he wants to come home. Embarrassed laughter. They break up at II P.M.

Leah is tired as she walks out into the cool night. Tired of anecdotes about kids, of moral questions about cosmetics. Young mothers always react that way to abortion, she tells me. She worries that she became impatient, interjecting comments when she should have been listening. Perhaps she was too "matronizing." But for all her frustrations, she will go back next week and the week after until the group is established. "The women's movement has been a life raft for me. I don't feel guilty about my life the way I used to." The tension in her voice dissolves into a hush. "I really believe I have a future now."

While we drive through the streetlit night I think of how her life has changed in the past few years and how my opinion of her has changed in the past few weeks. I can see beyond the idealism and the contradictions to a woman working for independence on her own terms. "I've changed my attitudes about what my kids ought to look like—the hair styles, the coordinated clothes. I used to think they always reflected me. Now I don't. This makes them individuals as well as me an individual. And you know that discussion about the horseback riding lessons? Alec said he would drive. He was dealing in terms of *his* responsibility to the child. He wasn't pushing it on me, which is the way I lived before."

She pauses. "You know people criticize the movement for being middle class. One of the reasons is that middle-class women are no longer deluded by the 'nice-house-and-family dream.' We know how *limited* it is. Another point is that I'm a woman just as much as a welfare mother, inasmuch as we're assigned certain roles by society. Just because I'm middle class, doesn't mean I'm not oppressed."

I turn to watch Leah accelerate the Pontiac Suburban station wagon. Back to her family, her dog who eats crayons, her sculpture. Back to that beige brick house in Willowdale where she's liberating at least one middle-class housewife.

Indian Women and the Indian Act

"Indian Women Love Their People." "Resurrect the Bill of Rights." We are marching in front of the Toronto-Dominion Centre, which shelters within its sleek recesses a branch of the federal Department of Justice. It is noon in downtown Toronto, where people usually walk briskly and anonymously past each other. Today they stop and gawk at the outdoor cabaret: sixty women—clerks in the latest Harridge's winter coats, radical lesbians in leather jackets and jeans, academic women in muted shades of wool. Some Indian women. Mostly white women.

The revolutionary young filmmaker, who appears at every political event with the appropriate companion, today brings along a certified Indian man, complete with tasselled jacket. The bulky gray-haired housewife, who writes letters to department stores about sexist toys, hands out leaflets. And of course there is Jeannette Lavell, the Indian woman who demanded that the Supreme Court reinstate the native status she lost when she married a white man.

Lavell, in her brown blanket serape, her hair pulled back in a bright band, is explaining to reporters how the Indian Act is sexist: it permits men who marry outside to keep their status and even bring their white wives into the band, but the Court decided that the sexual equality granted in the Bill of Rights is superseded by the Indian Act. So today women in Vancouver, Edmonton, Thunder Bay, and Halifax are marching before similar offices as part of this National Day of Mourning for the Bill of Rights.

Beneath the placards and the mimeoed handbills and reels of newstape lies a very complicated issue. The classic liberal dilemma: individual rights versus cultural rights. While Lavell and other non-status Indian women demand their recognition by the Supreme Court, registered Indians at Caughnwaga Reserve near Montreal insist on their ethnic autonomy by evicting Indian women with white spouses. Which side has priority?

This isn't a simple conflict between women's liberation and cultural self-determination. Lavell's proponents claim that the Indian Act does not reflect Indian

This essay is reprinted from *Saturday Night*, April 1974. In 1985, the Indian Act was amended by the removal of the section which stripped Indian status from Indian women who married non-Indians or non-status Indians. It also made it possible for women who had lost their status for this reason and for their children to apply for band membership and status.

attitudes. For instance, when the Act requires that a woman adopt the status of her husband, it contravenes many matrilineal traditions. They say the Act was conceived by paternalistic Anglos, ignorant of native custom, who invoked the most expedient method of exclusion. There's a singular irony in excluding women, since many of the rights "granted" with Indian status—land, education, resource assets—are compensatory measures. How can Ottawa say that women, of all people, should not be compensated for their oppression?

Meanwhile, other natives demand that the Indian Act be maintained. They say that it would be impossible to reflect both matrilineal and patrilineal cultures. They claim that Lavell's position means assimilation. The reserves would become overcrowded; the government benefits would be cut down; the blood line would be diluted. So *both* sides say they are fighting genocide.

There are several solutions to the problem, but none of them satisfies everyone. The Indian Act could be amended so that both men and women would lose their status. Ottawa could adopt the tradition of Australia, New Zealand, and the United States, where anyone with one quarter aboriginal blood is considered native. Or status could be determined by each individual band. The only area of consensus in the whole muddle is that the final choice must be made by the Indians themselves.

Whatever the decision, it must be made within the machinations of a distant bureaucratic democracy. The partisans must propagandize. So they create media events like this "Day of Mourning." The demonstration isn't held for the enlightenment of the Toronto office workers but for the CBC cameras and the *Toronto Star* steno pads and the CKEY tape recorder. Jeannette Lavell stands over to the side of the T-D bank with a tall, imposing interviewer in a gaudy green corduroy suit and one of those little tweed hats. "You remember me, Jeannette?" he says in his announcer voice. "I was in your house when this whole thing started several years ago . . . Now if you could just step over here so our sound man can catch your voice." She relates her story in simple, clear words, as one who has reluctantly become accustomed to journalistic mediocrity. She won her case at the federal level; she lost it at the Supreme Court. Lavell emphasizes that she doesn't want to be singled out. She is just one of 6,000 women who have lost their status in the last ten years. "I can't do any more through the courts. It's up to the Canadian voters now."

The scene around the interview is a collage of contemporary Canadians. The middle-aged organizer for the Committee on the Status of Women is handing out protest pamphlets next to her car, which is plastered with bumper stickers: "Save Our North; Stop Their Pipeline." "Boycott Dare Cookies." She tries to recruit a young secretary in a rain slicker carrying a white lunch sack. "Oh, no, people from the office would see me." While the organizer coordinates the distribution of propaganda, she introduces reporters to marchers and greets new participants, like the young lesbian photographer. "It seems a simple issue to me," declares the young woman. "Indian women are being oppressed by men. The Indian government; the white government—they're all run by men. If the Bill of Rights can be overturned on this, then it can be contravened by other legislation, in other issues pertaining to women."

I know what she means. But what started out as an article on the Jeannette Lavell case—an exploration of sexism in the judicial process—has evolved into an essay on the ambivalence of leftist commitment. My reflexive sympathies still go to Lavell, but as I talked to status Indian women I grew more concerned about native tradition. I became confused about my own priorities. I realized that the decision must ultimately be made by the Indians themselves. Any solutions I had at the beginning are lost in the quagmire of my research. I can only share some of my questions.

We are sitting in Frances Garlow's small dining room on the Six Nations Reserve, with Judy Jamieson and Sally English. Frances and her husband own Garlow Motors—"Joe's lemon yard," as her friends around Brantford, Ontario, call it— and we can see the heaps of Buicks and Chevies piled next to the corrugated metal garage through her filmy white curtains. As morning moves into noon, our aggravated talk about Indian tradition and women's rights is mellowed by sandwiches and tea and cake at Frances's plastic-covered table.

Frances, a Mohawk who became an Oneida when she married, has five grown children. This warm, modest, charitable woman is active in the local Pentecostal Church. Judy was a non-status Indian before she married. She belongs to the Longhouse and makes leather goods with her husband. They have eight children. Sally's only child married a white man, but she agrees that her daughter should be removed from the band list. She bears a proud, protective commitment to her people. She headed the Six Nations Community project which brought water to the reserve. We discuss the status issue in general terms—referring only occasionally to the Lavell case and the situation of Yvonne Bedard, a woman who tried to return to Six Nations after she divorced her husband. Bedard was ordered off the reserve under the same section of the Indian Act.

Sally looks down at the pad where she has cautiously prepared some notes. "This is part of the tradition. It has been from way back. We were told, as soon as we were able to understand the opposite sex, that if you took a liking to a white man and married him, you would lose your status. It's part of our tradition."

Judy adds, "If it weren't this way, soon we'd be overrun with non-Indians. And white men would be able to buy up and monopolize the land holdings because they have more access to capital. There are white people here already who shouldn't be."

Frances nods. "If the Act was changed, it would soon be so overcrowded. I enjoy going back to the woods and wandering around. I keep my boots by the back door so I can go out when I want. I don't want to lose that."

Judy laughs. "All we have left is our reserve, and our Indian summer. I guess they can't take that away from us." She explains that the Iroquois Confederacy revoked the status of women who married white men long before the inception of the Indian Act. "It happened when Pauline Johnson's father asked if she could bring her white husband onto the Indian list."

They don't sympathize with Lavell's and Bedard's loss of identity. "Once an Indian, always an Indian," they say. They can have their heritage, but not the land. It's a simple equation—more residents would mean less land for everyone. "They knew what they were getting into when they got married."

Sally taps her pen on the table. "You know, I think the white man has incited the whole problem. The only reason Yvonne came back to the reserve was that *one* reporter. He went to her place three times..."

"You know, I think so too," says Judy. "I know Mrs. Bedard and I know she isn't pushy. She's just a simple woman. I think it got out of her hands. I don't know how her case got so far. In the papers and everything."

The drama is surrounded by white concern: the government issuing decisions, the courts upholding them, the journalists reporting them. The whites wrote the script and the whites play all the starring roles.

Frances declares, "This issue is part of our political and cultural tradition." "Yes, we all want to remain Indians," says Judy. "I'm worried for my children, for my grandchildren. I want them to have a future."

They are simple women who want to be left alone. Although I am another white intruder, they are very hospitable and—once the initial defensiveness dissolves— friendly to me. The frailty of my feminism is all too apparent to me when I look around at these independent women. Here I am, the soft Ms. City Writer proselytizing for equality to people like Sally English, who shot three deer with a Winchester one day before noon this year. Their very presence takes an edge off what they call my "women's lib" position.

We are in the living room of Pauline Harper, a Cree Indian from Edmonton who married a Métis and moved to Toronto. Sitting under the huge red and white feathered headdress is Jenny Margetts, Pauline's sister, and Monica Turner, an Ojibway from Thunder Bay. Ethel Johnson, also an Ojibway, sits on the easy chair beneath the deer's antlers. Across from her is Nellie Carlson, another Cree from

Edmonton. As we discuss the various rights and assets they have all lost by marrying whites or non-status Indians, the tone moves from exasperation to outrage.

Pauline, Jenny, Monica, Ethel, and Nellie vehemently support the Lavell position. As we chat, children wander in and out. Pauline's husband, Vern, vice-president of the Ontario Métis and Non-status Indian Association, stops by for a chat. Several friends drop in to add a few words. The atmosphere is casual, but hardly relaxed. These women feel dispossessed. I feel more like an intruder here than I did with Mrs. Garlow's friends, perhaps because the Canadian government has ruled against their position. Their words are fiery. They hear my questions as challenges. At times I feel more like a captured enemy envoy than an allied feminist.

Nellie, a bright, sassy, middle-aged woman wearing an Edmonton Eskimos button, leans forward and declares: "In Alberta we have oil royalties on the reserve. A woman who marries into another band really loses a lot. A Blackfoot girl from Cardston or a Cree girl from Hobbema would lose thousands and thousands. There's coal in Blackfoot, too."

Ethel adds: "We lost health care, reserve status, government benefits. Indians can have a free university education."

"And you can bet the white women on the reserves grab it," interrupts Nellie. "The white women who come onto the reserve get all these benefits for free. They become status Indians and we have nothing. Do you know there's a white woman who is an Indian chief?"

"Shouldn't the Indian Act supersede the Bill of Rights?" I ask. "It was written first and it represents a commitment to the Indian people."

Jenny points out the Joe Drybones case. The Act was overruled there as racist in its restriction of the sale of alcohol to Indians. "The Indian men supported *that.* If they don't think the Indian Act is discriminatory against women, then it's because of their own bias, their own status. The Indian leaders are very threatened by our stance."

They deny that the Indian Act preserves native culture. Although they all came from patrilineal tribes, they insist the authority on their reserve is shared equally by men and women. Besides, the Act certainly doesn't observe the traditions of the matrilineal Haida, Oneida, Mohawk, Seneca. How could one law reflect all Indian cultures?

Ethel adds, in a gentle, determined voice: "You know the thing that hurts the most is when you go back to the reserve. Your Indian brothers and sisters frown upon you and say you don't have a right to ceremonial dress. But your white sister, who was made an Indian by the government . . . "

"With her blond hair and pink skin," says Nellie. "I've seen that and it really hurts. She can participate fully in the customs."

Keeping their Indian heritage is their main concern. I ask Monica if she wants to go back to the reserve. She shouts back: "That's a scare tactic. Most of us have no intention of going back to live! I *would* like to go back for a visit. But on some of the reserves you can't stay after five-thirty according to the rules."

"That's right," says Pauline. "My son is just now being sent back from Alberta, from visiting his grandmother, because the band didn't want half-breeds on the reserve."

"Look," says Monica, "We just want to feel like we belong. It's all part of that—what's the word for when you rub something out?"

"Erase? Eliminate?"

"Genocide?"

"Yeah, *genocide,* that's the key to the whole thing," says Jenny. "The Canadian Government is trying to assimilate us. Just like they assimilated other Indians by forgetting to put them on the band lists or by holding out liquor and voting as incentives to leave the reserve until a few years ago. If our children were registered it would make a stronger native society. It would strengthen all of us. But the government doesn't want that."

The ultimate injustice of their situation, I realize, is that they are treated like whites by the Indians and like Indians by the whites.

"In one sense it's hard to forget we're Indians," exclaims Monica. "You know, I went into a grocery store in Thunder Bay to buy vanilla extract for my daughter's birthday cake. The owner came up to me with an old ruling encased in plastic that said they can't sell alcohol to Indians. Of all the nerve! I had the darndest laugh. But it's not funny."

Nellie nods. "You know, sometimes you get so angry about the injustice of the whole thing, that you have to make your point. I was asked to translate tapes from Cree to English for one hundred dollars a week in a government project. I turned it down. I said, 'You've asked the wrong woman. Remember, I'm *not* an Indian.' Would you believe I turned down one hundred dollars?"

I feel I'm back where I began, marching around the Toronto-Dominion Centre. I agree with their arguments against sexism in the Indian Act. I sympathize with their loss of heritage. Meanwhile, I recall the chorus of "It's our tradition" from the women at Six Nations. The dilemma is more intricate than I had imagined. I just want to forget the whole issue. But, perhaps because I carry a white conscience, I can't dismiss it. I continue to look for someone with an equitable solution.

Mary Terwyn doesn't feel bitter. She left her Manitoulin Island reserve twenty years ago to get a job in the city. Now she is an assistant supervisor of keypunchers at Imperial Oil in Toronto. Her long dark hair hangs over the shoulders of her black sheath dress, fashionably accentuated with gold jewelry and jazzy black pumps. She is the classic assimilated Indian.

Mary lost her Ojibway status when she married a white man, but she doesn't support Jeannette Lavell. In fact, Mary opposes Lavell as adamantly as the women on the Six Nations Reserve. "We knew what would happen if we married non-Indians; we were expecting it. Now why should we bring white men on the reserve? Natives shouldn't lose what little there is left."

Mary can't sympathize with claims like full college education. "I don't know what they're talking about—free education. I had five years of school on the reserve and the teachers I had . . ." She shakes her head. "There was only one teacher that we learned from. One of my teachers was a drunk. We used to play volleyball all day. I mean, this is why I came to Toronto."

Mary took upgrading courses at a city school, worked as a live-in maid for two years, became a housewife for six years, started at Imperial Oil, and worked up through the system. "If someone has enough ambition, you can do anything you want. For some Indian women it's very hard in the city. Maybe they just don't get the breaks. Or maybe they don't have enough ambition."

She objects to the notoriety the issue has received through white feminist involvement. "I don't think Indian status has anything to do with women's liberation, really. Indian women don't want more rights; we're satisfied with our traditions. And those white women never cared about other Indian issues—the number of Indian women in jails and on welfare—why should they care now? They're just interested in getting their own ticket to enforce the Bill of Rights. This is an Indian issue, not a white issue. It's not their problem."

Mary visits her family on the reserve every month, but she would never go back there to live. She's too used to the city, now. Besides, how would she earn an income? Her position seems so inconsistent: the middle-class success story demanding her people's cultural autonomy; someone who says that she doesn't want to go back to the band but who insists that she retains her full Indian identity. Her criticism of women who want to return to the reserve is made from the comfort of hindsight and a decent standard of living. She says she just wants to defend her friends and family and heritage. Somehow, her support of the band seems a little late and distant.

Most other non-status women in the city want a stake in both societies. Mary says that's impossible. You take your step—in your chosen direction, "within the system."

"Indian Women for Indian Rights." The red ink blares out on the white poster under three large red handprints. Non-status Indians from all over the country are meeting today in a Canadian Legion hall in Toronto to discuss their land claims. It's a strange atmosphere—the slick color photo of Queen Elizabeth in her white satin gown and diamond crown flanked by Indian paintings of symbolic animals and the provincial and national flags. The conference leaders, an informally defined group, sit at the yellow front table where a small child plays with the coffee cups amid the clutter of letters and reports. The room slowly fills to fifty people. The conversation fluctuates between gossip and meetingese. Old women in bargain-basement dresses sit next to young girls in slick pantsuits. Everyone wears some Indian token: a pin, a beaded necklace. The pace of the meeting is slow and uneven.

The conference itself is a lesson in the political knots of the non-status issue. One of the first orders of business is a discussion of government funds. Ottawa supports the National Native Women's Association. The women here today claim *they* represent native women and they should be funded. Meanwhile, the Native Council of Canada supports their position. The National Indian Brotherhood opposes it. So who speaks for native people?

"Can't we possibly find an organization that will represent all of us?"

"You hear so many views from Indian men. Harold Cardinal said that we shouldn't lose our rights. He wrote a book, *The Unjust Society,* and then *he* came out against Lavell."

"Yeah, you should look how many of the Indian leaders have white wives and then you can understand their position easily enough."

"I get outraged when white people complain that Indians aren't together on this issue. How can they talk? Are they together with all the people in Europe? We are a nation of many peoples, many tribes."

Another typical white complaint is political perspective. When we can't discern who represents the Indians, we ask which side is conservative and which side is radical. Some of the women here today are ardent socialists. Others shudder at a mention of the Left. Meanwhile, some of their opponents subscribe to Red Power militancy, but the women at Six Nations say they're just trying to preserve tradition. Political affiliation remains as inconsequential to the Indians as any other white label.

The meeting moves slowly through the day with official business; a film by Duke Redbird; a potluck lunch of rolled bologna, cheese, salad, stacks of white bread; and a hundred interruptions by friends and husbands and children. No one wants to be here in this stilted, formal conference situation. But somehow, over the hours, as the memories and jokes mingle with the prepared reports and formal resolutions, the room feels more like a livingroom than a legion hall.

Late in the afternoon, someone at the back of the room announces that a non-status woman was just denied burial rights on the Caughnwaga reserve. They couldn't break tradition for her, as they do for the dogs and cats of white Montrealers who rent part of the reserve as a pet cemetery.

The women are indignant.

"That points up the whole question about where is our home."

"We don't have one even in death."

"I think we should send a telegram petitioning the chief to allow her to be buried there." The meeting dissolves into a discussion of how the message should be worded.

"What should it say—to have 'non-status Indians' buried?"

"No, *Indians*. We're Indians, like anybody else."

Enter the CBC, with bright lights and cumbersome sound equipment and intimidation. The non-conference is further disturbed as one of the leaders is called for an interview. Chairs and tables are rearranged so that, for the cameras, the meeting will look more like a meeting. After the CBC exits, everyone compliments the leader for making the evening news. It will be good for the cause. Maybe they will get some money from Ottawa.

The whole day has been an odd compromise between Indian tradition and white bureaucracy. "I was given Robert's *Rules of Order*," declares the chairwoman, "but we're going to disregard them and the white man's parliamentary procedure. We seem to be skipping all over the agenda—which is good—the beginning of the meeting is at the end and the end is at the beginning."

One woman announces the next general conference to be held in Vancouver. She raises the problem of recruiting participants. "The government pays people sixty dollars a day to go to their Indian meetings. How are we going to get people on our side when we don't even know if we'll be able to pay for the hall?"

The meeting has no end, just as it had no beginning.

I keep thinking back on that funeral procession for the Bill of Rights last fall. I wonder if we white academics and secretaries and social workers and housewives weren't just repeating a traditional mistake, coopting an Indian issue for our own. I remember one young woman eagerly passing out leaflets encouraging passers-by to join the march. This was her first demonstration. Yes, she saw both sides of the issue. "There is danger of infringing on cultural rights and I thought about that for a long time. But women get screwed up by every culture and my commitment has to be to women. The government has to protect individual rights. After all, they've taken away other rights from the Indians, the right to scalp people." I was as abashed by her naïveté as by the sexism of two men I met later. They couldn't understand the fuss. "But the woman who marries white gets to keep her husband's status. She is white. That's the way our society works. The kids are white. It all works out. There are the same amount of whites and Indians in the end." When I reread the handbills—"We mourn the ruling over Indian women," written in Ojibway and English by the egalitarian Committee on the Status of Women—I realize that their argument is still valid, but not comprehensive. I continue to support Lavell, but I doubt whether the opinion of any non-Indian matters.

The answer can't be drawn from simplistic priorities—sexism or racism. The solution must preserve both individual and cultural rights within the context of native autonomy. And because of that, the Indians themselves must find the answer. But who speaks for the Indians? The Native Council of Canada or the National Indian Brotherhood? Jeanette Lavell or Mary Terwyn? Perhaps the ultimate irony is that the government has so factionalized the Indians that there can be no representative answer.

Sisterhood Is Variable

Ms. and *Spare Rib* are as different as two sisters can be. Both magazines grew up with the same vocation to provide stimulus and support for the Women's Liberation Movement. They both offer forums for debate, testimony, and information. There the family resemblance ends.

Ms. is older, more professional and affluent. She is settled with, if not married to, the system. She is the kind of modern woman invited to trendy parties. Independent, but not strident. Provocative, but not offensive. A very successful lady in her own radical slick way. *Spare Rib* is fresh, direct, idealistic. She maintains a sisterhood with *Ms.* However, she has moved out on the system. "Success" isn't as relevant as "commitment." She translates politics as revolution, not as statistical representation. Unlike her sensible big sister, she is unequivocally socialist.

Ms. and *Spare Rib* reflect differences between American and British feminism. The United States has a "broader" if not "higher" consciousness. The radical dialectic is similar, but the American roots are spread wider in equal-rights legislation, feminist theater, self-help clinics, liberation bookmobiles, women's studies courses, cooperative daycare centers. The rhetoric is an articulate expression of the distinction. Last year, while Britons lobbied ardently for the use of "Ms" on passports, U.S. businesses were using it routinely. (The conservative publishing house McGraw Hill had directed editors to avoid "the fair sex," "the ladies," "housewives.") American feminists would never use *girl* to refer to adult females, although the word is current at Women's Liberation meetings here. The movement is more fully accepted *and* more easily compromised in North America. *Ms.* thrives with 120-plus pages and a circulation of over 100,000 in a country where feminism is actually an asset to congressional candidates. *Spare Rib* subsists within 47 pages and a 16,000 circulation in a milieu where feminism has the same suspicious overtones as psychotherapy. *Spare Rib* often seems to have more *potential* than *Ms.* simply because she isn't scarred by as many concessions.

Like *Ebony*, the glossy journal for Blacks, *Ms.* affects and reflects the creeping moderation of American protest politics. But she never claimed to be a revolutionary

---

This essay originally appeared in the *New Statesman*, 17 January 1975. Some of my predictions were quite wrong. The old *Ms.* died, while *Spare Rib* has continued to publish up to the present. A "new *Ms.*" was born in 1990 with increased international coverage and no advertising.

agent. She is a discreet chaplain to middle-income women who are working toward equality, which is different from change. *Ms.* is a symbol of the classic American compromise between idealism and affluence.

Spare Rib is less focused. She proposes to reach a wide spectrum of women: factory workers, housewives, radical professionals. But because women's liberation is less integrated here, the readers and writers are largely young, schooled, Marxist Londoners. The movement here is concentrated on the Left (as it was in the United States five years ago) for several reasons. Women's oppression is a compatible issue with Third World and working-class oppression. Also, women who sought a forum for their commitment often found the political groups themselves heavily sexist. Many remained within their Trotskyist or CP caucuses. Others went on independently to found crêches, health collectives, and magazines like *Spare Rib*.

Perhaps one reason why the movement hasn't spread beyond the Left is that women's status is institutionalized if not equalized in Britain. Women have guaranteed "places," for instance, as students and teachers in single-sex schools and colleges. Women have more of a tradition in *certain* mainstream activites like literature and politics. (Compare the renown of Lessing, Drabble, Spark, Murdoch, O'Brien with their American counterparts. Consider the remarkable political success of Bernadette Devlin, Margo MacDonald, Margaret Thatcher, Shirley Williams within established parties.) The British movement is subverted before it begins because middle-class women see little need for feminism. This illusion is magnified by reserve and formality. Despite the overtures to fair play, the sexism is more ritualized and more deeply etched here. *Spare Rib* does little to counteract the alienation of middle-class women from the movement. Her slapdash style and ideological earnestness are more "alternative" than professional, indistinguishable from *Women's Report, Red Rag, Shrew*. Duplicated energies are often wasted. Here they are siphoned away from a potentially large constituency. *Spare Rib*'s propaganda powers are as restrained by Leftist insensitivity as *Ms.*'s powers are coopted by capitalism.

Both magazines succeed in their coverage of the arts, acknowledging and stimulating "female culture." Their letters constitute a unique community bulletin board with requests for legal help, lessons of consciousness, notices about conferences and studies. The No Comment section of *Ms.* and "The Ones That Got Away" in *Spare Rib* expose media chauvinism and provide good sardonic relief. *Ms.* excels in her feminist round-up of the news. The "story for free children" is another valuable department. *Spare Rib*'s special features include the adventures of "Li-Shuangshuang," a Maoist feminist comic. And the medical reporting—long, personal coverage about subjects like anorexia nervosa and vaginismus—is consistently good.

The two magazines have chosen different priorities in the classic propagandist's dilemma: political fervor versus professional journalism. *Spare Rib*'s independence from the corporate media keeps her poor as well as pure. The five full-time collective members earn twenty pounds a week. *Ms.* is produced by fifty people, including an advertising department of ten. *Spare Rib* has the conviction; *Ms.* has the readers. The distinction becomes clear by comparing two fairly representative issues: *Ms.,* no. 40 (October 1974) and *Spare Rib,* no. 29 (Fall 1974). One begins with the admonition that it is too easy to be matronizing. Certainly they both deserve kudos for courage and hard work. They are also established enough to benefit from careful analysis. Anything less is condescension, not sisterhood. Support means candid criticism as well as renewed subscriptions.

Ms. sells a cover photo of Katharine Graham in pearls and a white polka-dot dress. Just a blush of makeup and a wide, amiable smile. "Meet the Most Powerful Woman in America." Packed into the same issue and laced in turquoise ink are "Surviving Widowhood," "The Patty Hearsts That Got Away," "Must We Be Childless to Be Free?" *Ms.* knows what will sell. Forty-seven-year-old Katharine Graham is an appealing choice for role model of the month. Graham is rich, bright, powerful, attractive, maternal. The vacuous content of the piece is almost as irritating as the slick style. This devoted mother managed a depressive husband until he committed suicide and now manages a media empire including the *Washington Post, Newsweek,* the *International Herald Tribune,* six broadcasting stations. But just what does she *do?* She is friendly with Truman Capote; she has met JFK and the Emperor of Japan. Where can the reader empathize? She is referred to as "Mrs. Graham" rather than as "Ms. Graham," or "Graham," which would be consistent with house style. How much of her treatment is related to her $20,000 investment in *Ms.?* There are plenty of gutsy women around. Why choose the owner of notoriously sexist publications?

Feminist is a word much bandied about by *Ms.* Like *liberal,* and *progressive,* it seems to be a virtue which would be uncharitable to measure or reserve. In America feminism is not only becoming a professional advantage; it is becoming a profession among women's studies instructors, women's liaison officers, women journalists.

In Britain, feminism is still more threat than promise. *Spare Rib* may be less compromised than *Ms.* but she is also less coherent, waffling between proselytizing to the masses and theorizing for the converted. This edition is a tentative notebook of good ideas. The black and white cover blurts out "Contraceptive C?n." The lettering has been squeezed from a tube of spermicide. The red subheads include "Women Workers," "Sex and Self-Hate," "Girlhood in the First World War." The image is angry, bold, sardonic.

"On the Bench," the account of the author's job at an electronics plant in Bradford, is honest: a middle-class woman's politically outraged and personally sympathetic view of the working-class women's situation. She tells us how hard they work, how little recognition they receive, how their exploitation continues at home. Feminism is as alien to them as the idea of asking their husbands to share the washing up. But what can the women's movement do for and learn from them? Perhaps all *we* can do is to be aware of their oppression in relationship to our own?

Granted, the energies of a small staff are finite, but *Spare Rib* doesn't bother to discern between documentaries and home movies. The feature coverage is insouciant, losing momentum after the idea stage. The article about Oliver Schreiner, the South African feminist, is a fine topic. The insipid format, however, consists of a stilted interview with Schreiner's biographer. The cover story on contraception is good investigative reportage, exposing inadequate information supplied with chemical contraceptives. The writers' coup is landing a copy of C-Film's confidential marketing reports that show an unethical discrepancy with their proposed sales pitch. The piece was taken from *Women's Report,* which again raises the problems of distinctive identity and duplicated efforts.

The "women's movement" is, of course, an ideal, a variable ideal. Both magazines represent and stimulate the movement within cultural limitations. They might well challenge and learn from each other. The U.S. struggle is three, four, five years ahead (fill in appropriate struggle and appropriate time), but the question is whether it is moving in the right direction. We should be wary of *Ms.*'s dimming sense of urgency. Meanwhile, *Spare Rib* is more likely to fade away than grow fat and complacent. Idealism isn't sustenance. She needs contributions from professional feminist journalists (perhaps a regular literary tithe?). Some people design better than they write; some people promote better than they edit. *Spare Rib* has to choose between being an ad hoc forum and a challenging, lucid magazine. She cannot survive on disco benefits and lapel-pin sales. We are told to trust in God: she'll provide. *Ms.* and *Spare Rib* are mixed blessings. At the very least, they're good answers to that inane question: "Do you belong to Women's Lib?"

Letter from Australia

Australian writers are tickled about being "flavor of the month" in American bookstores. The Australia Council proudly cites eighty-eight recent reviews of Australian books in journals ranging from the *Witchita Falls Times* to the *New York Times*. Some Australians say they owe their high profile to *Crocodile Dundee* or to the topicality of the white bicentenary. Most know that their visibility is enhanced by millions of government dollars spent promoting Australian culture here and abroad.

During my six months traveling throughout this exquisite and diverse country, I have been impressed by the enormous popular interest in serious Australian literature. Australian authors benefit from vigorous academic support for contemporary literature, a lively interstate series of readings, extensive exposure of writers in the media, and a concerted campaign to ensure international visibility. Meanwhile, the publishing industry is plagued by a surprisingly antediluvian branch plant mentality which allows British firms to select books entering and leaving the country. Despite traditional economic and cultural ties to Britain, Australians often seem more interested in being published in the United States. They imagine an American edition will bring substantial income and prestige. This year the Australia Council's Literary Arts Board and other government agencies are giving them a big bicentennial push.

The Board is currently funding a series of literary readings around the United States, including presenting ten Australians in the fashionable series at the 92nd Street Y in New York. They are sending Dorothy Hewett to the International Women Playwrights' Conference in Buffalo in October and then on to Rollins College in Florida, where she will be writer-in-residence, a position they regularly co-fund with the private college.

Other standard government sponsorships include a place at Yaddo Writers' Colony and a graduate fellowship to Stanford's Creative Writing program. The Board offers assistance to overseas publishers of Australian work; the initial subsidy went to Houghton Mifflin for poet Judith Wright's *The Double Tree*. They have brought over magazine editors and academics in hopes of cultivating attention for

This essay appeared in a slightly abridged form in the *Washington Post Book World*, 7 August 1988, ©1988, The Washington Post. Reprinted with permission.

"Auslit." This year they are paying for the visits of five American publishers (including representatives from Persea, Norton, and Abrams) to encourage U.S. editions. In New York, the Board hires a publicist who reports success lobbying for reviews in *Ms., Booklist,* the *Washington Times,* and other journals. While U.S. promotion is emphasized, the Board publicizes writers internationally. They have given translation fee subsidies to Swedish, French, and Italian publishers and have financially supported Australian inclusion in foreign anthologies. Qantas, the government airline, gave away free copies of Ross Terrill's *The Australians* to first-class passengers. On a more academic note, Antipodean tax dollars have funded the Chair for Australian Studies at Harvard University and have contributed to Australian studies centers at such places as Pennsylvania State University and the University of Texas at Austin. This year Australian literature will be on the bill at the Folger Library, the Smithsonian Library, the Chicago Public Library, and the Conference of the Modern Language Association in New Orleans.

Australians purchase more books per capita than Americans or Britons. As Susan Ryan, head of Penguin Australia, said in a recent *Bulletin* interview, "I think Australians are increasingly interested in Australia and in themselves, so Australian fiction is greatly in demand." One of the most highly praised novelists is Queenslander David Malouf, who told me that his novel, *Johnno,* put Brisbane on the map. "America has already been mapped in literature. But Australian fiction has the advantage of having a whole country to fill."

As I talked with novelists and poets around the country, I was pleasantly taken aback by the self-identification "full-time writer," a term one rarely hears in the United States. Indeed, many writers here can afford to be full-time because of increasing domestic and foreign popular markets for their work, use of contemporary literature in the schools, public lending right royalties, and generous allocation of fellowships. One snide critic recently suggested that every current Australian novel is preceded by a grant and followed by a prize. Australian publishing is marked by a stunning array of awards, travel burseries, residencies, and even pensions for deserving writers over fifty-five. The Board funds journals, publishers, and community arts programs in addition to individual authors. Over the years, one frequently sees the same names among the honored. Poets Robert Adamson, Robert Gray, Les Murray, and John Tranter have each received six or seven fellowships.

Writers say they don't know how they would survive without the government money. Les Murray was quoted in a recent history of the literature board as saying, "I think the Australian patronage system is quite good. . . . I don't think that patronage makes authors into appendages of the State, and it is certainly not a prize or privilege. If we are made part of the education of people, they owe us a living too." Thomas Keneally found the support "Absolutely essential toward my becoming a professional writer. It also enabled attempts at a different kind of writing than one would essay without the financial support of a grant." Novelist Frank Moorhouse had his own inimitable response:

> I would have done the writing somehow by using the methods as old as writing itself and which I used in my early career before new writer grants, i.e. writing in the employer's time (damaging to the spirit and the economy)— fraud, use of faked medical certificates to get time off, use of credit accounts to stockpile food which were never paid (damaging to the spirit and the economy)—use of accumulated sick and recreation leave (damaging to the health)—borrowed money which I was then unable to pay resulting in legal problems and garnishes. The fellowship scheme is therefore not only a more civilised way for the writer to work but less damaging to the economy.

Such government largesse, as well as the widespread sense of individual entitlement, is enough to inspire astonishment, envy, and admiration in the heart of a visiting writer. Australians, of course, are envious of Americans, imagining that if they lived in the United States, they would receive huge royalties and massive grants from private foundations. (They cite, for instance, fellowships from the Guggenheim and Ford foundations, unaware that those institutions fund far more academic projects than literary ones.) However, there is one consistent trans-Pacific parallel in literary sponsorship: women and minorities are underfunded. None of the current Australian senior literary fellowships went to a woman.

Not only do Australians want to read Australian books, but they want to meet Australian writers in person. Literary festivals and reading venues have burgeoned around the country. Audience enthusiasm is stunning. Over 20,000 attended Writers' Week, held at open-air tents in Adelaide's blistering March heat. Newer festivals—Brisbane's Warana Writers Week, Melbourne's Spoleto Festival, and Perth's Writers' Festival—attract smaller, but vociferous crowds. While Adelaide's Writers' Week was uneven in quality and maddeningly disorganized, the crowds were patient and eager. They sat for hours in the South Australian sun listening to favorite writers read from their works. The book tent did a rapid trade in Australian poetry and fiction. Likewise, the Sydney Writers' Week, held in mid-February, drew together a wide audience into the elegant Victorian Town Hall as well as to rowdy public readings at a pub across town.

With all this consumer and government support for contemporary writing, it's astonishing that Australia still suffers from a branch plant publishing culture. At writers' festivals, I was surprised to see panels dominated by British-owned houses such as Collins Australia, Picador Australia, Allen and Unwin Australia, and so on. Some of these companies have extensive local lists and claim to be editorially autonomous from their UK owners, but as the Canadians learned a long time ago, cultural imperialism is hard to shake. Ottawa passed laws limiting U.S. media and the Canada Council has strongly supported indigenous publishing. Generally, Australians harbor deep ambivalence about the British, whom they constantly disparage as "Poms" in conversation, but whom they officially invest with sovereign power over their country. As recently as 1975, Prime Minister Gough Whitlam was summarily dismissed from office by the British governor general.

Independent publisher Hilary McPhee, who with her partner opened McPhee Gribble thirteen years ago, told me, "The commitment of overseas publishers must be unstable because the local company is tied to the health of the parent company. Some of these firms are bought and sold with little notice. They cut their editorial staffs in half and put their lists on the market. We're delighted that Australian literature is so popular now, but like any intellectual climate, this literary taste is vulnerable."

Overseas companies not only influence what gets published in this country, but they affect what culture is imported. Internationally, English-language rights are divided between the British and American publishers with the same noblesse oblige which characterized the Pope's division of the world between Spanish and Portuguese colonizers. British companies effectively select American, Canadian, and British writers for Australian readers, determine which writers are translated, and are responsible for distributing their firm's international list here. As someone who has published five novels with a major British house, I have suffered the pitfalls of conglomerate distribution in each of the seven Australian states. My London publisher blames the Melbourne distributor who, in turn, blames the London publisher. In one sense I am lucky because I do have British publishers and a number of my books have managed to migrate over the years. American books which are not picked up by a British house currently have virtually no chance of exposure here. Books with strong U.S. regional voices, including books by Black authors, have trouble getting literary visas.

Some of the most provocative Australian titles are being offered by independent houses. McPhee Gribble has a particularly strong local fiction list. The University of Queensland Press in Brisbane has met great success with Rosa Cappiello's novel, *Oh Lucky Country,* a stinging exposé of Anglo-Australian treatment of Italian immigrants. Adelaide's Tantrum Press has just produced a brilliant audiotape of feminist prose and poetry from South Australia. Out West, the Fremantle Arts Centre Press, has won kudos for Sally Morgan's *My Place,* the autobiography of a young woman searching for her aboriginal roots.

No doubt the reputation of Australian literature will continue to flourish among a growing national and international audience. During the last fifteen years, the changes have been staggering. Veteran Sydney novelist Elizabeth Harrower told me, "Writers were thin on the ground when I began writing. The Australia Council changed all that. It's much easier now than it used to be. I didn't read Australian writers until I was in my early thirties. We looked in the opposite direction—toward Europe." In 1972 only 19 novels were published in Australia. By 1986, the number had reached 200. In 1974, 1,615 Australian books were published and by 1985 the figure was 3,570.

According to Elaine Lindsay of the Literary Arts Board, Australians wish the American government would send more writers over here. She did think that the exchange in terms of the printed word was evening out.

> The trade has been one way for so long that it's nice to be able to send our books to the United States. Some people say that exporting our literature is part of the "cultural cringe" because we need overseas approval to tell us it's good enough. But that's not what it's all about. It's just saying, "Here's some interesting reading." Aside from the economic benefits of exporting our literature, it's nice to be able to have something good to offer. It causes us to look at ourselves in a new way when people say, "Hey, this is different."

Reading along the Dyke

We walk barefoot along the stone wall which separates the mountains from the sea. Our balance is held by poetry, engraved into the top of the wall. We *feel* these words through our soles. They give us direction, courage, and momentum. We assume a confidence beyond our experience. We *know* with a collective consciousness that the wall does not belong between the water and the land. We who walk on the wall are called outsiders. However, because we are in between, we are inside(h)ers. On a round earth, those who live on the margins also live in the middle. We name ourselves after the wall on which we walk, the dyke which affords us perspective and holds our world together.

In these four recent volumes of lesbian feminist poetry, *Flamingoes and Bears* by Jewelle Gomez; *Borderlands/La Frontera* by Gloria Anzaldúa; *Trying to Be an Honest Woman* by Judith Barrington; and *Beautiful Barbarians,* edited by Lilian Mohin, we find poets writing on the edge. The dyke. The border. The boundary. Sexual marginality is a lens through which to consider other marginalities—national, racial, linguistic, economic. From such poetry we learn about uniqueness and commonality. The writers do not deny difference. Rather they relish individual identity and cultural distinctiveness while observing the similarities within the differences. They articulate a context of conflict and connection.

At a time when "postfeminist" values are chic, these poets persist in their social protest as well as their love for other women. Not surprisingly all the books here are produced by independent houses. While mainstream publishing does offer some radical material, that work is infrequent and often tokenized. Most conglomerate editors would have us believe that engaged literature is passé, that "serious" writing has turned back toward conventional notions of family, back toward a tedious, solipsistic aesthetic. The poets in these volumes not only *come from* but *bring forward* a range of races and nationalities—Black, Chicana, Asian, white, Scottish, English, Indian, Irish, Australian, American. These lesbian writers live *in* the world. They write with outrage, passion, street wisdom, and elegance. Their voices keep us alert.

This essay originally appeared in the premier issue of *Out/Look* 1, no. 1 (Spring 1988). Reprinted courtesy of *Out/Look,* the national lesbian and gay quarterly.

In *Flamingoes and Bears,* Jewelle Gomez bridges a variety of cultures. Her work is a provocative mixture of the analytical, the sensual, and the fey. A Black woman born in Boston, she now lives in Jersey City. She has emerged from a family of strong women with a forceful, delicate voice singing, wailing, laughing, scolding, commemorating.

Her politics move with clear-eyed fury in "Arthur McDuffie," the story of a Black Miami man killed by four white police officers; in "Housework," the tale of a domestic worker who deserts her duties; and in "Hiroshima Red in Black and White," the description of a photo exhibit of nuclear murder. Gomez exposes the razor edge where lesbianism and feminism meet in her poems, "Oral Tradition" and "Sir Raleigh." The latter is an amusing tribute to her Raleigh bicycle.

> the only thing a man ever gave me
> that was always good
> between my legs.

And she does not spare women her irony as she investigates the hypocrisies of sisterhood in "My Chakabuku Mama" and "Our Feminist Who Art in Heaven."

Gomez's erotic writing is infused with tender humor and constant watchfulness in such poems as "At Night," "Love Poem for C. C.," and "Hands." In "Approach," she writes,

> The perspiration on your leg
> where it meets mine
> is a conductor.

My favorite of the love letters is "For Mi Osita,"

> In sleep she arches a brow
> over her dark shadowed eye,
> causing ripples
> that move out from her center
> to encircle me.
> Light sneaks into our shuttered room.
> The scented air lingers on the copper of her skin
>
> and the coal black of her curls.
> Her sleeping hums in my ear
> closing out noise of the traffic below
> and Monday to come,
> harmonizing with the rustle of the sheet

as she turns her back to me.
An invitation I always recognize.

Gomez's title poem, "Flamingoes and Bears," is a playful excursion into the dangers and delights of perversion.

Flamingoes and bears
meet secretly
on odd street corners.
Horses and chickens
elephants and geese
look shocked and appalled.

But the Flamingoes and Bears learn to ignore the others. What was once kept secret is now flaunted. Gomez doesn't simply come out of the closet; she leaves the house. While some lesbian writers celebrate the naturalness of their lives, Gomez questions nature.

there's room in the world
for a bear who likes palm trees
and a bird who loves honey.

The poem is highlighted on the book cover, where bright flamingo pink stripes are crossed by a strong, bear black bar. Prison stripes are converted into festive fabric. Social stigma metamorphoses into social grace. Gomez's response to conservative outrage is to be magnificently outrageous.

Gloria Anzaldúa traverses many boundaries in her powerful *Borderlands/La Frontera*. The reader is directly engaged in emigration and immigration through her use of Spanish and English; through her constant reminders that she is both Mexican and U.S. American; through her passage from prose in the first section to poetry in the second. The Chicana journey is crystallized in her poignant "To live in the Borderlands means you."

To live in the Borderlands means to
put *chile* in the borscht,
eat whole wheat *tortillas,*
speak Tex-Mex with a Brooklyn accent;
be stopped by *la migra* at the border check-
points . . .

To survive the borderlands
you must live *sin fronteras*
be a crossroads.

Anzaldúa writes with impressive range in the 100 pages of poetry. This second part of the book, which I found more fluid and gripping than the prose section, has the drama of a serious historical novel. Her poetry couples uncompromising social critique with homage to personal heroism. For Anzaldúa, as for Gomez, the women in her family stimulate the ink in her blood. She ends the book with Spanish and English versions of "Don't Give In, Chicanita," an inspiring legacy to her niece. And she pays tribute to her mother in the heart-wrenching *"sus plumas el viento."*

> cutting washing weighing packaging
> broccoli spears carrots cabbages in 12 hours 15
> double shift the roar of machines inside her
> head. . . .

> She vows to get out
> of the numbing chill, the 110 degree heat
> If the wind would give her feathers for fingers
> she would string words and images together.
> *Pero el viento sur le tiro su saliva*
> *pa' 'tras en la cara.*

Her poem "Corner of 50th Street and Fifth Av.," about the harassment of a Puerto Rican by New York police, reverberates painfully with the incident described in Gomez's "Arthur McDuffie." Another vivid exposure of racist brutality is "We Call Them Greasers," a white man's account of running Chicano(a)s off the land, burning their homes, raping a woman and then murdering her by sitting on her face.

Born a Chicana on the Texas-Mexico border, Anzaldúa acknowledges many heritages. In "Holy Relics," she recounts how the Spanish church exploited the sainthood of Teresa of Avila.

> The good father drew near,
> lifted her hand as if to kiss it,
> placed a knife under her wrist
> and from her rigid arm he severed it.

The long, fever-pitched ballad reveals that priests continued to raid Teresa's coffin is search of first-class relics, appropriating her goodness for their own purposes. The poem is held together with a haunting refrain.

> We are the holy relics,
> the scattered bones of a saint,
> the best loved bones of Spain.
> We seek each other.

"Holy Relics" graphically documents the dismemberment of Teresa and testifies to the cultural dismemberment of Anzaldúa's people. This poem is a metaphor for the rest of this brave book in which Anzaldúa continually recollects and remembers.

In *Trying to Be an Honest Woman,* Judith Barrington creates graceful, urbane poetry, claiming respect with its distilled clarity and hitting the deepest psychological nerves. While Barrington's migration may first seem less dramatic than that of the previous poets, she also finds herself crossing difficult borders—as an English expatriate in Spain and then in the States; as a middle-class, white woman reduced to modest means; as the gentile partner of a Jewish lover. Inspired by Adrienne Rich's *Women and Honor: Some Notes on Lying,* Barrington attends to her ideas with scrupulous precision. Her honesty is not so much a penitent confession as a vibrant statement of liberation.

Six of her poems were included in *Beautiful Barbarians.* Under the title, "Four Days in Spain," these pieces trace a journey the poet took with her sister after their parents were killed. The Spanish trip symbolizes a passage from childhood to orphanhood. Barrington looks closely at herself, at her sister, at the two of them together and apart. The silence between these sad women strikes louder than the words. "Today we are sisters, lost in a rare world, / but we never mention the purpose of the trip" (p. 43).

Each time I read Barrington's book something new absorbs me. This encounter, it is the three poems, "How I Came to America 1, 2 and 3," the titles of which might be read as is or with quotation marks around the word *came* or around the words *came to* for these are poems of movement, of sex, and of awakening. In the first, the narrator leaves a London lover, who stands open-mouthed in the rain. In the second, she settles with a new lover in Oregon. Within three weeks she is out on the doorstep, having thrown away her old, red backpack for a suitcase. The final poem is a love/hate memory of intense London feminist meetings where "they all jostled in those smoke-filled rooms." The new world, she finds, is just a little too sanitary and efficient.

I crossed an ocean to escape the spiralling talk
and now I scan this clean air for some verbal passion
or even just an honest-to-god position

Barrington's scope is wide; this is the work of a woman who lives passionately: walking outdoors, reading books, making love, always watching for how to live a better life—more honest, more whole. Her last poem is well chosen for a book which celebrates the courage of continuing.

Anniversary Poem

Sometimes tolerated, rarely celebrated,
  we've chosen to return over and over
  to questions of how to love decently
  in a world polluted with its own fear
where only passion keeps the green coming
  as we circle and climb
  like the palms toward cleaner light....

We've sung Hebrew songs in a dark car
and changed our habits only when we had to
as we reached for enough room to be close.
Our anger was like hailstones
on new buds, too early in spring—
yet most of them bloomed, compelled by the sun
circling and climbing, climbing and circling.

In the context of so much lesbian literature where love flickers with phoenix-like rapidity, it is heartening to witness the commonplace rewards of loyalty. The poem also marks a blessed contrast to the lack of communication in "Four Days in Spain." On this anniversary, the women toast their differences, growing separately and together.

The sixteen poets in Lilian Mohin's startling anthology, *Beautiful Barbarians,* published by Britain's Onlywomen Press, savor the integration of politics into daily life. Two-thirds of these *Beautiful Barbarians* have settled outside their native lands for extended periods. This selection reflects the cosmopolitan nature of the British women's movement as well as the editor's personal sensibilities, for Mohin, herself, is an American who has lived in England for many years. The poets write with the tough wisdom of exiles and the poignant idealism of expatriates. While this is a consistenly fascinating book, I will highlight the work of five poets: Mary Dorcey, Jackie Kay, Sheila Shulman, Gillian Hanscombe, and Suniti Namjoshi.

Dorcey, a Dubliner now living in the West of Ireland, composes with a wry and elegant common sense. Her feminism is woven with unsentimental directness through "Songs of Peace," where she traces a heritage of women's antiwar activism. In "The Ordinary Woman," she responds to a reader who demands a poem about "the ordinary woman." Dorcey takes six pages to list all the ordinary women for whom she writes.

The woman who stays at home
The woman who has no home

The woman who raises children
The woman who can have no children
The woman who has too many children
The woman who wants no children. . . .

The naive woman   the paranoid woman
The passive woman   the dominant woman
The silly woman   the hard woman
The placid woman   the angry woman
The sober woman   the drunken woman
The silent woman   the screaming woman

Dorcey's love for women spans the shops, the streets, the prisons, the farms, the bedrooms. Lovingly fingering physical details, she investigates the fertile cracks in everyday contradictions. She tells us to continue beyond the despair. In "Beginning," she manages to write erotically about being abandoned.

[She] smiled at each woman she passed in the street
and asked nobody home
who might find out
that for months she still slept
in your blood stained sheets.

Sheila Shulman also writes about separation—of her Eastern European Jewish family from their land, of herself from the New York where she grew up, as well as from lovers and friends. The writing is rich with familiar, comfortable images of books and teacups and gossip. Her often untitled poems carry an intense emotional understatement, daring the reader to touch the fire beneath the surface. I cry every time I read "For Colleen (drowned April, 1980)," where Shulman considers a long friendship with Colleen, an expatriate from an unnamed country in Africa. The women support each other through loss and loneliness. Sheila survives. Colleen doesn't.

in the warm house   in big jumpers
you sat in your room   I in mine
we read   wrote
met for tea   for scratch meals
in the evening   we sat around
smoked   talked

we liked each other
I think we even liked ourselves
we were easy together . . .

I went to the Scilly Isles
you might have gone there

not to find you   but to say goodbye
in the place   that used to be called
the Blessed Isles   the Isles of the Dead

for form's sake   I asked
if anyone had seen you
old women   with kind blue eyes
wished me luck   gave me cups of tea

I looked for you
not for a body   but
for what you might have seen

that I had seen before   and loved
small gold shells   elephant rocks   tide pools
islands like dolphin backs   edged with spray
standing out   in the blue and friendly sea
if it had to be anywhere
I'm glad it was there

but birdbones   I wish I knew
was the water cold   and did your longing for
peace
carry you   or was it hard
and where are you now
and what the hell am I supposed to do
without you

Jackie Kay is a Black lesbian born in Edinburgh, a city more dour than gay, more orderly then ecumenical. Perhaps because my own mother is from this place, I am most touched by her very Scottish poem, "Some Nights in Brooklyn and the Blood." Adopted as a baby, she was raised "on cuddles and Campsie Glens / Burns suppers and wild mountain thyme..." Like Dorcey and Shulman, Kay is a refugee. For her the exile began in infancy.

I am like my mother and father
I have seeped in Scotland's flavours
sizzling oatcakes on the griddle

I am like the mother and father
who brought me up and taught me
not how to be Black but
how not to be grateful
and for that I am glad

we all have our contradictions
the ones with the mother's nose and father's
eyes have them

the blood does not bind confusion
yet some nights in Brooklyn
I confess to my contradiction
I want to know the blood from whence I
sprang . . .

I am far enough away to wonder
what were their faces like
who were their grandmothers
what were the days like
passed in Scotland
the land I came from
the soil in my blood

Kay also contributes to *Beautiful Barbarians* several poems from her 1986 play, "*Chiaroscuro*," which traces the struggles of four Black women to communicate. "Opal's Poem," about the isolation of a lesbian couple, reminds me of Kay's compassionate short story, "Since Agnes Left," in the recent Pandora fiction anthology, *Stepping Out*. At the age of twenty-six, Kay, the youngest poet reviewed here, reveals considerable talent for crossing genres.

Beautiful Barbarians concludes with a stunning section by lovers Gillian Hanscombe and Suniti Namjoshi, including poems by each of them as well as four collaborative pieces. Their joint work is impressive in a literary milieu where individualism is hallowed, writers claim an ownership of ideas, the academy discounts shared work, and critics personify art by identifying it by author instead of title. Namjoshi and Hanscombe have crossed over the threshhold of Holy Authorship and moved beyond the myth of solitary genesis. Namjoshi, originally from India, and Hanscombe, from Australia, live and work together in Devon, England.

II
A Difference

But surely, she says, there are some
                    you love, some you trust?
Me, for example. Think of me
          please as some sort of flower.
It's easy enough. We're sitting
                    on the grass.
She looks exactly
                    like a gigantic flower.
So I say to her,
                    but she still looks sad.
"There's a difference,"
                    she tells me gently,

"between a simile
and a genuine metaphor."

For Namjoshi and Hanscombe and most of the poets here, the lesson is that one continues to cross borders. Life is movement. Or, as Anzaldúa says, "You must live *sin fronteras*." Each of these books makes important contributions to the expanding discourse about difference. Among lesbians and gay men the early, unitary notions of gay identity are more and more frequently set aside for a richer understanding about the intersection of race, class, politics, language, and nationality in our individual lives and our community interactions. Few of us any longer can afford romantic notions about simple homosexual solidarity. These poets remind us diversity doesn't dilute gay culture, but rather strengthens it. "We are everywhere" and the "we" is a kaleidoscope through which to consider a complex daily reality rather than a telescope into an idealized future order. The experience of being sexually marginalized informs our appreciation for other identities within ourselves and each other. Balancing along the wall, living along the dyke, we see many sides of the story. We live *in* a world which pretends to segregate us. The popular imagination insists that we are one thing or another. Flamingoes or Bears. But the lesbian poets discussed here resist definition, insisting on claiming all their identities, creating a communal arcade from separate roots, reaching into their histories for visions.

Writing Fiction across Generations

Since I published *All Good Women,* a novel about friendship among four working-class American women during World War II, many readers have asked about the work of setting serious fiction in history. This essay explores some of the questions, dilemmas, and rewards of writing across generations.

As a Baby Boom daughter, born in 1947, I can claim to be a product of that war, but not a participant in it. I am very grateful to the many people who shared their first-hand experiences with me in interviews and in writing. A number of them, particularly members of my mother's generation, think of it as "their war," yet it is *my* war as well. Many of my ideas and values are legacies from the 40s—notions about territory, race, heroism, gender, nationality. Thus *All Good Women* is the product of contemporary questions *and* historical research. I find my distance to be a gift as well as a challenge in portraying the period.

The four characters in *All Good Women* meet in a San Francisco typing school ("Now is the time for all good women to come to the aid of their country") in the late 1930s and become close friends. Moving into a North Beach house together, their lives grow more closely involved. Then war breaks out. The war separates them, straining and strengthening their friendship.

In 1942, Wanda and her Japanese American family are interned in a camp in Arizona. Soon afterward Ann, the daughter of Jewish immigrants, goes to work with refugee children in London. Moira gives up her acting ambitions to join a shipyard. She has a baby while her man is in the Pacific. Teddy, also involved in war work, discovers she is a lesbian. Teddy and Moira hold the house together in San Francisco.

Through these lives I trace the impact that war had on women's feeling of possibility. Many war women, like the suffragists and more recent feminists, were pioneers. For many, war was a time without men. What did this do to their sense of self and community? Ultimately *All Good Women* explores the courage of continuing.

During the five years I was writing this novel, I was confronted daily with

This essay was originally delivered as a paper at the Berkshire Women's History Conference at Wellesley College in June 1987. It was first printed in *Sojourner: The Women's Forum* 13, no. 8 (April 1988).

questions about the intersection of art and history. Three of the most persistent were:

- Why do I—and so many of my contemporaries—feel compelled by World War II?
- What are the similarities and distinctions between exploring the past in scholarship and in fiction?
- What is the point of writing a fictional account of a period I never experienced?

The war deeply affected individual family histories as well as current American attitudes. World War II offered many women a route out of the home. It brought thousands of Blacks from the rural South to work in northern and western war industries. For Japanese Americans, who were interned in American camps, and for Jews, who struggled with Roosevelt to save their families from slaughter in Europe, the war intensified a sense of being "the other." For many Americans, the "good war" held the nation together with purposeful effectiveness. It encouraged us to identify as "leaders" of the "free world" (resulting in our tragic involvement in Vietnam and Central America). And perhaps, finally, World War II introduced the nuclear arms race. In *All Good Women,* I try to explore these broad issues while attending to the private stories behind them.

For me some of the most provocative dilemmas were the challenge of acting morally when one's idea of "civilization" is being destroyed; the pressure to convert to religious tradition and/or political activism under the threat of invasion and genocide; the fluctuating definition of family during a period of enforced separations; the strains between ethnic identity and patriotism; the deflection of personal goals for larger social ends; the intensity of the present moment at a time when the future could be nonexistent. All these questions remain alive for us today.

If these were the issues and dilemmas that stimulated the writing of *All Good Women,* there were also distinct literary impetuses. I wanted an adventure. I wanted to avoid the classic novelist's rut of writing the same book over again. The only directions left seemed to be the future or the past. I had no inclination toward science fiction, and I have always been interested in history. Little did I realize that writing about the thirties and forties would be like breathing the air of another planet. As much as I knew about that world, there was a great deal more I did not know. And unlike the writer of science fiction, I could not make up the details, for many of the inhabitants of my novel's world might read the book: indeed some might even review it. Certainly my other novels required research—about Ireland in *Blood Sisters;* about rape and sexual harassment in *Murder in the English Department;* about San Francisco's Tenderloin district and old age in *Winter's Edge.* But this was different. Writing *All Good Women* required study in language, music, food, sexuality, politics, geography from curious historical perspectives. More than once I cursed the adventuresomeness and the hubris which got me into this project.

I grew fascinated with the parallels and differences between writing history and writing fiction set in history. Both the historian and the novelist face the fact that most Americans over thirty have strong and often mutually exclusive images of World War II. Both of us have to ask—for whom are we writing? People who lived through the forties and have carefully constructed "memories" of the period or a younger audience for whom we might have to supply more documentation? And whose documentation do we *choose* in a field that is rich with scholarly debate? How do we use the wisdom of our hindsight while respecting the parameters of our subjects? How do we portray the racism and sexism of the period in ways that are not self-righteous, indeed in ways that are useful in informing contemporary reality with historical experience?

In addition to such questions of context and documentation confronted by *everyone* writing about the past, the novelist has some special quandaries. First is the task of marking the line between a story with its own integrity and a "fictionalized treatment" of the war. In the development of plot, how do you assure that the grand historical drama doesn't overshadow individual moral development? If the characters are inspired by friends or relatives or famous figures, how do you allow them to be people with lives of their own in the text? Several times I found that the plot shifted for historical accuracy. For instance, the first few drafts of the manuscript took Wanda from her home in California to the permanent internment camp in Arizona. When Sandra Uyeunten, an Asian American scholar writing about this period, read my manuscript she said she thought it was essential to describe the "transition" camp to which many San Franciscans were sent—a racetrack where they were required to clean the horse manure from the stalls before sleeping in them. I knew about the racetrack camp, but when Sandra reminded me, I realized that it would have been an important emotional experience for Wanda as well as a significant historical event. I added a chapter.

The novelist also faces particular questions about language. Although anyone writing about the past attends to the mutability of words and explores outdated terms, the novelist is surrounded by the period idiom within her fiction. There is no omniscient narrator in *All Good Women.* Rather it is written either in the internal monologue of the characters or in their direct dialogue—therefore *all* my language had to be genuine as well as accessible to the contemporary reader without the safety net of footnotes. It's chastening to realize how often I had to weed out current usages of such words as "ritual" and "fantasy." We have to excise anachronisms and recover speech that has lost currency. How do we develop an ear for this? How do we discern the common colloquialisms from the temporary vogues? And what idioms were regional? Did people really say, "She's a brick" in the United States, or only in England? When did the word *dyke* appear?

These questions grow more complex when you're dealing not only with temporal distances among writer and reader and character, but also with differences of race, class, ethnicity, and sexuality.

This is challenge enough in a contemporary context. When writing about the thirties and forties, one must remember that not only were the *words* different—*Negro*, not *Black*; *Oriental*, not *Asian*—but the attitudes were as well. Here in particular I was conscious of that crucial line between authenticity and stereotype.

Sometimes I got discouraged and would complain to my friends about the difficulty of obtaining adequate material about refugee children in England or the racial policy of the Emporium, a San Francisco department store, in the 1940s. "Well," many of them would shrug, "it is *fiction*. Can't you be a little free with facts?" I was horrified. While it's true that no one is going to read *All Good Women* for scholarly details in the development of a history Ph.D., I feel obliged to my readers and my "subjects" to make the novel as genuine as possible.

The making of art *is* different from the writing of history and the requirements of the narrative come first for me. The novel has to be an open-ended emotional and philosophical journey for the writer as well as for the characters or it will not work as vital fiction. Wanda, Ann, Moira, and Teddy are not historical figures and their house on Stockton Street never existed. I made up other settings—such as Ann's office in London and Wanda's internment camp. I was scrupulous in such instances to study other houses and offices and camps to provide the *spirit* of the experience if not a photograph of a specific place. I "created" the house and the office and the camp partially in order to free my imagination and to let the characters determine their own environments. I did it partially because if I did choose a specific house or office people would come up to me and say, "That's not the way it was. The door was green." No doubt I inadvertently have made some factual errors in the novel just as no doubt I have intuited the right color of a door when I simply thought I had made it up.

My original impulse in writing this book was to learn about my mother's generation and through that about my own identity as a woman and an American today. When I was a little girl growing up in Dumont, New Jersey, and Bellevue, Washington, I used to entertain a special fantasy before I fell asleep at night. I would imagine that I was in a bomb shelter leading people in song. The sanctuary was not the yet undug atomic fallout shelter in our backyard, but rather an Anderson shelter protecting me from VI missiles. And I was singing (although to this day I can't carry a tune) rather than fighting—because I knew that what mattered was not winning but surviving. Now you can attribute the dream in part to the fact that I was a strangely bookish Catholic child who read too many biographies of the saints. But why *that* war, the community of people, the woman leading them forward in spirit? Because so many of my attitudes about loyalty and courage and virtue were shaped by lessons from World War II. So many of my possibilities were founded on the courage of my parents and their peers. Writing this book was a searching for roots as much as traveling to my mother's birthplace in Scotland. When I mention roots, I'm not just referring literally to my own family history. Through this book I have adopted many mothers. Ann takes me to the England where I would live myself. From Wanda I have learned about the courage of being a writer at a time when fewer women were taken seriously. From Moira's job in the shipyard I gained a certain amount of physical courage. I often think about Teddy when I sit in a lesbian coffeehouse in the relative safety of 1987. Through all four I learned about the persistence of working-class people. Many today look back to the forties as a romantic time when life was simpler. That's not what I found. In certain senses the public forces of good and evil were sketched in stronger contrast. In some ways the personal choices were more dramatically opposite. But if life was more sharply defined, it was not any easier.

As much as I learned about these issues and these individual women, I learned more about Wanda, Moira, Teddy, and Ann *together*. *All Good Women* is—in the beginning and the end—a book about friendship. A friendship that is both more painful and more profound for its setting in World War II. It comes down to this: history is the inspiration and territory of this book. History is the fiber from which the story has emerged. History is the medium in which these characters have come to lives of their own, surprising me, disappointing me, delighting me in what has become not my mother's book or my book, but their book. I shall miss their friendship with each other and mine with them.

Journal Excerpts, December 1981 to August 1986

December 1981: I ask mother what it was like to be raising a small child alone in New York during World War II. She looks away and tells me about letters from my father. About his experience in the merchant marine in the Pacific and Atlantic. For the next five years I continue to ask questions about her experience and the conversation always returns to my father.

November 1982: In the magazine ads, so many people wear hats. There's a lot of smoking. And how do they get away with selling coffee as a health food?

March 1983: Were these characters older at twenty-two than I was?

June 1983: I'm meeting writers in China who like to talk about World War II because it was a time when China and the United States were allies.

July 1983: The San Francisco newspapers refer to the Japanese as "the enemy" as early as 11 December 1941.

August 1983: For Europeans, there have only been twenty-six years since the last war.

February 1984: Did women henna their hair during the war?

July 1984: When I ask my father about the war, he insists that the Japanese were much more brutal than the Germans. He does not mention my mother's experience.

October 1984: What did women do with their children when they worked in war industry, and why has it taken me so long to ask this?

November 1984: How different was the concept of family then?

January 1985: The soil gets redder as you travel west from Oklahoma City. Teddy would have been surprised by the winter fog in the San Joaquin Valley.

August 1985: When observing white people from Wanda's perspective, mention that they are white.

September 1985: The more I write, the more parallels I see between the experience of Japanese Americans and Jewish Americans.

As I write this they are bombing Rosh Hashanah services in Copenhagen. Japan is rearming. Thirty-five people were killed last night in a Philippine theater.

Wanda seems remote because the other characters don't understand her. Confront their stereotypes.

November 1985: Paula reminds me that they would have had to remove their bras for love-making. How could I forget bras?

February 1986: When we talk about the war today, we refer to the Japanese and the Nazis. Not to the Japanese and the Germans. Americans forgave the Germans by calling the criminals Nazis. We haven't "forgiven" the Japanese.

I am gaining weight. I feel as if the thickness of this book has gripped me around the hips.

March 1986: We are bombing Libya. I hear noises outside and think it is an air raid. It is our neighbor rototilling the garden.

August 1986: Lots of reflection. Not enough action. Perhaps because I know it only from hindsight.

I use the word *imagine* a lot.

II. Reading Lives

Twelve writers are considered here in biographical sketches, interviews, literary retrospectives, and essays that encompass several forms. As years pass, my focus shifts from the lives of the authors to their lives' work. The purpose of these pieces is at least twofold—to contribute to the visibility of a developing female tradition in contemporary literature and to discover models, mentors, and friends who teach me about the writing life.

The authors are novelists, poets, critics, and scholars from Australia, China, South Africa, Canada, and the United States. A number of changes have occurred since the original articles were published. Margaret Laurence died in 1987, but not before writing two more books—a collection of essays and an autobiography. Margaret Atwood has continued to go from strength to literary strength. The offspring she imagined in the article has been born and is named Jess. Abby Hoffman left the academy and is now director general of Sport Canada. Dorothy Bryant has been writing plays in recent years. Nadine Gordimer, Marge Piercy, May Sarton, Shen Rong, Thea Astley, Adrienne Rich, and Mary Daly have all published new books. Grace Paley has published a collection of poetry, *Leaning Forward,* and moved out of the Village for an almost full-time life in Vermont.

The work in this section was the most pleasurable and most difficult writing in *Rumors from the Cauldron.* I learned a lot about developing character—about developing my own character as well as about cultivating portraiture skills. When I look back at the "new journalism" pieces about Laurence, Atwood, and Hoffman, I shrink a little at the very visible young author who wrote them. Yet, that's what we were after in those days. As the coeditors wrote in the 1975 introduction to *Her Own Woman,* "Someone suggested that an encounter between us and other energetic, expressive women would make an interesting book, as much for the style of highly personal, involved, and opinionated journalism we would write it in as for the stories of courage and imagination the book would relate" (Kostash, McCracken, Miner, Paris, and Robertson, pp. vii–viii). Now, in retrospect, I wish I were a less obvious subject in some of those pieces. Of course, the profile is always about the journalist as much as it is about the interviewee. The impulse behind new journalism was to be a little more honest. Today, thanks to a range of influences, including feminist criticism, the increasing democratization of education, and deconstructivist theory, there is a wider reception of subjectivity in both the media and the academy.

In 1990, the Personal Narratives Group at the University of Minnesota published *Interpreting Women's Lives: Feminist Theory and Personal Narratives.* Their essay "Truths" discusses the crucial concept of plural truths.

> *Interpreting Women's Lives* has explored this dimension of plural truths, the truths of experience, history, and perceptions embodied in personal narratives. We have emphasized the multiple truths in all life stories. Only by attending to the conditions which create these narratives, the forms that guide them, and the relationships that produce them are we able to understand what is communicated in a personal narrative. These angles of interpretation not only provide different perspectives but reveal multiple truths of a life. . . . Therefore, rather than focus on the objective Truth, we focus on the links between women's perspectives and the truths they reveal. (P. 262)

Recently, the study of biography and autobiography has moved toward the center of feminist discourse as we locate experience as a crucible for integrating theory and practice.

In the earliest of these pieces I wanted to know how these women developed the discipline to write and if I could write. Laurence, Atwood, and Hoffman talked about the economic realities of creating fiction, poetry, and scholarship, about their balances between family and career, about persisting in a world inhospitable to independent women. Each steadfastly refused to offer me a blueprint. I later decided this was fair enough. I gained a lot through interviewing and writing about these women, but, understandably, there were places in their lives I was not welcome. My frustration with these closed doors led me to think more and more about someday creating fictional characters. In several ways, then, Laurence, Atwood, and Hoffman provided my momentum to write fiction.

As I began to publish novels, I became interested less in author profiles than in critical retrospectives. Now, I wanted to engage in a broader literary discourse about what the writers were writing. This hasn't always been easy because, despite the variety of subjects in this collection, I frequently encountered discrimination from journal editors who found the books I wanted to review too marginal.

Some day I would like to write a biography. These pieces are not biography nor are they academic literary criticism. Rather they are kinds of crossover writing related by a set of recurring questions: What does it mean to be a woman writer today? How did we get here? Where are we going? Who are we?

The Matriarch of Manawaka

At least Royland knew he had been a true diviner. There were the wells, proof positive. Water. Real wet water. There to be felt and tasted. Morag's magic tricks were of a different order. She would never know whether they actually worked or not, or to what extent. That wasn't given to her to know. In a sense, it did not matter. The necessary doing of the thing—that mattered.

—Margaret Laurence, *The Diviners*

Margaret Laurence, the writer, and Morag Gunn, the central figure in her new novel, are literary diviners. Once again, this year, Margaret Laurence's divinations have taken her back to Manawaka, Manitoba, that fertile town of her imagination and recollection where she set part or all of four earlier books. *The Diviners* is a cathartic sequel to those stories, a culmination in her series of female journeys to self-discovery. It is the semiautobiographical story of a forty-seven-year-old Scots Presbyterian prairie woman who finds herself in her writing. It is also a resolution between mortality and instinct, the chronicle of a woman coming to terms with her own strength.

I knew Morag before I met Margaret. When I left Morag, in the pages of *The Diviners,* she was walking up from a river that was obviously based on the Otonabee River, in Southern Ontario, to return to her cabin and write the last page of her novel. When I met Margaret, last winter, she was refurbishing her house near the Otonabee and waiting for *The Diviners* to be published.

A big, buoyant, booming woman: "Hi there, kid. Sorry I'm late. Say, have you had breakfast? That's an awfully long ride up on the bus from Toronto? Have you been waiting long?" Before I have a chance to reply—"No, thanks." "Not bad." "Not at all."—I'm sitting in an armchair, eating a ham sandwich and talking about my cat. Margaret says her son calls her the classic Yiddishe Mamma. Her sense of family extends past her own son and daughter to the troops of young Canadians who have crashed with her at the legendary Elm Cottage in Bucking-

This essay is reprinted from *Saturday Night*, May 1974. Margaret Laurence has remained one of my literary heroes. Since writing this and other early profiles, I am less determined to see autobiography (memory recorded) as the source of fiction. As a novelist, I now see that in my own writing autobiography surfaces more insistently as premonition than as personal history.

hamshire. She also maintains a strong sense of community with other Canadian writers. "Who influenced your style?" "Sinclair Ross, W.O. Mitchell, Ethel Wilson." "Who are your friends?" "Peggy Atwood, Harold Horwood, Don Cameron, John Metcalfe, Marian Engel." Her sense of fraternity was obvious in her recent efforts as the first head of the Writers Union of Canada.

We are sitting in the modern concrete cell provided for writers-in-residence at Trent University in Peterborough. The ambience starkly contrasts with the lumpy hominess of Elm Cottage. The apartment is spartan-chic: fireplace, warm rugs, sunken couch posed against cold concrete angles and slick bookcases filled with the predictable: *Taine's History of English Literature, Roughing It in the Bush, The Edible Woman, Love in a Burning Building,* tapes of Judy Collins, Dylan Thomas, Pete Seeger. The only room that looks livable is the small study where she reads manuscripts and encourages aspiring undergraduate writers. The academic blackboards are plastered with McClelland & Stewart posters: *The Temptations of Big Bear, Lovers and Lesser Men, The Energy of Slaves.* Surrounded by her colleagues on one side and by delicate drawings of Ontario flowers on the other, conferring with young writers, Margaret Laurence enacts a role for which she is uniquely suited— Matriarch of Canadian novelists.

As we talk, her exuberance fills the room. The wretched dustcover photographs (a coarse, blunt face—somewhere in the imaginative environs of Tugboat Annie, a Boxer dog, the Soviet Olympic discus thrower—what we called "a handsome woman" a few years ago when we were treading the fine line between truth and tact) fade in the light of her company. The cold, angular study is warmed by her vibrance, by her grand feelings, by her marble brown eyes and her gravelly, loud voice. She talks about her characters as though they were alive, about the restraints of fear and pride, about her gradual resolution and growing hopefulness for the Manawaka women. Hagar in *The Stone Angel* recognizing that pride was her wilderness, reaching out tentatively for love from her deathbed. Rachel in *A Jest of God* understanding that she could be accountable to herself and eventually taking the responsibility for her own mother. Stacey in *The Fire-Dwellers* digging down into her own neurosis to find that she wasn't a reed and then returning to her family with a larger sense of her own power. Vanessa in *A Bird in the House* breaking away from her patriarchal grandfather and going off to school. But *The Diviners* goes beyond the piquant vulnerability of the others' dilemmas to a plateau of inner strength when Morag decides to follow her own instincts about love and work. "My viewpoint generally comes down on the side of impulse or inner direction," Margaret Laurence explains, "provided that this can be followed with a minimum of damage to others—freedom doesn't mean doing exactly what you want, all the time."

Does *The Diviners* present an alternative to the Presbyterian strictures which hold back the other characters? "Yes, Morag comes closer to what might be termed the god within. Religion is a frequent theme in the novels. I don't have a traditional religion, but I believe that there's a mystery at the core of life." She says *The Diviners* is a statement of faith, a reflection of the strong sense of hope she now feels in her own life.

Then she asks if we can turn off the tape recorder for a while. It makes her nervous. And besides, she is keyed up enough because of the seminar this afternoon. "Something about literature and psychology. I'm getting the uncomfortable feeling that I'm going to be beyond my depth."

How can this big, strong woman worry about a group of students? As she walks around the study, straightening her beige wool pants suit—a concession to academic propriety; she's much more comfortable in baggy slacks and a poncho—fidgeting with her wrist watch, I remind myself that this woman has written ten books in the last fourteen years. "I always get nervous before these things. Oh, thank goodness, that must be Nancy."

She bustles to the door to hail a lithe, doe-eyed third-year student in blue jeans and Salvation Army fur coat. From the warmth of their greeting, I assume they are old friends. No, they just met a couple of weeks ago, says Nancy, trying to make her eyes less obviously wide. "There I was, knocking on this door and knowing that on the other side was *the* Margaret Laurence."

The Margaret Laurence, Nancy, and I squeeze into a blue mini car for a ride to Catherine Parr Traill College, located on the other side of Peterborough.

"Aren't we going a bit fast, Nancy dear?"

"Oh, no, I always drive like this. Now don't worry about the seminar. Everyone loves you. They love your books. They'll start asking you terrible questions like, 'Are you Hagar?'"

Margaret seems oddly comforted by this kid. A peculiar matriarch, she is as oblivious of the difference in age and prestige as Nancy is aware of it.

"I've had this incredible experience with your books lately," says Nancy, trying to sound as casual as she knows Margaret expects her to. "I was feeling so *down* in my position as a woman, about my own potential. But after reading about Hagar and Rachel and Stacey, I've begun to feel much better. I feel this tremendous survival instinct."

"Oh, wait till you've read the next one, then," answers Margaret, smiling broadly.

Margaret's knuckles are bleached white from the sharp turns and high speeds of downtown Peterborough by the time we reach the modern brick edifice grafted onto an old wood building, Catherine Parr Traill College.

Catherine Parr Traill—one of the obvious autobiographical traces in *The Diviners*. Morag holds an intermittent spiritual dialogue with that pioneer literary lady— seeking discipline and inspiration, trying to understand her Canadian heritage, her daughter's future, and her own potential. These conversations are woven through the time present part of the novel. But the flashbacks reveal an even closer resemblance between Margaret and Morag.

Born in a small prairie town. Orphaned at a young age. A lonely childhood, spent writing stories. High school during the war years. Reporting for the local paper. University in Winnipeg. An unsuccessful marriage to an academic man. A late start in a fulfilling writing career. A proud relish in her family. The Cancer Zodiac sign. ("And they always say lucky in career, but not so hot in love although oriented toward children and family.") A pilgrimage to Scotland to unearth the ancestors. A residence in England. A return to Canada via Vancouver. A distaste for city life that draws her to a small town in Ontario. A cabin. On a river.

But Margaret bristles at comparison with Morag. (She points out that Morag was raised by the local scavenger and his wife, whereas she was brought up by one of the leading families in her home town of Neepawa, Manitoba. And neither of her children is the illegitimate offspring of a Métis folksinger.) She says Vanessa, in *A Bird in the House,* is the only one of her characters whom she resembles. Although all the Manawaka protagonists except Hagar are written from her generation and idiom, she insists that she allows the characters to work out their own dilemmas. "I like to think I know who that person is, but I'm not manipulating her, she's free. I'm holding a dialogue with the character. In another sense, in the hours I spend each day writing about her, I become her. This is the sense one gets about leading a double life. When I'm putting the words down, I'm her and when I quit at the end of the day, I go back to being myself." She declines to analyze the spiritual relationship further, almost as though doing so would drain her powers.

When we reach the class, there is the traditional polite flutter. "Would you like coffee? How would you like it?"

"And do you mind if we smoke, Mrs. Laurence?" asks the solemn bearded undergraduate, drawing tentatively on his empty pipe.

"Oh, heavens, no." She pulls out her cigarettes. "I smoke like a train myself." She tries to make them all feel at home. "And please call me Margaret."

The questions are predictable. The answers are spirited and fresh. "No, I never knew anyone like Hagar. I had to start my Canadian work with the generation that shaped me. I didn't think it was proper to start with my contemporaries. My grandfather Simpson was the only person of that age I ever knew . . . I thought I knew him all too well at times. I didn't appreciate him very much when I was young. But I think *A Stone Angel* and *A Bird in the House* helped me to come to terms with him."

"That's what I was going to ask," says the professor. "I was wondering if writing was in any way therapy?"

"Oh, yes, it certainly can be. But if that's all there is to it, you should leave it in the drawer. It's a very legitimate reason for writing, but not for publishing. There are other things involved in writing, like caring for one's characters."

"What strikes me about Hagar," picks up the professor, "is that she had so many opportunities for helping people—for reaching out and touching them and she failed. She knew later that she should have done this or that . . ."

"And we *all* do that," adds an older woman.

Margaret nods, smiling sympathetically for Hagar.

The professor admits that he sang along with the minister's hymn at Hagar's deathbed. That he even began to cry.

"I know," nods Margaret, "I cried too."

"But there seems to be some sense of redemption at the end?"

"Yes, Hagar does do those two free acts. She gives the bedpan to the young girl and tells Marvin that she loves him. But after that, when the nurse tries to give her some water, she refuses it. She can't accept the love of another person."

"All the characters seem to have that Scots Presbyterian pride?"

"Yes, it's something I find in myself too. It gives us a tenacity and a will to survive. It also makes it difficult to reach out and touch people. Hagar was able to break out of it only in some ways."

In one sense, *The Diviners* is a cultural catharsis. Morag's personal alienation parallels the broader dispossession of the Scots and the Métis. Morag goes further than Hagar, Rachel, Stacey, or Vanessa in resolving the tension between pride and love, between the duty of the past and the instincts of the present. In fact, characters from the other novels are introduced and traced against Morag's development. The fire which kills Piquette Tonnerre must haunt Margaret Laurence because she describes it for the third time in this novel. She shows Niall Cameron, father of Rachel and Stacey and the local undertaker, assuming a communal sense of Scots guilt for the death of the young Métis woman. And she achieves symbolic absolution in the love between Morag Gunn and Jules Tonnerre. Their relationship mitigates the alienation of the two peoples. Their daughter, Piquette Tonnerre Gunn, represents a resolution of conscience, a new generation. And although Morag travels to Britain to find her roots, she realizes that she is essentially Canadian. "I found the whole town was in my head for as long as I live."

Morag also comes closer to a strong personal identity than the other Manawaka women. She finds satisfaction in her work as well as confidence in her relationships with her daughter and with men. Margaret tells me, "Inner freedom is the theme of the time present part of the novel. No one ever makes it in a perfect sense. We always have to carry along the baggage of the past. Certainly Morag will always go on worrying about her daughter. Everyone has worries. But she's all right. All right."

Nancy is leaning over, almost reaching out to Margaret. "You know this survival thing is something that impresses me about your work. I've been reading a lot of Sylvia Plath lately, and I wonder why you survive and she doesn't?"

Margaret looks pensive, very moved. "Well, that's interesting because when Sylvia Plath died, she was living in a grotty little Hampstead flat, just separated from her husband, with two children and trying to make it as a writer. That same winter I was living in a grotty little Hampstead flat, just separated from my husband, with two children and trying to make it as a writer. When I read about her suicide in the Hampstead and Highgate *Express,* I almost died. The situations were obviously so similar, but they were also dissimilar. It all goes back to your childhood. Hell, everybody had a terrible childhood. But mine was obviously much easier than hers."

"I don't know how you do it," answers Nancy. "I mean I have a rough time even handling my dog. How did you cope with two kids? I can't help but compare your survival with Sylvia's."

"But the damage was done to her so many years before. Personally, when I found myself on my own, I found the kids extremely supportive."

"Then there's the case of Dorothy Parker," remarks the older woman.

"Yes," sighs Margaret. "In some ways—and I hate to say it—it's a tragedy that she lived so long."

"Yes," nods the professor resignedly, "that she didn't end it."

Margaret winces, "You don't have to sit around with dog shit and empty whiskey bottles in a broken-down hotel room."

"Hurrah," exclaims the older woman.

Nancy persists: "But you don't feel a certain sense of aggravation, of anger, when you think about being a woman? I mean for a while I went around totally wrought up about the possibility of living my life out as a second-rate man. Do you encounter any of the problems of discrimination?"

Margaret laughs shortly, "I've often said that what every good writer needs is a good wife. I have many men writer friends who survive on the graces of their wives. They have lovely ladies who do their income tax for them and serve them tea on a tray. But it's hard for a heterosexual woman to write."

She says it isn't coincidental that all her Canadian protagonists are women. "I think my main characters will continue to be women. If the protagonist is a woman—even if she is very different from me in age, like Hagar—there are ways I can get to know her, understand her responses to life. Women tend to empathize more with women and men empathize more with men. There are a few exceptions— like Sinclair Ross's protagonist in *As for Me and My House*—but just a few. I also feel that someone has to write about the women. Most of the protagonists are men. And the thing is, people never notice that a man is writing about males. When a woman writes about women, people say, 'Isn't that odd? Doesn't she like men? Can't she do male characters?' They say your novels are 'women's novels.' It makes me wild with rage to be described as a 'female novelist.' You never hear people referring to male novels and gentlemen novelists. I'm a novelist and I'm a woman. I write about what I know."

Perhaps the strongest statement in *The Diviners* is Morag's growing autonomy as a woman, the discovery of her strength. Margaret Laurence is a vehement supporter of feminism. Like many women who found themselves before "The Movement" existed, her approach is less than rhetorical. Her writing assumes the necessary subtlety of fiction. Nevertheless, issues like physical exploitation, abortion, role playing are drawn in intricate detail in all the Manawaka novels, climaxing in Morag's self-definition.

Both Stacey in *The Fire-Dwellers* and Rachel in *A Jest of God* suffer from the physical put-down. Both are intensely aware of themselves as "imperfect." By the end of the novels, they accept their essentially "unglamorous" selves. In *The Diviners,* Morag decides that she will quit going to the hairdresser. She lets her hair grow long and straight. This decision is a proclamation of selfhood, taken in isolation, long before "women's liberation."

"On the abortion issue, a novel doesn't make statements the same way an article would," Margaret tells me. "I believe abortion should be freely open to any woman who needs or wants it. But a novel tries to say—'Look, here is the woman, in this situation and *this* is how she feels—draw your own conclusions, but for heaven's sake, *know* this is how she feels.' Rachel, of course, very desperately wants and needs a child. She is not willing to have an abortion, not because she disapproves of abortion, but because she wants the child. That isn't the way it works out for her, but her mind deals with various aspects of the single-parent dilemma—'You'd be responsible for a long time for this other person, etc.' She decides—having refused suicide—that she is able to take on that responsibility. Morag's situation is quite different. She bears a child to a man she cares about, someone who seems, really, almost related to her, someone who shares her past. But later, when she thinks she might be pregnant by a man she despises and fears, her main worry is that she may not be able to get an abortion. She is horrified to think she might be condemned to have *his* child, and to love and look after it for eighteen years.''

Morag's biggest step is her rejection of external roles. We see Hagar battling her father's expectations, Rachel fighting her mother's demands of propriety. Certainly Stacey is aware of role playing. Toward the end of *The Fire-Dwellers,* she is able to externalize at least some of her thoughts, to become a fuller person. Morag carries the whole process further. She rejects the traditional strictures of marriage, motherhood, and housewifery. She is able to level with people and to develop relationships of mutual affection and trust. Margaret explains to me, "There is a place for social statement in literature, in an indirect way. If you try to remain true to the individual characters themselves, and to portray them with as much understanding as you can muster, then this will inevitably involve a statement of faith."

A few more questions from the class about the how and when and why of writing. She discusses the concept of the Black Celt, a kind of Jungian shadow figure which haunts all her characters. It is a Scottish trait which balances despair with survival humor. "I think each of the novels—especially *The Diviners*—ends on a profound sense of hope. The Black Celt gives you a feeling of ambiguity, a knowledge that life in many ways is somber. You have to recognize this inner darkness so that you're not too threatened by it."

The professor apologizes for the redundancy of the questions. Hasn't she heard them all before? She only says, "I still care about my characters. It's good to have a chance to talk about them."

And we are off in Nancy's car to catch my bus back to Toronto. Margaret is pleased with the class and still nervous about Nancy's driving. I distract her from her white knuckles with a question about the hopefulness of *The Diviners.* She says that she feels happier now than ever before. She likes her work, is gratified by the critical acknowledgment, enjoys a large number of friends from several generations. She's hoping that the Lakefield house will attract the same brood who visited her in England so she can cook big meals and banter about writing and politics. "When you've got a full house of people who get along together and you are doing your own work and the household tasks are being shared—that seems a good scene to me. But I don't have this totally ebullient nature. I worry—a lot. I worry about everything. The basic nature of life seems tragic to me. And maybe the reason I am more happy now is that I see the limitations of life, the fact that what happens to us all is that we finally die. But all the same, life is alive."

I wave good-bye to Margaret, wishing I could be as open in my admiration as Nancy. Margaret Laurence is a kind of diviner, in the novels she writes, in the strength she shares. I feel as if I'm waving to Hagar, Rachel, Stacey, Vanessa, and Morag as well as Margaret.

Spinning Friends: May Sarton's Literary Spinsters

> In the mirror she recognized her *self*, her life companion, for better or worse. She looked at this self with compassion this morning, unmercifully prodded and driven as she had been for just under seventy years.
> —May Sarton, *Mrs. Stevens Hears the Mermaids Singing*

> She who has chosen her Self, who defines her Self, by choice, neither in relation to children nor to men, who is Self-identified, is a Spinster. . . .
> —Mary Daly, *Gyn/Ecology*

Spinning a web of literary friendship, May Sarton gives renewed grace and power to single women. "With a hundred threads binding their lives to hers," as she says of one character in *The Magnificent Spinster,* Sarton expands and interweaves the definitions of the words *spinster* and *friend.* May Sarton's spinsters are vital, often romantic women engaged in the world as teachers, writers, mentors, colleagues, and social activists.

Cam Arnold devotes herself to writing a biographical novel about Jane Reid as an act of friendship and communication in *The Magnificent Spinster.* Hilary Stevens befriends a troubled young man in *Mrs. Stevens Hears the Mermaids Singing.* Caro Spencer risks her own safety to protect another resident of her dreary nursing home in *As We Are Now.* These characters, like Sarton herself, are old women who have used their lives productively, indeed exuberantly. Although some might assume a tension between their friendship and autonomy, it is precisely the self-sufficiency of Sarton and her protagonists that locates their deep and lasting friendships as the source and expression of their best selves. Being spinsters has allowed them to give to their neighbors with time and spirit unavailable to many of their contemporaries who have chosen to reproduce and live in cloistered families.

The identity of the sisterly spinster is enacted in Sarton's own friendship with

This essay originally appeared in *Old Maids and Excellent Women: The Spinster in the Twentieth Century Novel,* edited by Laura Doan (University of Illinois Press, 1990). Parts of this paper were delivered on a panel at the National Women's Studies Conference in Atlanta in June, 1987.

her characters. Their stories raise provocative notions: spinsterhood as a vocation of social responsibility; companionship as an alternative to motherhood; lesbian bonding as an alternative to marriage; friendship as an alternative to any sexual partnership; and writing as an act of friendship.

In this essay, I explore the uneasy borders between fiction and memoir by observing reflections between the characters in Sarton's novels, *The Magnificent Spinster, As We Are Now,* and *Mrs. Stevens Hears the Mermaids Singing,* and the spinster self-portraits in her journals, *At Seventy, Journal of a Solitude,* and *I Knew a Phoenix.* In particular, I am interested in Sarton's representation of the lesbian spinster and the literary spinster.

Friendship between Author and Character

May Sarton manages to create a special familiarity among writer, protagonist, and reader because of the way she balances her work on the boundaries of autobiography and fiction. "I think of myself as a maker of bridges—between the heterosexual and the homosexual world, between the old and the young," Sarton tells Karen Saum in an interview for the *Paris Review* ("The Art of Poetry XXXII," p. 86). The flexible forms of Sarton's fiction allow unique access to all involved. Each of the three novels under discussion engages the audience in questions about purpose, process, and style of writing.

The Magnificent Spinster is a novel about Cam, a retired history professor, writing a novel about the life of her teacher Jane Reid. Here we learn not only about Cam and Jane but about the intricacies of conveying the qualities of a long friendship in fiction. Sarton is at her best shaping the distinctive temperaments of these friends—balancing Cam's rash enthusiasm and Jane's measured graciousness—revealing how the women complement and confound each other. *Mrs. Stevens Hears the Mermaids Singing* is an account of an extended interview with Hilary Stevens, an acclaimed old poet, in which the skeleton of her biography is constructed by the questions and answers, while the rest of her story is fleshed out by her own dramatic internal flashbacks. During the interview, Hilary Stevens reflects on past friendships while developing an incipient friendship with the interviewer, Jenny Hare. *As We Are Now* is a novel written as a journal to be published after Caro Spencer dies. Of these three protagonists, Caro most closely resembles the stereotype of the spinster as an isolated, single, old woman, but the greatest drama of the book takes place within the friendships of her last months and in the fire she sets, destroying her grim nursing home and herself. Caro's final legacy—the journal—is a celebration of those precious relationships as well as a customary gift to those who might follow her into rest homes.

It is easy to find the seeds of these novels in Sarton's life. Jane Reid in *The Magnificent Spinster* is consciously modeled on Sarton's old friend and teacher Ann Longfellow Thorp. Thorp is lovingly described in *I Knew a Phoenix* and *Journal of a Solitude*. Sarton proceeds to discuss the difficult process of writing the novel about Thorp in *At Seventy*. Like the protagonist in *Mrs. Stevens,* Sarton lived for a time in England, where she found great artistic nourishment. She, too, had romances with both men and women and found women to be the sustaining muse for her poetry. The inspiration for Caro Spencer's decline in *As We Are Now* can be traced to a visit Sarton makes to a nursing home in *Journal of a Solitude*. Indeed, she has Caro's friend repeat the words of Sarton's friend Perley Cole from *Journal:* "'I never thought it would end like this'" (p. 23). All these women share Sarton's white, middle-class, New England background.

Although Sarton's fiction is autobiographical in the sense of memory recalled, it is also autobiographical in the sense of premonition. She relates to the characters in her novels as friends and models for her own life. Mrs. Stevens, a poet verging on seventy, is finally receiving the acknowledgment Sarton desires for her own poetry. The novel, published when Sarton was fifty-three, allows the author to try on the kudos, to see how she would feel looking back at her life from the distance of seven decades. (The name of Hilary Stevens's protégé, Mar, is not so different from the name of his creator, May. Mar's name and personality signify the anger with which Sarton so closely identifies.) This book also permits Sarton to watch Hilary come out as a lesbian in her narrative, before she herself comes out in her journals. Once Sarton reaches her own seventies, she chooses the character Cam, a seventy-year-old woman, to write a novel about Jane, to teach her how to write the novel she herself wants to write about Ann Longfellow Thorp. One step further into old age, Sarton creates *As We Are Now,* an unflinching study of rest-home existence. In *At Seventy,* she writes about putting a deposit on a modern, flexible retirement community, no doubt partially in response to her experience struggling with Caro's limited choices. It is useful to remember that the Sarton portrayed in the journals is also a persona shaped by the author. Just as her fiction is autobiographical, her autobiography is a creation of imagination. No doubt the May Sartons who emerge in the work of those who dare to write biographies of this formidable woman will be different characters altogether.

Sarton, then, develops a unique intimacy with her characters, between her characters, between the characters and readers, and between herself and readers. All her prose—fiction and journal—is rendered in a straightforward yet elegant style. Although some may regard her commitment to realism as old-fashioned, I see it as yet another gesture of friendship because she makes her ideas accessible to a broad range of readers.

Social Vocations

May Sarton's spinsters forgo marriage for a wider province.[1] Like Louisa May Alcott, they believe that the pursuit of good work and public service is "a better husband than love" (Cook, "Incomplete Lives?" p. 5). These middle-class women are friends rather than wives—friends over the back fence and in the public arena. Sarton, whose work seems more Edwardian than contemporary, grew up in an era of strong single women, both literary figures and political activists. In Britain as well as the United States, single women were among the most visible early twentieth-century feminists—working in settlement houses, living in single-sex communities, and campaigning for female suffrage. Sarton's mother was English and her father was Belgian. She comes from a bourgeois European background noted for championing eccentricity. Given her girlhood acquaintance with genteel, socially concerned women in Cambridge, Massachusetts, it is not surprising to find that her stories focus on the contributions of publicly generous, personally modest women. In addition, her place as an only child probably helped cultivate an affinity for spinsterly solitude. In Sarton's recollections about her youth, one detects a pleasure in her own company and an aptitude for independence which prepared her for spinsterly success.

Her characters are solitary figures only when narrowly viewed. They are deeply engaged in serving others through education, social activism, and the arts. In *The Magnificent Spinster*, Cam challenges sexism among her contemporaries and fights against fascism in the Spanish Civil War. Both she and the subject of her novel, Jane, are dedicated teachers. Jane works with French orphans after World War I and helps Germans reconstruct their lives after World War II. Later Jane confronts Boston racism—and her own bigotry—through her growing friendship with Ellen, the African-American director of the Cambridge Community Center.

Sarton's spinsters are often understated about their social contributions. Not all her spinsters are as comfortable with singleness as Jane is. For instance, Hilary Stevens describes her spinsterhood as deviance in her interview with the young writers Jenny and Peter: "'For the aberrant woman art is health, the only health! It is,' she waved aside Peter's attempt to interrupt, 'as I see it, the contant attempt to rejoin something broken off or lost, to make whole again'" (*Mrs. Stevens*, p. 190). Earlier in the novel, Hilary reassures herself that life is not as bad as it might be, that she did not turn out like Aunt Ida, an artist who was institutionalized because she was suicidal: "Nevertheless, young Hilary reminded old Hilary, you have not done too badly, old thing. You did not break down like Aunt Ida; you kept going; you have worked hard, and you have made a garden, which would have pleased your mother; and once in a while you have been able to be of some use to another human being—Mar for instance" (p. 71). Despite her self-effacing presentation, Hilary has had a very successful writing career and is a stimulating, encouraging friend to numerous people, especially Mar, the defensive young artist. She also inspires her interviewer Jenny: "'For some odd reason you've given me courage,' she [Jenny] said, 'courage to be myself, to do what I want to do!'" (p. 197).

In *As We Are Now,* Caro Spencer questions the value of her own life after she is put out to pasture:

> Did they always hate me, my family I mean, because I was different, because I never married. . . . A high-school teacher in a small town is (or was in the years when I taught math) not exactly suspect, but set apart. Only in the very last years when I was established as a dear old eccentric did I ever dare have a drink in public! And even among my colleagues, mostly good simple-minded fellows, I did not quite fit in. They had their own club and went off fishing together and on an occasional spree to New York, but of course they didn't want an old maid tagging along. . . . (P. 20)

Caro's tightly corseted self-image conceals the cosmopolitan attitudes she has developed in her wide travels and forty years of teaching. Precisely because of her reserved nature, her expressions of loyalty—such as defending a colleague facing dismissal for his homosexuality—are acts of courage. Once in the nursing home, she becomes friends with Standish Flint, another resident. His mistreatment makes her strength flare. "Yet, Caro, remember that anger is the wicked side of fire—you had fire and that fire made you a good teacher and a brave fighter sometimes. Fire can be purifying" (pp. 43–44). It is this sacred fire which fuels the keeping of her diary and allows her to leave the world of her own accord.

In the journals, Sarton portrays *herself* as someone for whom solitude is a respite for nurturing social contribution—whether this is her art; her philanthropy to adopted families and needy friends; her support for HOME, a progressive housing project in Orland, Maine; or her advice to young writers. In *I Knew a Phoenix,* she honors spinsters who have influenced her life, including her teachers at Shady Hill School and the actor Eva Le Gallienne, who inspired her to give up college and join the theater. Like Sarton, these spinsters may be suspect in the outside world but only because their participation in that world is veiled by stereotype.

Alternatives to Traditional Motherhood

Because these women are unmarried, their class and generation dictate that they also be childless. For some, this state is a failure; for some a relief; for some an opportunity to "mother" in unique ways. The identity "childless" has taken on various meanings during their long lives. Sarton and her fictional spinsters grew up within an ethic which defined nonmothers as unnatural or barren. They have survived both world wars, experiencing the absence of men on the home front as well as the baby booms following the soldiers' return. They lived through eras when feminists questioned the maternal imperative and celebrated selfhood. More recently, some have found themselves in a period when women—including single heterosexuals and lesbians—are having a renewed romance with biological motherhood. Since Sarton and her characters are all WASPish women, under no pressure to compensate for the genocide of their culture, many would observe that their first contribution is the decision not to add to an already overpopulated world. Perhaps these women don't suffer the impulse to reproduce biologically because they have found other venues for self-creation.

In *Journal of Solitude*, Sarton describes Anne Longfellow Thorpe:

For her, life itself has been the creation, but not in the usual mode as wife, mother and grandmother. Had Anne married she would have led a different life and no doubt a rich one, but she would not have been able to give what she does here and in the way she does. . . . Here is a personal largess, a largess of giving to life in every possible way, that makes her presence itself a present. . . . Perhaps the key is in her capacity to make herself available on any day, at any time, to whatever human joy or grief longs to be fulfilled or assuaged by sharing . . . [or] longs to pour itself out and to be understood. So a teddy bear will materialize as if by magic for a one-year-old who has stubbed a toe; so a young woman who cannot decide whom to marry can have a long talk in perfect peace; so a very old lady can discuss with gusto the coming presidential election and feel a fire to match her own rise up in Anne's blue eyes. The participation is never passive, shot through with a sudden gust of laughter as it often is, always vivid and original. (Pp. 172–73)

In contrast, Hilary Stevens is painfully conscious of her abnormality:

"No, the crucial question seems to me to be this: what is the *source* of creativity in the woman who wants to be an artist? After all, admit it, a woman is meant to create children not works of art—that's what she has been engined to do, so to speak. A man with a talent does what is expected of him, makes his way, constructs, is an engineer, a composer, a builder of bridges. It's the natural order of things that he construct objects outside himself and his family. The woman who does so is aberrant." (*Mrs. Stevens,* p. 190)

Near the end of the book, Hilary says to Mar, "'No, I think I would have liked to be a woman, simple and fruitful, a woman with many children, a great husband, ... and no talent!'" (p. 219, Sarton's ellipsis).

But Sarton's portrayal of the spinster or lesbian as perverted softens with the years. *Mrs. Stevens* is the earliest of the three novels discussed here. By the time readers meet Caro and especially Cam and Jane, the portait of the spinster as an estimable figure of solitary strength is less qualified. If one accepts the threads connecting these books, one detects three distinct moods—anxiety in *Mrs. Stevens,* fury in *As We Are Now,* and tranquility in *The Magnificent Spinster*—revealing a marked emotional movement. Perhaps the self-criticism so raw in *Mrs. Stevens* is due to the fact that this was Sarton's "coming-out" novel, and the writing process was filled with special conflict. Perhaps, too, she came to a greater peace about her own identity as spinster and lesbian in the years between this novel and the other two.

In *As We Are Now,* spinsterhood is portrayed both as freedom and loneliness. Caro doesn't think much about children, but, from her attitudes regarding marriage, readers gather that her independence from men and children comes from the same instinct for self-containment. When Anna asks Caro why she never married, Caro pauses, "It was a hard question to answer. How could I tell her, perhaps that I am a failure, couldn't take what it would have cost to give up an authentic being, myself, to take in the stranger? That I failed because I was afraid of losing myself when in fact I might have grown through sharing an equality with another human being. And yet ... do I really regret not marrying? No, to be quite honest, *no*" (p. 95, Sarton's ellipsis).

Similarly, in *The Magnificent Spinster,* Cam describes Jane's spinsterhood in terms of potential: "she did not resemble anyone's idea of a spinster, dried up, afraid of life, locked away. On the contrary it may have been her richness as a personality, her openness, the depth of her feelings that made her what she was, not quite the marrying kind ... a free spirit" (p. 60, Sarton's ellipsis). And, like Caro and Hilary, Jane serves many different people with her "extra" time. Long after she quits teaching, Jane makes a point of inviting children to her family's country retreat.

Sarton's journals also reflect an active relationship with younger people. One of the most touching parts of *At Seventy* is Sarton's description of a visit by "little Sarton," a girl named after her by parents who fell in love while reading her poetry.

She also discusses the satisfactions of her friendship with a young scholar named Georgia:

> What is wonderful for me is to be with someone whose vision of life is so like mine, who reads avidly and with discrimination, who goes deeply into whatever is happening to her and her family and can talk about it freely, so it feels a little like a piece of music in which we are playing different instruments that weave a theme in and out, in almost perfect accord. I had this experience always with my mother when I came home and we could talk. And I feel so happy that perhaps I can be that kind of mother for Georgia. (P. 145)

The spinsters in these books are parents in the sense of being mentors and confidantes. While they lack some maternal satisfactions, such as the pleasure derived from physical resemblance between oneself and one's own offspring, they are freed from certain kinds of maternal guilt and legal responsibilities. In *The Magnificent Spinster,* Jane gently directs Cam. Both Hilary Stevens and Caro Spencer can look back to spinster aunts as inspirational yet admonitory examples. In her journals Sarton emerges as a wise, generous persona, a model for her readers.

In addition to the gratification of reproducing, mothers often look forward to being cosseted by their children in old age. What does a spinster do? Sarton offers various possibilities, from Jane, who is surrounded by loving friends until the end, to Caro, who creates her own end and arranges her own cremation. Caro's death is admirable, tragic, and—in keeping with Mary Daly's glorious self-definition of spinsterhood—transcendent. "Spinsters, too, learn to be at home on the road. Our ability to make our spirits our moving shelters will enable us to dispense with patriarchal shelters, the various homes that house the domesticated, the sick, the 'mentally ill,' the destitute" (*Gyn/Ecology,* p. 395).

For each of these characters—Hilary, Caro, Cam, and the Sarton of the journals—the absence of one's own children is a blessing and a loss. Each in her own way expresses ambivalence and conflict about this aspect of being a *single* woman. The childlessness is one more instance of her autonomy from the family, if not from the society.

The Lesbian Spinster

Lesbian friendship is a sanctuary and a stigma for Sarton's spinsters. One conventional definition of spinster is a "woman who has rejected or who has been rejected by marriage." Today, however, marriage is so broadly rejected in favor of live-in, unmarried partnerships between women and men that the definition is outdated. If one reads "male-linked" for marriage, one has a clearer sense of the current popular definition. All lesbians, whether coupled or not, might claim to be spinsters. By choosing women, they have remained "unmarried" to, and unprotected by, male identity. (While many heterosexual feminists have fought for autonomy within their individual partnerships, they do have privileges unavailable to women who forgo such bonding with males.) Spinsters have historically been identified by what they are *not* (married) just as contemporary lesbians are ostracized for what they are not (male-linked). This "identity by lack" leaves room for the cultural imagination to conjure new labels. People often seem more threatened by dismissal of patriarchy than by antagonism to it and thus turn the sin of omission into a sin of commission, transforming the medieval spinster into a witch (consorting with the devil is more easily imaginable than not consorting with males at all) and the contemporary lesbian into a pervert. Witch-hunting spirals into gay-bashing. While few of today's lesbian spinsters are burned at the stake, they suffer enormous discrimination in employment, housing, and health care. To be a lesbian in the United States is to be "illegitimate," to be substantially without civil rights. Lesbians are declared unsuitable as teachers in certain areas and unfit to immigrate to this country. When lesbians aren't attacked, they, like other spinsters, are often ignored. Individually, some heterosexuals find lesbian bonding so threatening that they refuse to see it, and in an ironic twist on my theme, they interpet the intimacy between longtime partners as a tamer "friendship." Such women, particularly the older ones, are identified in their jobs and neighborhoods as "spinsters."

These novels reveal a multiplicity of lesbians, from Cam, who has a long-term relationship with Ruth in *The Magnificent Spinster,* to Caro, whose last great love is Anna ("I myself am on the brink of understanding things about love I have never understood before" [p. 98]), to Hilary, who struggles with her aberration. Writing *Mrs. Stevens* was a profound psychological and professional risk for Sarton, as she explains in *Journal of a Solitude:*

> On the surface my work has not looked radical, but perhaps it will be seen eventually that in a "nice, quiet, noisy way" I have been trying to say radical things gently so that they may penetrate without shock. The fear of homosexuality is so great that it took courage to write *Mrs. Stevens,* to write a novel about a woman who is not a sex maniac, a drunkard, a drug-taker, or in any way repulsive; to portray a homosexual who is neither pitiable nor disgusting, without sentimentality.... But I am well aware that I probably could not have "leveled" as I did in that book had I had any family (my parents were dead when I wrote it), and perhaps not if I had had a regular

job. I have a great responsibility because I can afford to be honest. The danger is that if you are placed in a sexual context people will read your work from a distorting angle of vision. I did not write *Mrs. Stevens* until I had written several novels concerned with marriage and family life. (Pp. 90–91)

In fact, Sarton did lose teaching engagements as a result of the book's publication. Her poetry has been censored from school texts, not because of explicit sexual references but simply because she is now widely known as lesbian.

On the other hand, this visibility has brought many lesbian readers. The revelation also has freed her to write more openly about her own relationships in the journals. In *Journal of a Solitude* and *At Seventy*, she looks back on her primary partnership with Judith Matlock, an English professor. Matlock, lover, friend, and Friend (a committed Quaker) lived with Sarton for fifteen years.

Sarton, however, is not doctrinaire. The lesbian connections are honored without any of the throat-clearing fanfare of more didactic lesbian novels. Moreover, just as she poses lesbianism as an alternative to marriage, she poses nonsexual friendship as an alternative to sexual partnership. Comrades and companions are often valued over lovers. Sexual relationships are often set in the past or in the background of a story. The strongest relationship in *The Magnificent Spinster* is between Cam and Jane—a friendship of cherished mutual development. In *As We Are Now*, Caro's current friendships with Standish, Reverend Thornhill, and Lisa are more important than any sexual partnership. *Mrs. Stevens* ends as it began, showing Hilary cajoling young Mar. The last scene is filled with affection, hope, and a provocative sexual energy: "For a second they confronted each other, the bold blue eyes of Mar and the hooded gray eyes of Hilary. Then at the same instant, each reached for a pebble and threw it down. The two pebbles struck the water about two feet apart, and they watched avidly as the two great widening ripples intersected" (p. 219).

In Sarton's journals, the sexual partnerships are also masked (as in the reference to "X" in *Journal of a Solitude*) or set in the past. Sarton is at her most vital when greeting friends in her house in Nelson, Massachusetts, or York, Maine. She frequently complains about her voluminous correspondence with people she has met through her books, but, of course, the descriptions of such correspondence are what prompt so many fans to write.

Writing as an Art of Friendship

Like spinning wool or silk or webs, writing is for Sarton a process of *conserving* the essential while transforming it into something useful for herself and others.

Sarton spins her stories with intelligence and craft. Much as early spinsters turned their wheels, she uses her hands and wit to recycle raw experience.

Cam describes her impulse to write about Jane:

> What then has driven me so late in life to write a novel? Quite simply the unequivocal need to celebrate an extraordinary woman whom I had the good fortune to know for more than fifty years until her death a year ago. . . .
>
> I realized that in a few years everyone who knew Jane would be dead. Who would remember her? In fifty years who would know she had existed? She never married. There would be no children and grandchildren to keep her memory alive. She was already vanishing like sand in the ocean. . . . Then, almost without thinking, I went into my study, forgetting all about lunch, and began to write. (Pp. 13, 14; third ellipsis Sarton's)

In *As We Are Now*, the most meaningful and candid connection Caro has is with readers—of her letters, her imaginary letters, and the journal which she intends to be read after her death. The journal is an epistle from hell. Her last act of friendship before setting fire to the rest home is to hide the journal in a refrigerator where it will not burn, where it will be preserved for others.

For Sarton, literary friendship is an *exchange* involving various levels of inter-action with members of her audience as well as with her characters. She is neither puppeteer nor omniscient benefactor. She needs her readers. Sarton's most popular work is her journals, which resemble long letters addressed to a broad-based audience of friends. Indeed, many pages contain fragments of letters she has received from her readers or descriptions of feelings these letters have evoked. The personal connections become even more direct. Sarton reclaims storytelling as an oral form in offering readings all over the country to standing-room-only crowds. She does booksignings where people wait two hours to exchange a word and get an autograph. She describes one of these events in *At Seventy:*

> At three the next afternoon she drove me to a very different part of the city, a slum that is being rehabilitated, and there I found myself among "my people" at the Crazy Ladies—a subway crush of young and old but mostly young in blue jeans and sweaters, crowding around to get *Journal of a Solitude* signed (that is one for the young) and of course *Anger*. Some had brought a great pile of my books from home. Many had things to say to me, but it was rather a rush as the line was long and the time short. At the end of two hours when I had not stopped making my mark, it looked as though the bookstore may have been saved (they are having a hard time), and everyone

was happy. And on the way back to the Regency and Heidi, two women from the cooperative told me they thought they had sold $1,500 worth. Once more I felt lifted up on all the delightful caring of these people who read me.

It cannot be denied that it is these days a very good life for an old raccoon of seventy. (P. 210)

Such encounters buffer Sarton against the pain and fury about what she considers the unfair treatment—not just negative evaluation—of her work by the reviewing establishment. She describes two more personal exchanges earlier in *At Seventy:*

When Webster was here last winter he asked me shyly whether I would be willing to give him a signed copy of *A Reckoning* in exchange for the work done. I told him he was getting the lean end of the bargain, but he insisted the book would do it.

In the same order of good happenings, Bob Johnson at the florist's left a round planter filled with spring plants, a hyacinth, two yellow primroses, and some lilies on the terrace, this time with a note to say how he felt about *Recovering.* What do critics matter when workmen and florists are moved to respond with their gifts to mine?

I sometimes imagine I am the luckiest person in the world. For what does a poet truly want but to be able to give her gifts and find that they are accepted? Deprived people have never found their gifts or feel their true gifts are not acceptable. This has happened to me more than once in a love relationship and that is my definition of hell. (P. 45)

May Sarton's spinsters are friendly women. Being spinsters allows them time to attend to numerous and often unlikely people. Like that legendary spinster Charlotte, who rescues her friend by spinning magical words, May Sarton's spinsters tend to their friends *in* their writing and *through* their lives.[2]

NOTES

1. For an excellent study of single women, see Martha Vicinus, *Independent Women.*
2. This reference was inspired by Mary Daly. Generally, I found Daly's work to be very provocative in the writing of this essay.

Atwood in Metamorphosis:
An Authentic Canadian Fairy Tale

I take this picture of myself
and with my sewing scissors
cut out the face.

Now it is more accurate:

where my eyes were,
every-
thing appears

—The Journals of Susanna Moodie

Once upon a time there was a writer who played make-believe. She had many roles. And there was a journalist who came to take a photograph of the writer. The journalist could not find a good likeness because the writer mistrusted cameras and kept changing her image. So the journalist came away with several photos and she made a collage.

Margaret Atwood is the archetype of the elusive writer, used to submerging herself in her symbols and characters. A classic protean personality: woman, artist, academic, wild creature. A fairy-tale princess in her pre-Raphaelite hair and piercing blue eyes and Boticelli pink skin, running away from the wicked camera.

Snap: Drinking home-brewed beer and eating home-baked chocolate cake at the farm near Alliston, Ontario, where she lives and works. Feeding the chickens, tending the forest of indoor plants. The satisfied rural Ontario farm woman.

Snap: Frenetic hippie in Afro-auburn hair, blue jeans, and orange Indian overblouse sitting at a black Selectric typing out novels in an upstairs room. She is the recluse writer—laconic, brusque—the prodigy who won the Governor General's Award at twenty-seven, the literary celebrity of the moment at thirty-five.

Snap: The trenchant scholar. English instructor at Sir George Williams Uni-

This essay is reprinted from *Her Own Woman,* published by Macmillan, Canada (1975), and available in a Goodread paperback from Formac Publishing, Halifax, Nova Scotia. The book emerged from my first writers' group, which included Myrna Kostash, Melinda McCracken, Erna Paris, and Heather Robertson. We each wrote two profiles and helped to edit each other's work.

versity, the University of British Columbia, York University. She is the respected literary critic and staunch apologist for nationalism orating at the Federation of Ontario Naturalists and the Empire Club. She spins out her sentences, catching her audience in her similes. Sardonically cool and professional.

Snap: The mythically free animal of her imagination. The six-month infant being carried into the Quebec North Woods; the teenage "nature girl" explaining frogs and toads to summer camp children; the university student more comfortable in the Lake Superior bush than in the Toronto classroom. She grew into the red fox-woman of her musings.

Snap: Successful, independent person who has made it with a strong sense of herself as a woman. Well loved at home. Successful in her career. An example for the feminist movement, an ideal from whom all of us can draw confidence. She is a "role model."

But ultimately the role model identity fails, because in emulating her, we lose focus on our own strengths and we distort her individuality. I didn't realize it, but I was looking for an elusive self-image in Margaret. So the last photo is an optical illusion, because I was pointing the camera at someone who was standing in front of a mirror. When I developed the story, I not only had photographs of her, but pictures of myself taking the photographs. This piece is about Margaret and about me and about the two of us together.

In the spring of 1974 I took the Canadian Pacific Railway over the Albion hills to ask Margaret why and how and where and when she writes. And if I was eager to find a role model, she was equally anxious not to be found. Margaret's defensiveness is legend. She's revealed it on CBC programs, even in her conversation in *Eleven Canadian Novelists* with Graeme Gibson, the man she lives with and knows and trusts. Still, I was surprised when she proved to be the most evasive subject I have ever interviewed. It's easy to write about politicians or businesswomen or scientists or sorceresses because I don't want to be a politician or a businesswoman or a scientist or a sorceress. But I am a writer, and I was frustrated when Margaret didn't empathize with my standards and goals. Meanwhile, she had come to be wary of reporters arriving on the Vista Dome bearing cameras.

Margaret and Graeme pick me up at the station in their clanking, mud-streaked Rambler. As we drive over the hills to their small farm, we talk about the escalating price of alfalfa and oats, about the ominous threat of a commuter train piercing the privacy of Alliston. One reward for living fifty miles from Toronto is that people are inhibited by the long distance telephone charge. She shares a six-party line and only has to answer after one long and one short ring. "You have no idea how pleasant it is to know that the call isn't for you each time it rings."

She doesn't mind being a successful writer, but she does mind being famous.

She never anticipated the money or the public recognition. She thought that being successful in Canada meant getting your books reviewed in the *University of Toronto Quarterly.* "But now I feel I can't be myself in public. People think that you're indomitable, invulnerable. They wouldn't think that about me if I didn't have this big reputation. *I'm* not intimidating. But because I'm a writer, people care whether or not I'm paying attention to them. They are afraid, in love, or hostile. They feel there are certain things they can't say or certain things they *have* to say, because only I *can* understand.

"Sometimes I would just like to be able to walk down the street and have no one notice me. But in Canada people talk to me on the airport bus, while I'm taking a quiet pee in Eaton's, when I'm walking down Bloor Street." In the end, she says, it's all superfluous. "The only important thing about being a writer is what you write." That's why she admires Beatrix Potter so much. When she was tired of writing, she refused to talk to anyone about her work and started a sheep farm. Margaret toyed with the idea of raising cattle some day—until she tried it, and quickly tired of chasing escaped cattle through thunderstorms. Meanwhile, she carries around a "fetish" Graeme made for her—a small wooden figure saying "no" to the students wanting advice, reporters wanting interviews, editors wanting copy, and academics wanting lectures.

A writer has to invent a public persona or go underground. Alliston is on the road to Margaret's underground.

> When we were in it we were very small very
> small, at least we thought we were small
> and it was giant it was too green
> for us it was like living
> on the surface of the sun (green)....
>
> *(Procedures for Underground)*

The Kodachrome slides of Peggy and her brother Harold growing up in the woods show them paddling canoes, picking berries, bathing by the lake, chopping wood, catching pickerel for dinner. Carl and Margaret Atwood carried Peggy into the Quebec North Woods when she was six months old. The family spent half of each year in the woods—mostly in Northern Quebec—where Dr. Atwood did research in forest entomology. They lived in tents and rough cabins which they built themselves. According to Dr. Atwood, "Tradition has it that no hireling lays a finger on an Atwood operation."

Her Maritime background is important to her although she grew up in Quebec and Ontario. She is proud of the heritage of severity, frugality, honesty, hospitality, shrewdness—almost preoccupied with her roots. One of her ancestors was Cornwallis Moreau, the first white child born in Halifax, the son of a monk expelled from his order in France. The original Atwoods sailed over to Massachusetts in 1635 and later came to Canada before the Revolution. On her mother's side there were the Killams who arrived in Salem, Massachusetts, in 1637. And there were family stories about the Websters and their descendants—Noah, the dictionary man, and the witch, who after she was hanged for casting a spell, got down from the gallows, cut the rope from her neck, and walked away to live another eleven years. There was also the French Huguenot Louis Payzant who was killed in an Indian raid in 1756, four of his children escaping Mahone Bay to propagate and tell the story. . . .

Story-telling was an ancient, respected family tradition. Margaret Killam Atwood loved to read aloud from the Brothers Grimm and Beatrix Potter. Since their company was restricted to family, Peggy learned to be self-sufficient inside her imagination. Harold, two and a half years older, taught her to read when she was four. Together they wrote comic books. And they made up stories for each other when they went to bed, adding a chapter each night, radio serial style. Soon Peggy began to write for herself. Her mother remembers one night when Peggy was squirming into her pyjamas. "Hurry, Mummy. I'm telling myself a story and I can't wait to find out how it turns out."

In the woods outside their cabin Peggy enjoyed wheeling Buglie, the faded, eyeless panda bear, around in a six-quart apple basket. For pets, Harold and she had the Canada Jays who ate out of their hands, the frogs, the toads, the snakes, the crayfish. When they grew older, they built an Indian tepee out of birch bark and made maps of the woods, naming the uncharted lakes and rivers. Later, when a much younger sister had appeared on the scene, Peggy created fairy villages for her out of moss and lichens and stones.

Peggy was never treated like a little girl, but like a smaller person. You couldn't wear pink dresses into the woods—if you didn't have overalls and a healthy dose of her father's homemade Pyrethrum repellant, you weren't likely to survive the blackflies. Her mother wasn't a delicate female figure. She never liked housework, so she didn't mind living in tents or cooking outside. She never cared about clothes. Since her husband was away researching for weeks at a time, she took the children on wildflower hunts, picnics, and blueberry-picking expeditions. "All my city friends thought my mother was horribly courageous. I just thought she was normal. I mean, we came from a long line of strong-minded women. The basic thing in a woman's development is how the parents treat the girl child. In Nova Scotia the image of the female is the hard worker, the good manager." Grandmother Killam went to Toronto from Nova Scotia to become a typist, which at that time was quite an adventurous thing to do. Aunt Kay was the first woman to earn an M.A.

in history from the University of Toronto. Her mother's younger sister Joyce became a newspaper columnist. So the family didn't find anything peculiar about Margaret Killam Atwood's independence in the bush.

Margaret Killam, a vivacious tomboy, a rider of horses, was a little too fun-loving for her father, a country doctor, to send her to college. So she taught elementary school for a few years—riding her horse to and from classes—to save enough money to send herself to Mount Allison University. Meanwhile Carl Atwood, the son of a Clyde River, Nova Scotia, sawmill operator, had gone to the University of Toronto to become a scientist. They got married and went off to the bush together in 1932.

But they never lost the Maritime heritage. Their daughter explains, "If I have any religion, it's a strong Nova Scotia moral code. We are against *waste* in all forms—from not wasting organic materials—I put it on the compost heap—to not wasting your talents or your time, to not wasting human life, which is why I'm against wars."

The Atwoods moved into the city each winter, from the first snowfall in October or November until the ice melted in March. The transitions—back to Ottawa and Sault Ste. Marie before she was six, afterwards to Toronto—were always dramatic. Peggy remembers her startling encounters with flushing toilets and sucking vacuum cleaners. But what alarmed her most was the way people changed their appearances; especially her mother, who put on nylons and dresses and hats and gloves and makeup when they came south. They had one identity for the city and one for the bush. She says now that the rhythm of going back and forth made her slightly "double-natured."

Peggy and Harold were different from the other kids. For one thing, they talked funny: complete sentences, precise grammar, Novia Scotia flat *a*. They had been isolated from the slang of most childhoods. But what distinguished them most of all was their story-telling parents. The evening reading became a neighborhood ritual. First a couple of friends asked if they could come over, then a few more started sitting in. Sometimes, the Atwoods had twenty children and tag-along parents sitting in their spare living room, listening to *The Tale of Benjamin Bunny* or *The House at Pooh Corner*.

Another weird thing about the Atwood kids was their understanding of nature; Peggy had a pet cabbage butterfly and a praying mantis named Lenore. Dinner table conversation focused on topics like how long it would take a pair of fruit flies, multiplying unchecked, to cover the surface of the earth twenty-two feet deep. The kids were always reading from the bulging bookcases.

Peggy was a gregarious child. She was usually the youngest in the class, the fragile girl with the flushed cheeks and the clear blue eyes and the long dark curls,

Botticelli even then. Her friends had heroines like Esther Williams and June Allyson, but her own were imaginary. And often they were animals; her first novel was about an ant floating down a river on a raft. She was "engaged" at age eight. She landed her first job that year: wheeling a baby carriage for twenty-five cents an hour. When she was eleven, she managed to knit an entire layette for her new sister, Ruth. Several years later she was the hit of the neighborhood when she opened her own puppet troupe and—for money—gave performances at birthday parties.

She says she didn't really have an adolescence. "I stopped writing from age eight to grade twelve. I consider it my sterile period," she says ironically. "I came into being when I was born. I had a temporary lapse in high school." The Leaside Collegiate yearbook portrays an All-Canadian girl: basketball team, UN Club, Citizenship Award. She belonged to the Triple Trio which went around to Rotary luncheons singing songs like "Come and Trip It As You Go." She entered the Unitarian Church in grade eleven, a dramatic philosophical commitment for someone brought up an agnostic. And she continued her eclectic employment career as a census taker, a waitress, a nature instructor at Camp White Pine "where the sun forever shines," a Jewish coeducational camp in Haliburton. She concealed her intelligence in the classroom like most girls. Her early pioneer impulses were submerged in teenage anxieties about balancing on high heels. She shopped in Kresge's for her purple nail polish and orange lipstick. She made her own pastel formals for the school proms where she danced to "Tutti Frutti" and "Blue Suede Shoes."

But she also maintained a critical, defensive social and academic distance. "I was very sarcastic to people so they wouldn't mess around with me too much." She decided to major in home economics because of all the positions the guidance booklets suggested for girls—teaching, nursing, typing, homemaking—it seemed the most profitable and the least obnoxious. Once when she disliked her grade twelve home ec. assignment of making stuffed animals, she replaced it with an operetta about synthetic fabrics. (She wrote about Sir Wooley who had a blot on his character. He had to sell the girls Orlon, Rayon, and Nylon that he shrank from washing.) She claims in *The Edible Woman* that high school was just a walk-through for her—that she didn't develop the role seriously.

She turned her head and examined her profile out of the corner of her eye. The difficulty was that she couldn't grasp the total effect: her attention caught on the various details, the things she wasn't used to—the fingernails, the heavy ear-rings, the hair, the various parts of her face that Ainsley had added or altered. She was only able to see one thing at a time. What was it that lay beneath the surface these pieces were floating on, holding them all together? She held both of her naked arms out towards the mirror. They were the only portion of her flesh that was without a cloth or nylon or leather or varnish covering, but in the glass even they looked fake, like soft pinkish-white rubbor of plastic, boneless flexible. . . .

"*The sexual awakening* wasn't that important to me. The only thing I regard as important was the moment I realized I wanted to be a writer. I even remember the first poem—about a desert. It was terrible. All my early poems were terrible, but that didn't matter. At that time I felt I couldn't get married and have kids and be a writer too. A pretty heavy acknowledgment for a sixteen-year-old girl. It seemed to me that getting married would be a kind of death. Society didn't provide alternatives then. There was no Women's Lib telling you that you could do both. I didn't feel guilty *as a girl* about wanting to write because at that time *no one* wanted to be a writer." But of course it wouldn't have mattered if anyone had objected. As her mother comments now, "No one guided Peggy. I don't think anyone could *guide* Peggy."

Carl and Margaret Atwood are still as bright and audacious as that couple who took Peggy and Harold into the bush. The house in Toronto where they have lived since Peggy was in grade three is spare, but warm. Durable tweed and Naugahyde chairs are set around a blazing fire. The mantle is clear except for candlesticks and cherrywood carvings made by Grandfather Killam. The hardwood floor is uncarpeted. Historical maps of Scotland and England hang unframed on one wall. Every open space is used for a bookcase or a planter. They see their daughter once a week on her treks into the city; they talk about books and Nova Scotia relatives and gardening. "We didn't intentionally raise Peggy in any specific way," says her father. "The marriage market just didn't make sense. Independence and freedom rate very high with us. One of the reasons we liked life in the bush so much was that it presented problems we had to settle without outside aid. We were on our own a lot."

Peggy got her first real recognition at the University of Toronto where she studied English with Jay Macpherson, Northrop Frye, Kathleen Coburn, Millar MacLure. She was an excellent student, was active in the drama group, and had male friends and boyfriends in spite of her seedy gabardine coat, her prim tortoise-shell glasses, and the long, frizzy hair captured by bobby pins at the back of her head. The real hallmark of her college career was publishing—poems in *Acta Victoriana*, the *Canadian Forum*, the *Tamarack Review*. Most of her peers were indifferent about her writing ambitions, but she remembers one conversation with a date in the Toronto subway. "He thought it was all right for me to write, but to *publish?* His attitude was nothing new, in fact it was a hangover from the Victorian idea that there's something vulgar about a woman's name appearing in print. A lady is someone whose name is published three times: when she's born, when she gets married, when she dies. I didn't see why I should have to deal with that shit. A lot of women stopped writing because they felt this irrational guilt. I felt very alone, but I didn't feel guilty. Guilt just isn't my thing."

Nor is intimidation. When one of her University of Toronto professors advised that she be a wise girl and get married after her B.A., she ignored him and applied to Radcliffe. She did her Master's and then moved over to Harvard for her Ph.D. She left school to write and to earn money to finish her studies. She taught at Sir George Williams and the University of British Columbia and York University. But she hasn't yet finished her thesis on the metaphysical romance. After she won a Governor General's Award for poetry in 1966, her writing began to absorb more and more of her time.

Other people were beginning to recognize what Peggy had known since that grade twelve poem, that she was a writer. Critics. Students. Reporters. They all asked why she wanted to write: "I don't care *why* I want to be a writer. It's such a Puritan question. It implies that you have to have some reason, some excuse to do something that isn't concrete. I suppose I've had my questions, my periods of severe depression, wondering whether it was any good, whether I could keep going, whether I was going to starve, whether I would live until thirty. But I never serously thought I was going to *stop.*"

Life with Graeme in Alliston is somewhere between the Atwood version of *Roughing It in the Bush* and her youth in the yellow brick house in North Toronto. Their old white farm house is the kind of unself-conscious home where the pipes are exposed in the half-formed bathroom, where *The Feminine Mystique* and *Canadian Dimension* are tossed next to the toilet, which only works when you descend your hand into the cold, murky waters of the tank and pull up the algae-covered plunger. The guest room is cramped with a freezer, sewing machine, fermenting bottles of homemade beer, and a dusty Zenith portable TV shoved behind two huge sacks of Vermiculite Garden Treat. The living room–dining room is the center of activity in classic rural Ontario style—a cowgirl calendar from the Friendly Corner Store, a china cabinet with bits and pieces of place settings, a cupboard with a built-in flour sifter. We spend the evening sitting around the old round wooden table warmed by Graeme's hearty lamb stew, the wine, and the fire in the Franklin stove.

Margaret's relationships haven't always been so comfortable. In fact, most of the poetry she writes about men is troubled, heavy stuff: the exploited, martyred woman versus the uncommunicative distant man. The photos of high school and college were relatively easy to collect. But as we focus on the present, I find her backing away from the questions. She is close-mouthed about all her relationships. "The good ones I remember with gratitude. The bad ones I'm glad are no longer going on, but I can't talk about them. The people are still alive. It wouldn't be fair."

Margaret was raised outside the conventional bond between guilt and sex. She knew virginity was the bargaining point with most women in the fifties, but since she wasn't aiming at marriage, it wasn't an important asset. She did have one moral stricture—honesty, a directness which threads through her life. There were no patterns to her relationships with men—some were grizzly; some were good. Several engagements broke up because of her writing. "The men who didn't want me to write—who felt threatened by it—entrenched me in my belief that I wanted to write. Nothing else had as much meaning for me. It would be impossible for me to live with anyone who didn't allow me to be a writer. Repressing that part of me would lead to more misery than it would be worth. Tough for him. And for me. No one would have said to a man, you can't be a doctor, you've got to get married. I didn't see why I should give up writing. But it cost me a lot of blood, let me tell you. I missed out on a lot of things other women had— children, a husband for a long time. Now I know that I may not have missed anything at all. But the point is, I *thought* I did. It always hurt to say good-bye."

She didn't marry until she was twenty-seven. Not until, as she had promised herself, she was a writer. She married a fellow Harvard graduate student. They separated in 1973 for what she says tersely were "personal reasons."

> Marriage is not
> a house or even a tent
>
> it is before that, and colder:
>
> the edge of the forest, the edge
> of the desert
>   the unpainted stairs
> at the back where we squat
> outside, eating popcorn
>
> the edge of the receding glacier
>
> where painfully and with wonder
> at having survived even
> this far
>
> we are learning to make fire
>
>   (*Procedures for Underground*)

Perhaps the most gossiped about of her private relationships was a rumored

affair with a young poet during the last part of her marriage, and which was
reflected to some extent in *Power Politics.*

2

I approach this love
like a biologist
pulling on my rubber
gloves & white labcoat

You flee from it
like an escaped political
prisoner, and no wonder

3

You held out your hand
I took your fingerprints

You asked for love
I gave you only descriptions

Please die I said
So I can write about it

She used to be afraid of putting men down, but she doesn't submerge her
talents any more. There aren't too many men who are secure enough not to feel
intimidated by her. She says it's important to wait for someone who can handle
it. Otherwise relationships are charades.

Life with Graeme is congenial, supportive, relaxed. Their work is similar
enough to generate advice, different enough to obviate comparison. She insists that
they're not in competition, that people who like Graeme's experimental novels
would consider hers overly popular, a somewhat dubious assertion considering her
critical acclaim. They go out of their way to ignore her reputation.

One evening after supper, Graeme entertains us by reading selections from
the ever-proper *Pears Cyclopedia.* We laugh at the almanac's sensible advice on obesity,
neurosis, masturbation, happiness. We spend the rest of the evening talking, and
leave the dishes until morning.

"There's a lot to be said for my life right now. Here I am living with someone I
get on with. I don't have to worry about money. I'm having a better time. I think
I'd like to have kids; if I don't now, I never will. The 'purpose' of having kids
is the same as the 'purpose' for writing. The theory is that you will enjoy it."

I sat in the house, raised up
between that shapeless raging and

my sleeping children
a charm: geometry, the human
architecture of the house, square
closed doors, proved roofbeams,
the logic of windows.

(The Journals of Susanna Moodie)

Her writing conveys a strong sense of female heritage, a spiritual, cultural kinship with other women. Her career is a statement of her confidence in herself as a woman. Like many pre-movement feminists, Margaret supports women's liberation, but it isn't the passion of her life. She never collected the linen or the children or the china, so she doesn't feel the real energy of bitterness that motivates many feminists. "Since I never felt my life was taken away from me, I don't have all that distilled outrage to devote to the movement. I don't mind playing roles— as long as I can determine the roles."

She notices a marked difference now in women's response to her work. She no longer senses the competitive hostility of those college cocktail parties where the girls always wondered why she wouldn't join them to talk about place settings. In fact women today are effusive in their encouragement. It is the men—those who used to pat her on the head and say, "Yes, dear, do go ahead and try to write," who feel threatened by her success. She says that she feels closer to women writers, that any rivalry is likely to take the form of wanting—or expecting— them to write better. She is more critical of women's work than of men's—more aware of their flaws and achievements.

Her books themselves could sustain a course on women's literature: *The Edible Woman,* a comic novel about Marian, a young college graduate who suffers Anorexia Nervosa at the prospect of being contained in a marriage with a sterile young lawyer; *Surfacing,* a novel in which a young woman's search for her father serves as a metaphor for her search for sanity; *The Journals of Susanna Moodie,* a collection of reflections on the Canadian pioneer's life ranging from "The Disembarking at Quebec" to "The First Neighbours" to "Death of a Young Son by Drowning" to her resurrection as a contemporary old woman on "A Bus Along St. Clair." The other poetry collections are eloquent in their statement of female identity from the bitterness of *Power Politics* to the warmth of the poems about her mother and sister in *Procedures for Underground.*

Margaret writes about women simply because she is a woman. She says that she can empathize with, but not identify with male characters in books. She has no particular models. But perhaps her confidence derived from a youth immersed in Victorian literature: George Eliot, Christina Rossetti, the Brontës, Emily Dickinson. "The important thing is that women are right there in the foreground—

you don't have to go out and dig them up. If they are *there* then you don't have to think it's curious that you're a writer. It doesn't matter so much what they write or what they are like personally, but just that they are there, so you know it's possible for you to be there too."

As we sit on the Mexican sun blanket which Graeme brought back from Oaxaca, she crochets white and blue and gray flowers. One after the other, alternating colors. She doesn't know what she will do with them—make an afghan or a coat or a... but she doesn't want to waste time. As I sit listening to her, I feel she is making pronouncements. She often interrupts questions, ignores ones she doesn't want to answer, answers ones she's not asked. I feel more like a disciple than a reporter.

This is not a unique reaction to Margaret. At parties, she's often the focus of attention, or adulation or hostility. According to one source, she has on occasion been known to sit and hold forth at length. Tonight, we're in one of those optical illusion scenes where I see as much of myself as I do of Margaret. She laughs, "I guess this is kind of a defense. Like when I was sarcastic in high school. I still have some of the sarcasm left over. But my distance from people is more often disguised as wisdom of a spurious kind. Also, now people's attitudes toward me have changed so that those I meet usually want something from me. They don't give me the business, so I'm not as likely to give it back."

Her main aversion to radical feminism is that a didactic, one-dimensional critique will develop: women will praise women's books just because they are women's books, as a backlash to the predictably one-dimensional male reviews in which bad writing is somehow related to femininity and good writing is sexless or "male." "There's also the sexual compliment put-down, where a critic will comment on the cute cover photo and dismiss the contents of the book. A hard-hitting piece by a male writer is described as having 'balls.' But have you ever heard of work by a woman described as having 'tits'? Some feminists insist that my works, things like *The Edible Woman* and *Power Politics*, stem from the women's movement. But they didn't. This isn't to disparage anyone's politics. It is merely to indicate that parallel lines do not usually start from the same point and that being adopted is not, finally, the same as being born."

Margaret works in a small second floor study, just big enough for her huge desk, her bookcases, and a couple of chairs. The desk is cluttered with her thesis, with letters from her New York agent about the screen rights to *Surfacing*, with spray paint, a measuring tape, a bottle of Johnson's baby lotion. On one wall hang her own diffuse watercolor paintings and a carefully executed sampler, "Blossoms and Birds and Budding Trees. Thank God We May Be Sure of These," made by her sister.

She is reluctant to discuss her work. She insists that her job is to write her poetry and fiction, not to do the definitive criticism of it. She does say that *The Edible Woman* expresses her own early fear of marriage and her distaste for the pompous, neurotic graduate student ethic. And *Surfacing* is set in the bush, written partly from childhood memories and subsequent observations. The protagonist has a dominant, severe father; by contrast, Margaret's father is affable, outgoing, fond of jokes, and energetic. "As far as what I've done, I'm more like my father, immersed in all sorts of projects and procrastinating about each one. Very rational. But spiritually, I think I'm more like my mother." As we talk, she digresses about her astrological sign, Scorpio, which is sceptical, and about her life-line, which has recently rejoined. "It would be quite possible for me to stop writing and go off in some opposite direction—something that would be an internalizing, rather than a pouring out. I think I have another life to live. . . ." She stops abruptly, as though concerned about gaining a public reputation as a purveyor of mysticism. She repeats that all she has to say, she expresses in her writing. It's her work that's important. Not her analysis of it or her personal life.

She bristles when I ask about the Yeats line, "How can we know the dancer from the dance?" "The only time a writer is in a dancer-dance situation is when he is writing the book. After that, it's cut loose, sent out. You change. I'm not the same person I was when I wrote *Surfacing*. The only thing that makes a book tolerable is the thought of finishing it. The final connection is between the reader and the book. You get a whole other sense of the work if you think of it as a thing apart from the author."

"Simplistically, any writer writes biography. But on a more subtle level, you also act like a lens, a movie camera. I project my energy into my characters. I'm not writing down the story of my own life, but I'm imagining myself in certain situations in which I haven't been before. Fictions are possibilities."

They can't be trusted. They'll mistake me for a human being, a naked woman wrapped in a blanket: possibly that's what they've come here for, if it's running around loose, ownerless, why not take it. They won't be able to tell what I really am. But if they guess my true form, identity, they will shoot me or bludgeon in my skull and hang me up by the feet from a tree. (*Surfacing*)

Margaret has been intrigued by metamorphosis since her childhood. Animals are a form of mask. Another role. Another image. Another identity. Wilderness is a pervasive theme in her work. So is madness. Both wilderness and madness are retreats from a pressurized world which threatens to contain or manipulate. Escapes from claustrophobic urban life. Disguises.

She still feels more at home in the Quebec bush than she does in the streets of Toronto. She goes canoeing every year, and she is an honorary member of the Federation of Ontario Naturalists. She still talks about moving farther away than Alliston once her career settles down. Margaret spends most of her days on the farm with Ruby, the ancient matriarchial tabby, and Patience, the precocious black Persian, two Irish wolfhound pups, and the ducks and the chickens and the sheep and the peacocks. The animal she identifies with most is the red fox. Some friends insist that she's a silver fox or an otter or a hare. But the image is consistent: clever, quick, sprightly. Her very appearance flouts urban sensibility. She dashes around to Toronto editorial offices in blue jeans and loose Indian overblouse, her electric hair coiling from her scalp, her skin just washed and flawless except for those forehead lines that the Atwoods seem to be born with. It's quite a metamorphosis from that prim young student in the muted wools who pulled her hair back in a frizzy French roll. She looks like the untamed creatures of her poetry.

Another escape-retreat from the claustrophobic rationality and sterile stability is madness, a theme she explores in much of her work. She has a neurosurgeon's skill with her succinct, terse sentences. She creates an individual dream world in which change and reorder are a nebulous constant. It is a universe where people drift in and out of madness, where the reference points between sanity and insanity are always shifting. One critic acutely described her as "a psychological iconoclast." Madness and wilderness come together in the animal fantasy of *Surfacing*. The protagonist goes through a role of a wild animal to distance herself from the neurotic people around her and to get in touch with her own fears.

Margaret's personal fear is chaos. "It's triggered off by having to deal with a lot of shit from other people. Sometimes I think I'll never get out from under it." She also tries to avoid situations in which she can be contained or limited by other people's expectations, political, moral, or literary. "One thing you don't seem to grasp," she tells me in an irritated tone one day, "I don't think in terms of 'usual' and 'unusual.' *Of course* it was unusual for me to do a lot of things I did in other people's terms, but not in mine."

Her sense of stability is an individual one, distilled by her early experiences in the bush. In her life she keeps a fine balance between urban culture and natural environment. She still mistrusts machines and is only now learning to drive. When she flies, if she is close to completing a book, she will mail a copy of the manuscript to her home address in case the plane crashes. She describes herself as "depressingly sane. I've had it checked out. I went to a therapist when my marriage was breaking up, mainly to talk over things like how long I should keep the house. After a while, he asked me what I was doing in therapy. How I feel depends on the circumstances. When things are OK, I'm OK. If they're not, then I'm not. I'm very susceptible to input. That's why I moved out of the city. There was too much input."

"I think madness is a kind of escape valve in our society. It is symbolic of whatever is bothering a person. Our society makes it easier for women to crack up. Women are taught to fear, to think they need refuge, to believe they need to be taken care of. It renders them childlike and helpless." In *Surfacing,* she leaves it open to the reader whether the protagonist is crazy, or right, or crazy and right.

In the evening I make a different lair, further back and better hidden. I eat nothing but I lie down on the rocks and drink from the lake. During the night I have a dream about them, the way they were when they were alive and becoming older; they are in a boat, the green canoe, heading out of the bay.

The collage is finished. A composite of disparate images. Some more sharply focused than others. Some candid. Some posed. Some double exposed. No one representative. Duck eggs and crocheted flowers and fairy-tale figures and mad women. Metamorphosis in the bush and metaphysical romance. The Connecticut witch's descendant. The child pioneer. The contemporary celebrity. As for the future . . .

Who is Margaret Atwood? The mirror cracked a long time ago and I still don't know. I climb on board the CP to take me back to Toronto and my typewriter. She gets in the old Rambler and heads back along the mud ruts to her tower in Alliston. And if she doesn't live happily ever after, at least she knows that every time the phone rings, it's not for her.

(The photograph was taken
the day after I drowned.

I am in the lake, in the center
of the picture, just under the surface.

It is difficult to say where
precisely, or to say
how large or small I am:

the effect of water
on light is a distortion

but if you look long enough,
eventually
you will be able to see me.)

(*The Circle Game*)

Living the Free-lance Life: A Portrait of Abby Hoffman

"All Star Defenceman Turns Out To Be Girl," blared the large banner headline on the *Toronto Telegram*. The kid with the boy's haircut and the boy's dash on the ice had fooled them, the paper's 8 March 1956 edition continued in amazement. Eight-year-old Abigail Hoffman had made it halfway through the season before they realized she was a girl. What was worse, by the time her secret was discovered, she had been invited to compete on the all-star team in Maple Leaf Gardens, and it was too embarrassing to kick her out. In the marshmallow world of the mid-fifties, Abby proved a cause célèbre for papers from the *Grand Forks South Dakota Herald,* to the *New York Times,* to the *Montreal Gazette.* By the next year, when the media had moved on to Sputnik and there was no room for cute masquerades, the Tee Pees dropped their hard-hitting defensewoman.

The newspaper photos of the spunky little girl with the brush cut and the baggy Tee Pee uniform are yellowing now—replaced with half-tones of a strong, slender, intricately well-modeled woman moving down a track with force and grace. The leg muscles are taut; the arms move back and forth like gears in a Swiss watch. The brown Brillo hair is blown back by the wind, the gray eyes stare straight ahead, oblivious to the stands behind her which are filled with a popcorn blur of people. The twenty-seven-year-old woman is pushing, pulling, running—lithe, strong, determined, and alone.

This recent photograph is Abby's self-image—the athlete detached, developing, racing for the sheer satisfaction of effort. Today she is one of Canada's hopes for the 1976 Olympics although she is nearing the end of her athletic career. She placed seventh in the 800 meter races at Mexico City and eighth at Munich. She garnered gold medals at the Pan American Games and the Commonwealth Games. She has served on more international track and field competitions than any other living Canadian.

Although Abby and I are the same age, she seems much more free—from the judgments of tradition and the claims of the future. I wonder if she is the certified

This essay is reprinted from *Her Own Woman,* published by Macmillan, Canada (1975), and available in a Goodread paperback edition from Formac Publishing, Halifax, Nova Scotia.

"liberated woman"—the kind of individual my imaginary daughter might become. It seems too late for me and for most other women of my generation who were socialized into the "woman's role." But Abby grew up without the feminine constraints about dress, behavior, worth, and power. Her family encouraged her to set her own standards. When she was little, she was called "off-beat." Her mother was called "eccentric." The cliché today is "liberated." The cost has been reduced from ostracism in the fifties to mere detachment in the seventies. Abby says she doesn't mind the isolation; she has always been an outsider.

Abby considers herself primarily an athlete, but she has also surfaced with an independent identity as a university teacher and a political activist. The eight-year-old nonconformist has grown up to be a vehement critic of commercial sport exploitation, of sedentary university society, and of colonialism in the Third World. She is, perhaps, a woman of our generation in her ambivalence about a single career. But she is almost unique in the degree of her success. She seems unburdened by the traditional anxieties about her strength and ability.

Abby lives outside the mystique of the female body. From a distance, she is an androgynous figure. She never wears dresses or makeup. She is unfamiliar with the prescribed feminine gestures and accoutrements. Her hand movements are precise, not delicate. She strides rather than walks. In fact when she goes into Eaton's, she is often greeted with "May I help you, Sir?" "Oh, yeah, it happens all the time. I just take it as part of my absurdist view of the world."

Abby is proud of her body, liberated with it in a sense most of us could never imagine. She says, "I don't care if I fit the social stereotype. An athlete learns just how superficial those definitions are. You know what your body can do. You're aware of fitness and form." Although Abby would cringe at being called a "beautiful woman," she is a sensual person: vibrant complexion, fresh, bright smile, clear eyes, well-toned limbs. Her lithe movements remind me of a bird—not a delicate sit-in-her-nest type of bird—more of a searching, swooping bird of prey. Maybe an osprey. She is stimulated by physical challenge. Her very presence is a subtle admonition. She makes me all too aware of my futile attempts to hide or shed the extra seven pounds of flab. I mean, there she is—someone who is in tune with her body, someone who doesn't feel weighed down by the classic dichotomy between a woman's sexuality and her intellect. Abby says, "I can't relate to not relating to by body. I don't know why I'm different from other women. I guess it's my general orientation to the world—'Screw you.'"

She grew up in that weird corner house on Glendonwynne Road in Toronto where you could look right through the drapeless windows. The neighborhood kids always wondered why there was no TV in the living room. Queerest of all: there was no living room, just a large, empty, terrazzo tiled area with cupboards along the wall chock-full of sports equipment—an indoor hockey rink. When property tax officials tried to assess her for running a school, Abby's mother explained that she wasn't running an institution, just a home, thank you. Nobody seemed to understand why the idiosyncratic Hoffmans drove around in a blue panel truck when everybody else was flashing two-tone sedans with V-8 engines and fancy tail-fins. They couldn't appreciate why the Hoffmans spent evenings together in the workroom, painting, and modeling, and reading, rather than watching "Perry Mason" and "Gunsmoke," or why they took rock hunting hikes in the summer instead of driving down to Miami's air-conditioned, cut-rate motels. The closer they came to this household, the more eccentric it seemed. Sam Hoffman shared the shopping and cooking and cleaning. He washed his own clothes by hand. They didn't have a washing machine or an electric mixer or a vacuum cleaner or . . . because they spent their money on books and a country cabin. There wasn't much money, anyway, from Sam's salary as a paint company chemist and Dorothy's income as a nursery school teacher, especially since Dorothy paid the housekeeper a little bit more than she earned herself. The neighbors couldn't understand that at all. . . .

Dorothy shaped Abby's independence. Dorothy Medhurst, swimmer and basketball star, the artist who dropped out of Central Technical School to work at the Art Gallery of Ontario with Arthur Lismer and later became a teacher without any professional training. The handsome blond woman who wore rimless glasses and straight wool suits in the petticoated fifties has always retained her maiden name. She didn't see anything peculiar in having a job. She came from a long tradition of working women. Her grandmother had always worked as a tailor's assistant. How else could she survive after she shed her worthless husband? And Dorothy's mother established herself as a bookkeeper after she, in turn, left Mr. Medhurst. Dorothy grew up in twenty different rooming houses in Toronto's Cabbagetown. Dorothy always felt lucky to spend so much time with her mother— much more than the kids with two parents—reading and talking and going to movies. And her mother genuinely valued her freedom. She said that she paddled her own boat and that the sinking or swimming was up to her. Her Scots Presbyterian independence supported most of the unpopular causes of the day. She read Simone de Beauvoir, Eleanor Roosevelt, Agnes McPhail. She passed on her own temperate feminism to her daughter and granddaughter.

The Hoffmans were a close, but not affectionate family. "We never spent a lot of time hugging and kissing," declares Abby with traces of little girl distaste in her voice. Paul, Muni, Abby, and Benny were all encouraged to compete in organized sport. It drew the four diverse personalities together—Paul, who wanted to grow up and become a solitary geologist; Muni, the sociable kid with all the girlfriends who wanted to be a garbageman with five children; Abby, the indomitable sprite, who looked forward to making a fortune as a gold prospector; and Benny, who declared that he would like to become a cloud. The family's self-sufficiency lessened the need for outside social life. Throughout school Abby was always on the periphery. "We were taught that the other circles weren't important, that you had to have your own circle, your own set of principles." So began Abby's race against her own standards of perfection.

As we sit in her downtown Toronto apartment, Abby shows me another news photo from her large, blue scrapbook—a grinning four-year-old girl treading water in the Humberside Collegiate pool. Sports constitute her earliest memories and she says she will always define herself as an athlete. "It's very hard to explain; there's just something in my personality that draws me to sport." The stimulation and determination and discipline have clearly shaped her self-image. On the table next to us are piles of Xeroxed papers for her socioeconomic study of Canadian women's sports. Scattered on the makeshift couch are several articles about political exploitation of sport in South Africa, the topic of her Ph.D. thesis. She hands me a copy of "Super-Jock in Decline: Liberating Sport from Sexist Stereotypes," which she has written for *Canadian Dimension.* Four gold medals are hung casually on the doorknob.

Abby played most of her early hockey on the terrazzo front room floor or at the artificial rink across the street. She would race home for lunch, slurp down her soup with the skates still around her neck, and run back to the ice. Her energetic family encouraged her hiking, swimming, hockey, running. Abby always wore trousers, partly because of these activities and partly because of Dorothy's pragmatism. Why shouldn't girls wear slacks? Their legs get cold in the winter, too. Besides, there were so many perfectly good corduroys in the house. The only dress Abby would wear was her Brownie uniform, much to the indignation of her teachers. And on several vacations, she and her mother were evicted from campground washrooms because they were mistaken for men in their short hair and pants. Abby recalls, "That hurt, because when you are six, you're insecure enough about reaching the door handle without someone telling you that you should be in the men's room."

Abby didn't have many girlfriends. "Girls are dumb in the head," the star Tee Pee defensewoman told the newspaper interviewers. No doubt the idea originated with her brothers, but she developed her own disdain for girls' docility. "They got in the way of the hockey puck and they cried when you threw snowballs at them." The first girlfriend she remembers is someone she tied up with skipping rope. She was alienated from girls because of their lack of skill as much as because of her lack of enthusiasm for Jr. Pillsbury Cookbooks and Betsy Wetsy dolls. In school, she was separated from most of the other kids because of her sports prowess.

She began competitive swimming when she was six. In junior high, she was distracted from the traditional preteen anxieties and activities by preparing for the Ontario Swimming Championships.

Abby never considered herself a female jock—just someone with a different interest. Once before a high school race, a woman approached her and warned that track would hamper her chances of having children. She told the woman to go to hell.

If the other kids thought that the Girls' Athletic Association was weird, she made equally devastating judgments about the inanity of their party scene. While most of her peers were struggling with the latest dance steps or the new cheerleader routines, Abby was testing *her* coordination for the Tokyo Olympics.

What you feel at the beginning of a race is a great deal of strength, a great deal of speed, a great deal of power and dynamism. The fear you had—the apprehension—is dissolved when the gun is fired. Now almost each tenth of a second is an exercise in total concentration. It's a question of internal harmony. You program yourself to hear your coach's signal, the cadence and breathing of the other runners. Similarly you focus your eyes like a camera lens—ten feet ahead—and you don't take in anything else. You're consistently aware of your position. You have to know who's in front of you and who's behind. Who's moving. Who can't handle the group. Who appears to be running smoothly. You're also aware of how you feel physically. Most of the fear is gone. But if someone does something unexpected—someone is running faster than you anticipated—you say, 'Christ, I can't keep up. That has ruined my tactical plan to run the race.' Or you may begin to wear out before the end of the race, at the final kick. You may reach the lactic acid saturation point.

The first sensation at the end is relief. If the race has gone well, with a great deal of concentration, you should feel like it has taken two hours instead of two minutes. The change you've put your body through is fantastic—from the point of being able to do anything to the point of being physically incapacitated. After a race, you just stand and put your hands on your knees for a few seconds, until some of the lactic acid has cleared out of your body. You warm down for a few minutes to get yourself back on the regenerative cycle. If you have done well, you are exhilarated. Regardless, you have a tremendous feeling of relaxation. You have no inhibitions of letting your body act of its own accord. You can't imagine feeling any more lack of control, any more intense release.

Abby was shaping her own priorities when most of us were still scrutinizing *Mademoiselle*'s "Twelve-Hints-To-Attract-A-Neat-Date" articles. Today she doesn't seem the least bit nostalgic for her missing Shelly Fabares youth. She dated a few times, had a couple of friends, but she wasn't one of the bevies of Canadian girls who spent their afternoons in front of the TV gossiping and guzzling Coke. Athletics provided her with too many alternatives—traveling, newspaper coverage, physical stimulation. "Sure there were days when I said, 'Shit, I wish I was a cheerleader . . .' or 'I wish I had *her* looks,' but there weren't many." There was enough satisfaction in sports and in that perennial intervening variable, her family.

She said it never bothered her, the way it worried the rest of us academic wallflowers, that she didn't get invited to the Junior Prom or the Senior Ball. She would have had a harder time explaining to Dorothy how she got talked into the bourgeois affair than she had facing her own romantic rejection. She wasn't one of us who spent hours before the mirror, struggling to get the eyeliner straight, mixing white with pink lipstick for just the right frosted shade, or blushing on Revlon's natural tone. She just washed her face in the morning before she went to school. What would she say to Dorothy if she came home with a little plastic makeup kit?

She didn't spend hours in Eaton's agonizing over the neatest colour of Shetland mix-and-match sweater to go with her Capezio shoes. She did face one crisis, however, the catastrophe of frizzy hair. What do you do with a Brillo pad when the other girls have such straight, sleek manes? She even went to the local drug store to inquire about a hair-straightening kit, but she couldn't figure out how to use it. Besides, how could she explain it to Dorothy? "I would have been laughed right out of the house if I had done any of those soppy teenage things," Abby says, laughing now, herself. So Abby was too busy, too perceptive, too isolated for the adolescent anxieties which confined most of our generation.

In university she continued training for the Mexico City Olympics. People questioned her combination of athletics and academics more than her status as a woman athlete. Her University of Toronto friends couldn't understand why she ran, and track friends couldn't relate to her studies. But their lack of empathy never bothered her. "Most people don't talk to me at all about my sports. They don't say, 'It's weird that you do all this running my dear.' That may be a sign of being odd in itself. I mean, who knows how to carry on a conversation with a female runner? Christ, there aren't too many of us around." The only confrontation between the individualist athlete and the traditional university occurred at the Hart House track during Abby's first year. She knew it was reserved for men, but she thought she'd try it, anyway. When she was thrown out, she didn't complain— she had survived the Tee Pees and there was no moral support from a women's movement then—she just found another place to train. The discipline and routine of studying added to the discipline and routine of sports, distancing her further from other people.

"I guess I use the isolation of sports as an excuse to stay apart," she tells me one day. This is an unusually introspective response from Abby. Ironically, the closer I come to her, the more distant I feel. I am at ease in her social ambience—the academic subsistence level life-style. Her old flat reminds me of my own, ten blocks away in the same immigrant neighborhood: the clinking debilitated radiator, the cheap furniture, the stacks of books and records, the same magazines lying open on the floor. As we sit on her cheap kitchen chairs, I realize that as much as I identify with her domestic surroundings and political reference points, I am very detached from her. Her independence is sustained by a concentration on work. She does not diffuse her energies into personal relationships.

She enjoys running for the sense of harmony with other women as much as for the competition. "One of the reasons I like being in a high level contest is the feeling of group rhythm. It becomes difficult to distinguish myself from the other members of the race. When I was in the Munich Olympics, the difference between the first person and the last person in the final was 1.7 seconds. Obviously we went around the track with a great deal of harmony. You feel like all the runners are tied together on a string. It's a psychological and physical relationship. You could be very far behind, but if you're accelerating and decelerating with that lead person, you feel like you can reel her in. You're always aware of trying to beat the others. But everyone wants to put in a good performance together. It's a paradox: the group concept heightens the competition. I finished last at Munich, but I felt a great sense of satisfaction at the end because I had run my best personal time and because the race had been of such high caliber. I don't think I would have felt much more exhilarated if I had won."

As Abby approaches the end of her competitive years, she considers an advisory career in sport. Her current absorption is a book about the history of women in Canadian sport. She will discuss, for instance, the 1920s and 1930s when the media coverage of women's athletics was similar to the press attention now focused on men's organized sport. There were regular women sports columnists. The softball games at Toronto's Kew Beach were broadcast on the radio. Many of the participants were working-class women in their twenties. The popularity petered out in the mid-thirties as part of the conservative backlash of the depression, when women were persuaded to leave their jobs. Then the newspapers were crammed with reactionary articles declaring that sport wasn't healthy for women. "We're still recovering from the stereotypes," declares Abby. "We associate sport with men, with masculinity and masculine qualities. We have to break that down."

Abby becomes more and more animated as we move from her personal relationships to her social criticism. She leans the wooden chair against the counter of the persimmon and plum kitchen cupboards, pacing her quick comments out with her thin hand. Perhaps this is her most natural milieu—this world of sociopolitical hypothesis. As we drink tea from rough, handmade mugs, I wonder what Abby Hoffman is doing with the mundane sink-side accessories of Power Plus and Javex. Indeed, from *any* point of view her private life—the clutter of the kitchen sink or the raw edge of her emotions—seems spare in comparison to her public image.

Her most vociferous complaint about athletics focuses on a problem shared by men and women: commercial exploitation. She says professional athletics uses the talents of a few players and the interests of thousands of spectators for corporate profit. She complains that the distinction between participant and observer just encourages "sloth" (one of her favorite pejoratives), "sloth" and "indolence."

At first I was disturbed by her kinetic personality. Obsessive compulsive? No, that's a fatuous, even jealous, observation. More probably she just inherited a healthy respect for effort from her active family. In fact, her whole energy is stimulated by and calculated for achievement. "People only use about half their body IQ," she admonishes with almost evangelistic fervour. "You can't accomplish anything if you sit around all day. In fact I think my mental capacity is only about three hours a day. If I don't get some exercise, I'm no good at academic work."

Assistant Professor Abby Hoffman teaches in the concrete, characterless Arts edifice which looks down over smaller, graceful buildings at the University of Guelph in Southern Ontario. This traditional Aggie campus, defined by flush-faced farm kids and housewives in homecoming buttons, seems an ironic contrast to Abby's radical urban sensibilities. But she likes the openness of these students. She sits confidently at the front of the room—behind one of the large white tables joined in a square. Her students don't call her "Professor Hoffman," nor do they call her "Abby." Somewhere in between, she holds their unclassified respect. Abby is scholarly but not esoteric, demanding but not authoritarian. As she lectures, she draws in her breath, setting a hard edge to her voice. Her directness is a kind of reserve in itself. It inhibits people, establishing a protective distance.

Today in her seminar on Africa she is discussing "a typical example of the hysterical over-simplified coverage you get in *Time*," an article predicting the decline of apartheid in South Africa. She easily draws out her students' opinions, closely leading, but not impeding the discussion. When one fellow asks, "Aren't they offering the Blacks more jobs to increase their buying power?" she answers excitedly, "OK, OK, but what are they giving the Blacks really?" "Nothing, I guess." She continually refers them back to the other readings—encouraging one student to answer another. The spirited discussion closes with characteristic cynicism. "See, you have a great deal of fun when you read *Time* slowly."

We walk up to her office in this corporate academic building with its sleek elevators and carpeted hallways. Abby looks more like a frenetic student than a dignified scholar. She enjoys the classroom interaction as much as the academic preparation. She grins slyly as she admits the controversy she has created by teaching her classes on the Third World as studies in capitalist exploitation. Guelph is a conservative campus where professors tend to subscribe to the "All's right-with-the-world, colonialism-was-good-for-the-savages" theory. Obviously benign neglect was never one of Abby's philosophies. She prefers to teach part-time; she has no aspirations to professional prestige. She isn't dedicated enough to the institution of the university to care whether her students borrow essays. She just hopes to stimulate her classes sufficiently to do their own work. She prepares lectures diligently, leads class discussions enthusiastically, listens attentively to students' questions during office hours. But academia remains only one part of her free-lance life along with her running, her CBC work, and her political concerns.

The clutter of her small office illustrates the challenge of fitting together her jigsaw puzzle schedule. "Go to the book store at 3:00" is scrawled on an index card in the dial of the ringing phone. The small blackboard is cramped with scribbles, "See Bruce about study group." Piled on the floor are Xerox copies of an article, "Castro Has Evidence that U.S. Took Part in Coup," which are to be distributed in class. A map of the University of Guelph is falling off the back of the door. Her flip calendar is dated eleven days ago. Her jacket hangs on a wall peg—two felt pens sticking out of the pocket—convenient to grab when she dashes out the door.

Abby is the only female professor in her department. She says some of the women students relate particularly well to her, but she bristles at being called a card-carrying "role model." She has no qualms about women's ability. She declares vehemently that women are better organized and quicker witted than men—a reflection of her own self-image. The only discrimination she has encountered has been a reluctance to give her some of the department's busywork. But she doesn't want to climb Guelph's academic ladder, anyway. Perhaps the clearest indication of her immunity to academic chauvinism was her initial job interview. She wasn't asked any of the customary "female" questions about home and family. "There's something in my manner that's sufficiently intimidating that I don't get questions like that very often."

Her penchant for politics was stimulated, predictably enough, by the little Lenin library on Glendonwynne Road. Both parents were active in the Progressive

Movement during the thirties; they were stomped by RCMP horses in Queen's Park in 1939. Just as Abby models her independence on her mother, she inherited her keen critical mind from her father. Sam Hoffman, who was once described in the *Toronto Telegram's* inimitable phrasing as "a retiring sort," exerted his influence around the household through passive resistance. He would proffer opinions about Continentalism and Stalinism and the ravings of Joe McCarthy—inconsequential platforms for domestic decisions, but formative stimuli to his children's analytical minds. Abby was taught to observe and interpret politics for herself.

At age five, she entered the University of Toronto School where she benefited from the close student-teacher rapport. At Humberside Collegiate, where she was tracked into the "brain class," her favorite subject was history. She joined the model UN and became disillusioned with the liberal ideal of world government: "The kids at Upper Canada College always got to be the United States or Russia and the kids from schools like mine got to be Chad or Gabon. I'd say that's a pretty realistic lesson about world power. The rich wind up with all the territory." When she entered university, she wanted to study political science and become a diplomat or a civil servant. Like many of us who started college as liberals, studies radicalized her beyond the compromise required by government service. Instead, she opted for the detached role of political analyst.

Abby was never involved in the student movement at university she says, "because it was controlled by a small group of relatively incompetent men." Despite her parents' example, she has never participated in a demonstration—prime distinction between Abby's individualism and my idealism. At Berkeley I transferred the passionate righteousness of my conservative Catholic home to "the movement." We Catholics had an edge on revolution anyway, because of our pervasive guilt and our potent free wills. My emotional commitment—to antiwar protest, the California Grape boycott, Third World autonomy—preceded my academic analysis. I wonder if I was not more representative of our generation. Abby's involvement was strictly intellectual. Sure, the "revolution" was ephemeral. But while I imagined myself in the vanguard, Abby was reading about the movement in the *Varsity.*

Today she infuses her ideology into her teaching, articles, and speeches. Abby describes herself as "definitely more radical than NDP," but she's alienated from the socialism that has splintered into the absurd, indistinguishable abbreviations of the New Left. "I guess you could call me an anarchist. I'm a nationalist, but I'm not naive enough to be fooled by the self-interest of some people's patriotism." She concedes, somewhat reluctantly, "I see a real benefit in making people believe in the perfectability of man. It makes life less hostile. But basically I believe that things are pretty screwed up and they're going to stay that way." Her politics, like her athletics and her academic career, are defined from the periphery.

Abby has to get back to Toronto to do a radio show the next morning, so she offers me a lift down the 401. Her old red Volvo bears no proclamations on the bumper. The only evidence of ownership is the eclectic mess inside—a shoebag and an electric kettle tossed on the back seat with *Only One Earth,* an ancient red sweater, and a yellowing *Globe and Mail.* Our conversation about politics has led to an argument about women's liberation.

Abby challenges the movement's political priorities. She says that capitalism—not sexism—should be the prime target in developing countries. She also complains that within Canada itself, sexism is just a middle-class issue. "Society has got to change the role of women, but that's not the first thing you change. Sure, the basis of capitalism is the family and therefore the exploitation of women, but I can't place women at the beginning of my political analysis."

"But wait a minute," I interrupt, "Don't you realize that in any oppressed country, the most exploited people are the women? They have the lowest status and the least opportunity. They have to take orders from the men. They do all the shitwork."

I'm enjoying the sensation of having a spirited discussion rather than a detached interview with Abby. The relationship model and more of a . . . no, "sister" isn't the word, even I cringe at the sentimentality, more of a . . . contemporary.

"No, women *have* had a chance to contribute," she says. "Always. They've been in the background in the past. But that's changing now. . . ."

"Oh, really? How many women MP's . . ." It seems ironic to me as I look out the window, feeling our isolation from the other darkened cars and our own familiarity, that *we* should be arguing about feminism. The dispute belongs in the vw bug with the middle-aged man and his wife, or in the Buick station wagon with the graying mother and the teenage daughter, or behind any one of the hundreds of other sets of whizzing headlights, but not in the old red Volvo with the two radical young women. Again, I feel the paradox of being near Abby. We are brought together by circumstance and life-style and ideology, but are still divided by her sober individualism and my passionate idealism, by her rational Presbyterian reserve and my romantic Catholic commitment.

"Yes, yes," she concedes. "I agree with that and I would think women have a lot to offer. I could see a lot of good coming from women's involvement in sports and politics."

It's another clash of style. She agrees with the end, but not with the means. Abby will never carry a picket sign outside the Department of Justice to demand Indian women's land rights or hand out leaflets at a beauty pageant. She has been tempted, she says, to accept an invitation to address a right-to-life rally and then to declare her support for abortion on demand. Although the suggestion is sardonic, her conviction about abortion is deep and personal. She had an abortion last year in New York State. Since then, she has been battling with the Ontario Medical Health Insurance Plan to give her coverage for it. "It's the principle of the thing—not the money—I'm doing it on my own, making phone calls, writing letters to officials. Maybe if I get coverage for it, some other women will too. But that's what the women's movement doesn't seem to understand—you can be doing something on your own. You don't have to wave around a placard."

She doesn't want to talk about the abortion, because, she says, it is just a personal matter. I try to convince her that unless more people speak out, the laws won't change. I explain that after I had an abortion, I found it helpful to share the experience with other women. She still refuses. The persistent journalistic fear that one is trespassing into private territory precludes further discussion.

Abby's distance from the movement is measured by the difference between most women's vulnerability and her own self-confidence. While she is increasingly aware of cultural and professional discrimination against herself and other women, she doesn't suffer much sexism in her personal life. If liberation is the development of independent identity, she underwent the process during her preadolescent years. Predictably, she is disappointed in the progress of other women, and rejects the stereotype of females as victims, "I don't relate to myself as a person who has been discriminated against. My self-perception as a woman isn't the traditional one, and it's not the one seen by the women's movement either."

Her relationship with George, the man she lives with, is unconventional, even for a generation pretending to thrive on the other side of marital convention. She spends half her week at the cabin near Guelph and the other half at the Toronto apartment. They both come and go as they please. Abby enjoys their brief times together. She declares that she could never have a traditional marriage or live with anyone over a protracted period of time because she is too wilful.

George and Abby share the household chores. "Cleaning is a joint activity; that means nobody does it." They wind up in some traditional roles by default. One afternoon George doesn't know what to do with the chicken wings, so Abby cooks dinner. Meanwhile, she can't figure out what's wrong with the Volvo, so he spends half an hour outside repairing it. They share all the decisions. She explains, "At first I thought it would be good for the man to decide things, I guess because it always was the opposite when I was growing up. I let it go like that until he made a few wrong decisions. Now we're fairly egalitarian. I mean, much more so than in most households where the decision-making goes according to the economic contribution. I bring in most of the money here and I don't treat George like a wife."

Their relationship started with an intellectual attraction and their domestic atmosphere is one of ideological and temperamental confrontation. "I have the feeling that if I were around any more we wouldn't get along. Sometimes we ask each other, 'Don't you want to go on a trip or something?' We never gave it much thought when we moved in together. I mean we never thought it was forever or that it would restrict either of us. George socializes separately. I don't, but I go where I want and when I want. I stick with the guy because I really like him. We enjoy a lot of things together. We both have a sense of the absurd. We like to laugh at how fucked up the world is."

Abby has had several relationships with men but wouldn't consider lesbianism an extension of her body's liberation. "Goodie for the radical feminists, but I'm not interested in a homosexual relationship. I could tell you that running around the track with other women was a sublimated sexual experience. But that would be the biggest bunch of bull I ever fed anybody. Many people think sports is a replacement for sex. Well, you get kind of a catharsis from sports; it's a cleansing, stimulating thing. I don't want to carry the analogy too far, but I guess you could say there's a building up to a climax, a getting lost in it, a feeling of release. I wouldn't say that athletics is a replacement for sex. I do think that a certain kind of personality—a self-contained individual—is going to be more attracted to athletics. Someone who is very dependent on other people isn't going to go in for it."

Marriage promises little emotional reward to Abby. Convenience would be her only rationale for succumbing to a contract. "Maybe if the man I was living with was rich and it would make things easier legally...." Abby is ambivalent about motherhood. She would like to be a parent in about ten years, but worries she will be too old then to bear healthy children. And kids do bring hassles: the expense, the life-long commitment, the chores. On the other hand, she would enjoy the experience of watching someone develop and grow, of having someone around when she was older. She wouldn't care if she had sons or daughters.

Abby still sees her own parents at least twice a week. Her mother is her only close friend besides George. "Dorothy is energetic, entertaining, one of the most interesting people I know. She can talk about anything from the snakes of North-eastern Ontario to the Bauhaus. She's almost sixty and she goes on a three-week canoe trip every summer. She puts effort into everything she does. Next to her, I'm an indolent, slothful person."

The admiration is mutual. Dorothy respects Abby's humor and drive and athletic prowess. Dorothy gave me an interesting perspective into Abby's future, since the daughter is almost the mirror image of the mother's youth. All the edges have softened with Dorothy. Her bright blue eyes are cushioned with smile creases. Her lean body is kitten-limber as she sits on a first grade stool, her head on her hand, the elbow resting on her raised knee. Dorothy still wears the rimless glasses.

The bright purple and pink smock shows that the bookkeeper's daughter has brightened and relaxed over the years. Through Dorothy, I can see Abby's sometimes abrasive arrogance developing into a graceful individualism. Abby, who was made in her mother's image, admits that her parents' expectations are the only ones which still affect her. I feel more comfortable with Abby, seeing her reflection soften with the years. If she keeps stride with Dorothy, she will finish alone, perhaps, but not so isolated.

Meanwhile, aside from George and her mother, Abby has three or four other friends whom she sees during the course of her working day or if they happen to trip through her apartment. She doesn't go to parties or make luncheon dates or visit other people's homes. "I find friends a real burden, actually. I don't get a great deal of pleasure discussing my affairs with other people. Everybody is going through exactly the same shit. I don't want to impose my troubles on other people and I don't want them to bum me out with their problems.

"People think that if you're not particularly gregarious, you're some kind of misanthrope. It seems necessary to justify the pleasure of one's own company. There is a lot I like to do on my own. The athletics. The reading. And I find it much easier to deal with the world alone. There are some practical explanations, too. I've always been doing something different from most of my contemporaries. My family got me used to a nonexistent social life. It's not a question of making an overt choice to be detached. I'm not really conscious of what the alternatives are."

So Abby spends most of her time alone—long morning drives to the university, afternoons jogging in the park, evenings studying and correcting papers. She goes to films by herself; walks around for hours in the solitude of the Toronto Islands. She spends her life trying to meet her own standards.

We are approaching the Toronto exit and the end of our last talk. I wonder if I, Valerie Miner, the free-lance journalist, know Abby Hoffman, the free-lance person. I see her striving for intellectual satisfaction in her politics, for physical satisfaction in her athletics. These goals are her raison d'être. She gauges herself by the running rather than by the winning. Effort is her strongest moral imperative. She explains. "Athletes have to set high expectations to reach high levels. Even though most of the time these expectations are absurd, you realize that in the past it was possible for you to do this completely unrealistic thing, so you have to keep trying." She says I'll never understand her unless I can sympathize with the runner who trained for ten years to improve her record by a tenth of a second. I mention the obsession to write one simple, perfect sentence. She accepts the analogy. She says that she doubts whether anyone could express her character on paper when she can't even analyze it herself. If her arrogance is the victory of time over space, mine is the synthesis of perceptions and words. She nods and says I have come as close to her identity as possible.

I ask her why she let me get so close. "That's a good question," she laughs. "Ego and curiosity maybe. I say, 'Ah, the fuckin' interviewer's coming.' But I do care what other people think about me. I guess I'm not nearly as good at telling people to get lost as I fancy myself. And there's the social thing. My social interactions are quite structured. This started out as an interviewer-subject thing, but it could develop into kind of an accidental friendship. To the extent that I like communicating with other people, I like structured situations. Being interviewed is OK." I've never been called a "fuckin' interviewer" before, but I don't mind it from Abby. It implies a certain intimacy in her absurdist coterie. I would like to think she's right about an accidental friendship, that, some day, I'll be one of those people tripping through her apartment. But right now I can't think of any more structured situations for us.

I wonder about that imaginary daughter of mine. I would like her to be as "liberated" as Abby. I would like her to play hockey and argue politics. It's too late for me to act so freely with my body, to feel so uninhibited about my appearance, to be unrestrained enough to say "Screw you" as much as I would like. Abby's sense of freedom is a model for my someday child. However, I hope she will share some of my empathy and gentleness. I want her to realize, as I eventually did, that Abby is an individual as well as a prototype. She can emulate Abby without copying her. Hopefully, then, I won't find it so hard to be close to my daughter.

When I think about Abby now, I don't focus on any of the times we had together, the visits to each other's flats, or the telephone conversations, or the twelve reels of tape. I don't dwell on the photos in the blue scrapbook, the Tee Pee hockey player, or the high school swimmer, or the adult Olympic runner. I think of her in the future—ten years from now—running around High Park; lithe, strong, determined, and alone.

An Interview with Adrienne Rich
and Mary Daly

Valerie Miner: Let's begin with a general question about how feminist books are reviewed in the press and how that affects their success. Perhaps we could also make the distinction between feminist books and books by women.

Adrienne Rich: I think that distinction is extremely important. What I see happening in the establishment press is that a lot of women reviewers are being used to trash feminist books. There is also a fair amount of favorable reviewing—of books by women who are in no way feminists. There are virtually no feminists who are asked to review for the establishment. There is a decrease in the notice of feminist books at all. There is an increase in having them attacked, trashed, when they are reviewed. A few years ago, I was able to review *Woman and Madness, Beyond God the Father.* I could ask for a feminist book and review it for the *New York Times Book Review* or *Book World* in the *Washington Post.*

Mary Daly: There's another point, Adrienne, that nonfeminists are labeling themselves feminists. There's the infamous example of Francine Du Plessix Gray who reviewed *Of Woman Born* in the *New York Times Book Review.*

VM: Why do you think times are harder for feminist books now?

AR: I think the establishment press feels increasingly threatened and that there's a backlash. I don't like the term *backlash.* It's been a concentrated historic effort to blot out women's work, to blot out women's truth, to blot out women's experience. I think there have been periods of permissiveness and then the same thing reasserts itself.

MD: I think you have to see other analogues in society. Academia is the same. There are plenty of courses in women's studies taught by women who call themselves feminists.

VM: How do reviews affect the success of books?

AR: I think the *New York Times* has an inordinate amount of proliferative power

This interview originally appeared in the *San Francisco Review of Books,* October 1977.

given the kind of rag it is. My publisher told me that after the *New York Times* review came out, TV shows canceled who had been interested in interviewing me. There is a tendency in the rest of the establishment press to follow the *Times Review* and not to review the book. (I don't think that most book reviewers read books.) So, yes, it can adversely affect the success of a book. As can the non-notice of a book—sheer blocking.

MD: I think that silence has a very important effect.

VM: Do you write book reviews?

AR: I recently reviewed a book by Gerda Lerner in the *New York Times Book Review* partially because it gave me a chance to quote from a lot of early documents that I wanted people to be aware of. Right now, I'm desperately trying to make priorities and get into another prose book and put together a book of poetry. There's always just that pressure to get one's own work out.

VM: When you do review, do you feel any loyalty not to criticize a sister? Do you only say good things, encouraging people to make their own decisions after they buy the book?

AR: I think we have to be critical. I think you have to weigh how and where you are critical. But it's a myth that feminists are uncritical. Mary did a critical review of my book for the *Boston Real Paper.* She was distinctly critical of specifics in that book. We all have got to feel able to give books that serious kind of reviewing. But at the same time there is that problem of speaking in hostile territory. In territory where you are misquoted, quoted out of context, mangled and that is a very real liability.

MD: One of the techniques of subliminal advertising is juxtaposing material with something that is totally contradictory to the material. For example, candy manufacturers often ask that their ads be placed next to articles about dieting, to play on people's self-destructive impulses. I noticed that the first page of my review in the *Real Paper* occupied the top half of the page and the bottom was an ad for *Titters,* this book of alleged women's humor. The phrase that hit the eye right away was "Girl Talk" that stays with you. I think that it's important to watch for these things because the media—these rags—do not direct themselves to the conscious intellect.

VM: How do you feel about the choice between feminist presses and large houses? You've both published with large houses. What do you think of Daughters, Feminist Press, Diana and the others? June Arnold's piece in *Quest* said that she thinks women get better distribution, better treatment, and better money if they publish with feminist presses.

AR: I'm absolutely against anyone trying to dictate to any writer where she should publish. I think that's up to the writer to decide, depending on what kind of work it is, her individual financial situation, where she is in a great many senses. I don't believe in that kind of dictation. I also believe that the growth and the strengthening and the maturity of the feminist presses in America is a necessity. It is something that is in process, that all of us should support in whatever way we can—reviewing those books, publishing with those presses, donating money—in a variety of ways. The existence of those presses is making it possible for a lot of us to think about writing books which in the next couple of years, we're pretty sure are not going to be published by the establishment. I'm not talking about the feminist presses as an alternative to us when we think we're not able to publish with Doubleday, etc. Rather, they are a stimulus to possibilities within us.

I do think that the feminist presses have to prove themselves capable of providing the economic condition within which writers can survive. I feel very strongly that writers have to be able to do their work with some kind of guarantee of a livelihood.

MD: Here's another case where the parallels with academia are clear. There are certain feminists who say one should not even give a lecture in a university owned and directed by men. For example, I shouldn't give a speech at Radcliffe or at Yale. There's a lot of dogmatism.

AR: When I first read Judy Grahn's *A Woman Is Talking to Death,* when I first read Susan Griffin's poetry, it was through the feminist press. That work has meant a great deal to me in my life. In my work, it has challenged me and stimulated me.

MD: There's a problem of anti-intellectualism among feminists. It may not manifest itself so much against poetry and fiction, but in philosophy, it's there. Abstraction is bad.

VM: What do you think is happening with women's studies? It sounds like a lot of the coopting we've been discussing in publishing is possible there.

MD: I can't think of any simple way to talk about this. I was teaching at Boston College, which is run by Jesuits, teaching theology, being anti-Catholic and anti-Christian. I was teaching feminist studies. I think that's the problem, that exactly where you'd expect to find women's studies courses, you're likely to find them extremely insipid—Women in Literature, Women in History, Women in Yawn. You might find more feminist content in a theology department in a Jesuit university. The most creative women I know are unknown. They are my own students. My file cabinets are filled with their unpublished papers which are far more interesting than 90 percent of the alleged feminist articles and books. I don't even like the expression, "women's studies."

AR: Too often, that's precisely what it is, the study of women, not from a particularly feminist point of view.

MD: Gynocentric studies would be so totally spaced out from that, that there's no language to express it.

VM: Let's talk about how *Beyond God the Father* and *Of Woman Born* were treated in the press. With your book, Adrienne, almost everyone commented on the mother-daughter cathexis. Most reviewers were moved by that and your relationship with your three sons. The objections centered on the historical background and your extensions to contemporary times.

AR: Yes, I think there was a desire to chop the book in two. They said there was this really beautiful book written by a poet coming out of her own experience with these lyrical passages and there was also this attempt at analysis, at political theory and historicity, the contextual placing of this personal experience. That has been criticized as being unscholarly. They say, "Why doesn't she go on being a poet and write it personally, the way women are so good at writing." Very few reviewers wanted to see the book as a whole, wanted to see the interconnections, the interpenetrations.

For me the book is absolutely a whole. There was no question of writing a purely scholarly book or of writing my memoirs of motherhood.

There seemed to be an overall desire for the personal confessions which could be dealt with on that level: this individual woman had these pains and experiences and at the worst they so embittered her that she turned into a man-hating, ranting feminist. A desire not to see the book in the context of other feminist books. (Which is something that gets done to us over and over and over. It's as though we have just written the first piece of feminist theory.)

Much of the analysis in my book is a synthesis of work I've been reading a long time. The references are there, the footnotes are there, but these are ignored. It's treated as though it's come full blown out of my own traumas.

MD: I think that kind of split interpretation is to be expected in a schizophrenic society. A similar thing happened with *Beyond God the Father.* One reviewer said it was for two audiences, for the academics and also for women.

VM: Do you remember the *Commonweal* review?

MD: That was savage. The most vicious reviews came from a woman who should have been extremely qualified and who made it her business to review me in three different journals. She felt a competition with me. This is another strange phenomenon, but everyone seems to have a sort of shadow, Athena shadow lurking who's professionally competent, but is right there to attack. She's the fembot of the boys.

VM: The what?

MD: Fembot. Like Robot.

VM: What do you say to the critics about the scholarship?

AR: I said in the book that male scholarship is incredibly inaccurate as far as women are concerned. I suppose I could have stated that a good deal more strongly. I think that the book that Mary's writing now is such an exposé of that.

MD: I think we have to deal with a certain timidity, not only among other women, other feminists, other lesbian feminists, but also in ourselves, about criticizing male scholarship. The best of them are not good. The best of them are idiotic when it comes to talking about women, which is the only thing that matters. This is really true. One can take Joseph Campbell and show the illogic. I think that women, having been admitted to this realm of biblical texts, feel so awed that somewhere there is a fear of criticizing.

VM: Do you find a big difference between how your books are reviewed and how they're received by women generally?

AR: Women in general responded strongly to the whole question of anger, the whole question of violence. That last chapter ("Violence and the Heart of Maternal Darkness") made reviewers freak out in some cases. They said, how can one even talk about infanticide in relationship to motherhood? Or about the mother feeling, let alone expressing, anger in any form? This has been one of the taboos for a long time. A lot of women have written to me and said that for the first time they not only thought their anger was legitimate, but was going to be used for survival. The notion that anger could coexist with love was opening up for them a whole new way of living. Some women told me that the chapter on mothers and sons was also helpful to them, not only in their attempts to live with their sons, but to live in the male world.

VM: Why do you think that the cathexis between mothers and daughters has been ignored in literature?

AR: First of all, I think that all relationships between women have been seen as unimportant in literature, in the social sciences, so-called. The primary relationships in literature have been seen as either heterosexual romance or male-to-male competitiveness, aggression, father-son relationship, the golden bough, the son must kill the father and so forth. The mother-daughter relationship has never been perceived as crucial or as partaking of a kind of spiritual reality that's important to explore. Also, the kind of worldly power which fathers have been able to pass on to sons and in some cases, to a certain extent to their daughters, is not passed on by the mother. Mothers pass on a very different kind of power to their daughters but that has always been obscured.

MD: And in addition, mothers have been made into the torturers of their daughters. I think the increasing horror with patriarchy is when we see more and more the gyno(homo)cidal intent. Mothers are made murderers of each other. In China, through foot-binding, it's the mothers who crippled the feet of the seven-year-old daughters. In India, the mother-in-law is supposedly in the position where she had to encourage the burning of the daughter-in-law [when the daughter-in-law was widowed]. At present, there's mindbinding. Women are encouraging their daughters to stunt their minds, to be fashionable. In African countries, it's the women who perform the genital mutilation, the clitoridectomies on the young women. I think there's always a tendency to spatialize things to particularize things because the overall horror is too large. But when we look at these things, we have to make the connections, through the thousands of years and millions of women.

AR: I just want to go back and say one more thing about the mother-child relationship. It is through the mother, through the power of the mother-child bond, that patriarchy is able to control people. It is through that first relationship, that intimate relationship between mother and child, that patriarchy is able to warp bodies and minds.

VM: What were the responses to the physical references to mothers—the quote from Susan Silvermarie about how making love with a woman was like re-entering your mother and your comment that lying beside your husband, at times, you thought of your mother. Were people frightened, threatened, provoked in any way?

AR: The NY Times reviewer referred to what she called the most lyrical and clinically interesting passages in this book.

MD: That review was clinically interesting.

AR: Many women have responded strongly to that part. I found it rather unnerving to write about. I think that it's partly the taboo against erotic feelings between women. To write about those very primal feelings we have had about women's bodies immediately throws you into the taboo.

VM: In Mary's book, there was a sense of moving toward androgyny.

MD: There was. But I don't want to get into the details about what's wrong with androgyny. I would never use that word again. It was politically wrong, historically wrong. I think women, despite the word, saw how I was going to go beyond *Beyond God the Father.* I was trying to talk about an integrity. And as far as I'm concerned, that integrity has nothing to do with men. There is no man within me. There is no male necessary to my integrity. It is a womancenter becoming. That was the traditional word hanging around. And when I came to think about why I used it, it was very mind blowing. It was a conversation over the telephone with a very prominent male professor who slipped that word into my mind. I never would have used the word if I had not talked to that old fool. It wasn't natural to me at all. Androgyny always meant that for a woman to become complete, she had to become a man. For a man to become whole, he had to develop his feminine side. And of course that's what transsexualism is all about. And I suppose if you were a man, that might seem like a reasonable option. Androgyny is a completely fucked-up expression.

VM: How does your writing affect men?

MD: I don't care. When women enter our own space, we are present to ourselves and therefore absent to men and men in dresses, token women. (I would really stress the token women.) We become absent to those who would use us. And that power of absence is—not because we intended it to be—an invitation to men if they can fall into free space. When I become present to myself as a woman, it's not for the intention of avoiding men; it's just a by-product. I don't expect men to accept that.

VM: Both of you write about the international nature of women's oppression. What about the international nature of feminism?

MD: Everywhere I traveled in Europe, I met women who were close to my same space. They may have been fewer; they may have been farther apart from each other. But they were there. You have to look closely at what calls itself feminism. In London, for example, if you were looking for a feminist place, you might run into a bunch of women who were primarily socialists. I don't think one can judge by what labels itself feminism or what labels itself the "movement," because I think movement is movement and it's happening in secret places. The network is not easily describable. We may not know each others' names, but that sisterhood, that female friendship, that sense of reality exists.

VM: Should American women be making stronger ties with feminist groups in other countries?

MD: Personally, I think that books are important. Françoise D'Eaubonne wrote a book called *Feminism or Death* and more recently she wrote *Feminism before Patriarchy* which has a lot of interesting material. This woman creates new words, sparks. There's another woman, Benoite Groult, who wrote *Ainsi Soit-Elle*. In French, the word for "Amen" is *ainsi soit-il,* so it's a play on that. She had a very important chapter on hatred of the clitoris.

VM: How is your writing affected by your feminism?

MD: To me, anything I do, whether it's teaching or writing, is feminist. I don't particularly like the word *feminist,* but it's what we're stuck with at the moment. Woman-identified is perhaps better. I could not teach straight philosophy any more—Aristotle, Descartes, and Kant. It colors one's world view. I couldn't do a feminist book this year and the year after do one on Kant and the year after do a history of philosophy. There's no way. "Feminism" is my soul, my integrity.

VM: Adrienne, one of the things you discuss in *Of Woman Born* is having creative energy, not just time, but energy, drained by kids. Now that your three sons are grown up, do you feel you have more creative energy?

AR: I certainly think that part of my current energy has to do with where I am now. It's coming from a lot of sources. I certainly believe that children demand day-to-day constant attention that is a tremendous psychic and physical drain. Despite the childcare arrangements that women are able to create for themselves—always at great trouble—that psychic toll is always there. The primary responsibility is always with the mother. I don't see that changing despite all the changes women are going through.

VM: Do your feminist activities also drain energy from your writing?

AR: There's a constant struggle to try to create priorities that make sense. Certainly, I'm learning a lot from these activities and getting a lot of energy back. But there's always the point when a writer, as opposed to a full-time activist in another sense, has to get back to that room, to that typewriter, to that absolute solitude. You have to clear your head of all the voices that are in it and start listening to your own inner voice.

MD: If you think that your most lasting form of expression is your writing, that gives you your primary feminist activity.

AR: Yes it is, yes. We're living in a very anti-intellectual era. Not just among feminists. The entire society is increasingly so. With all the talk about how TV is taking over, audiovisual aides, etc., whenever anybody really wants to disseminate ideas, they write a book. I just read in the *Chronicle* this morning that Anita Bryant is about to write a book. Whenever any kind of propaganda is being disseminated, a book is written. The printed word is still considered to be essential. Writing has tremendous power.

VM: How are your friendships affected by the fact that you're writers, that you are mobile, have access to more means of communication?

AR: I don't feel that I have a community of writers so much as I have a community of women. I feel that I have come to know the minds of certain women through their writing before I have met them. The friendship came out of the rapport with their writing. However, as far as writing letters goes, I have become an absolutely terrible correspondent. Somehow communications go on. It's almost like a lightning thing that when I meet with people I haven't seen for a long time, the conversation begins right there and it's about essential things.

MD: Because they've read your books.

AR: Or because I've read their books or because we've had conversations before that were very crucial. It's an ongoing dialogue.

MD: There's also the point that one might really respect a book, but have a personal dislike for the writer. And still I think it's important to know that that book probably represents a primary and best aspect of a personality.

VM: Is feminism politics or philosophy? How does your writing affect working-class women in this country?

MD: I consider myself part of the working class. It's laughable that for years I used to fall for that question. Women in audiences would say, "With all these big words, how can you address the common woman?" Then I sat down and thought to myself, my father finished the eighth grade, my mother finished two years of high school. I had worked my way through every one of those goddamned degrees, never had it handed to me. I asked what kind of working class they were talking about. Usually the women who were doing this had big trust funds.

After I talked at Rutgers, a woman came up to me and said that it was the first time she realized she was a feminist. It was because she thought that feminism meant the ERA. Well, I don't. I'm bored by the ERA. I don't give a shit about women senators, presidents or generals or college professors for that matter. The word *politics* is a dirty word anyway. It was synonymous with the word *Jesuit* for centuries. It just smells bad.

AR: I think that the word that turns me off the most is *revolution*. It's so limited in comparison to what I consider feminism to be about. Which is a really total transformation.

MD: Revolution means spinning your wheels. Coming back to the same place.

VM: Talking about feminism and philosophy, Simone Weil seems the next likely subject for discussion.

AR: I found her work fascinating because she seemed to be trying—without succeeding—to make some of the very connections we've been trying to make. Especially in her notebooks, she had flashes of illumination that never got worked through. There was tremendous self-hatred, self-denigration, a lot of attributes we're used to seeing in brilliant women who simply feel unable to follow through with the power of their vision. But I agree with you that she's being made into a cult figure and people are not really reading her. They see the suicide, the victim woman, the woman who failed, who did not come through, that whole suffering, asceticized aspect of her. That's not what interests me about her.

VM: Why wasn't she more of a feminist?

AR: There are some very interesting little episodes in the Petrement book [*Simone Weil*]—like her reaction if a man even touched her, which was visceral. There was a kind of pattern if you read it from a feminist point of view. But there's no conscious feminism. Something like the essay *On Human Personality* was very valuable to me in a prefeminist stage because it gave enormous insight into questions about survival which I was trying to work through. The interesting thing to me is that you have two Simones both in the same class at the Ecole Normale, and one becomes the writer of *The Second Sex* and one becomes the writer of *Waiting for God*. Both come out of middle-class French intellectual backgrounds. What are the forces that are playing on these two women? I'd really like to see someone deal with that.

VM: What do you think of her emphasis on will, on morality coming from will? There seems to be a real strength in her that's uncorruptible, that she uses to destroy herself.

AR: I think she is unfulfilled—in the feminist sense—so full with potentialities and yet still so unfulfilled. I wish I could explain it. I think the kind of will she's talking about is very patriarchal.

MD: The concept of will is very patriarchal. She had been studying Aquinas and he always divorced it from intuition and emotion.

VM: Do you see the direction of women's writing as making connections, as refining the complaints and outrage and womanspirit of the last decade? Where have we moved from *Sisterhood Is Powerful?* Are we trying to understand patriarchy more thoroughly, trying to synthesize alternatives?

MD: It is developing. But I do have to return to all those brilliant papers from students in my files. There is no reasonable outlet for most of these in this society. When you talk about feminist writing, you're talking about a lot of stuff that isn't going to get published.

AR: I guess I'm more and more optimistic than you. In the past four or five months—four new magazines—*Chrysalis, Heresies, Conditions,* and *Sinister Wisdom.*

MD: But the articles I'm talking about are much better than the articles in these magazines.

AR: They should be sending them out.

MD: But these women are not known, they don't have connections. There is a built-in elite. I'm all for perfectionism. I'm not saying that everything a woman writes is philosophy; I don't use the word cheaply. But prominence isn't necessarily an indication of excellence.

VM: Is there a feminist metaphysics being developed? It seems so in *Of Woman Born, Beyond God the Father,* and in Susan Griffin's book in progress, *Woman and Nature.*

MD: I think it's important to use the term *metaethics.* Metaethics means getting at the hidden messages of myth and language which color all thought and all behavior. You have all these prominent men who consider themselves ethicists who talk about what's ethical about the neutron bomb and what's unethical, what's ethical about genetic engineering. All of those are foreground issues. And in the background [is the fact] that all mental processes are subliminally controlled by men. Language itself is so very controlled. If you make a study of the dictionary you'll see that almost every word has a history of opposites.

AR: What increasingly fascinates me is the saturation of the lie into the texture of things. The lie. The small lies. The secrets. The silences. In the effort to construct experience as it has been lived, it's the blank spaces that we have to be looking out for. In writing any kind of history, it is what is omitted that really counts. In reading the male texts, you're looking for what is left out more than what is being said. Even the little that is said is a lie.

MD: Sometimes women say they have to do more research. And that word *research* exposes just what they're doing. They're not searching. They're constantly just recovering what they did before. And then researching it and then recovering it. And then researching it and then recovering it.

Common Sense Waged and Earned:
The Work of Grace Paley

Grace Paley traces the lines between heart and conscience in her life and in her stories. She is one of this country's best writers. At sixty-two, Paley is a tough, shy, friendly woman. If you saw her on the street, chewing her ubiquitous wad of gum and schlepping groceries to her Greenwich Village apartment, you would hardly pick her out as a member of the prestigious American Academy and Institute of Arts and Letters. Rather, you might stop and ask directions because of her intelligent face. (Smart, not intelligent; her characters would say smart.) Sometimes I think of Paley's stories themselves as directions, practical lessons for the rest of us who have lost our common sense about people.

Paley provides something desperately needed in American fiction—a moral vision refined by practical experience and political sophistication. At a time when work cranked out of the creative-writing-school mill rarefies clever ennui, Paley writes with passion and conviction. She describes everyday people encountering death, love, motherhood, desertion, cultural exchange, growth. She often considers inequities of race, class, and sex—but never rhetorically, always within the common fabric of her characters' ordinary lives. Paley is a close observer and empathic listener who sighs her way to the bright side of life by early evening. Her stories are rooted in deep emotional movement, eschewing the paralyzed self-obsession of more voguish writers. Her social activism provides the clarity, vision, and optimism in her fiction.

The recent publication of *Later the Same Day* will delight admirers of her two previous story collections, *The Little Disturbances of Man* (1959) and *Enormous Changes at the Last Minute* (1974). Fans will also be pleased by the new edition of *Little Disturbances* and the current release of the movie, *Enormous Changes at the Last Minute*.

The reader is an active participant in Grace Paley's fiction. She stops in mid-sentence to tell you something, to ask, to demand, to explain a sudden transition or—more likely—the lack of one. In the narrative itself, she confides about the act of writing. "Then, as often happens in stories, it was several years later." She

This essay originally appeared in *Mama Bears News and Notes,* a community newspaper published by Mama Bears Bookstore in Oakland, California, in April–May 1986.

ignores almost all safe boundaries between artist and audience. In the final paragraph of "Listening" (*Later the Same Day*), Cassie complains to the narrator, Faith, that she hasn't appeared in any stories, "You are my friend, I know that, Faith, but I promise you, I won't forgive you, she said. From now on, I'll watch you like a hawk. I do not forgive you."

Later the Same Day features tales about Faith, a Jewish New York mother-gadfly-writer, who does and doesn't resemble Grace Paley. Like her other books, it's impossible to get through this volume without crying and laughing out loud. What a treat to read—or reread—Paley's collections in order of publication because *The Little Disturbances of Man* and *Enormous Changes at the Last Minute* introduce characters encountered in *Later the Same Day,* such as the seductive Dotty Wasserman, the nosy Mrs. Hegel-Shtein, and, of course, Faith and her family. We first meet Faith in *Disturbances,* where she is struggling to raise two sons on a slim typing salary. She is still trying to make ends meet in *Enormous Changes.* Now, *Later the Same Day* shows Faith coping with her adult sons' love affairs. "The boys were in different boroughs trying to find the right tune for their lives. They had been men to a couple of women and therefore came for supper only now and then. They were worried for my solitariness and suggested different ways I could wear my hair."

In *Later the Same Day,* Paley's characters are always in *some* social context, even in the first-person pieces. ("Somewhere Else" begins, "Twenty-two Americans were touring China. I was among them.") These stories are so artfully constructed that often a single aphoristic sentence or phrase can crystallize characters. "'Madame Nazdahova, our editor from *I BesseRe Zeit*—did you meet her.'—she listens like a disease.") or a theme ("Though the world cannot be changed by talking to one child at a time, it may at least be known.") Always she is playing with language. In "The Story Hearer," Faith says, "I haven't needed to iron in years because of famous American science, which gives us wash-and-wear in one test tube and nerve gas in the other. Its right test tube doesn't know what its left test tube is doing."

Paley's sensibility in *Later the Same Day* is more distilled than in her previous books. Her language is more fun, her truth is more steady. While she includes stories about other characters, the Faith pieces are my favorites. Older and more wry now, Faith remains brave and determined. Her edge is sharp, but no longer jagged. Although she frets about the planet's survival, Faith is certain about her right to a decent place in the world. ("Although" ... "but" ... "however"— Faith's reality is rarely without conjunction and never simple.) Life doesn't get easy; however, it does become more settled, as Faith observes. "Hindsight, usually looked down upon, is probably as valuable as foresight, since it does include a few facts."

The story "Friends" is a brilliant retrospective of the common sense Faith has waged and earned over the years. It is also a generous testimony to the survival of friendship. Faith, Ann, and Susan visit their friend Selena, who is dying. "Our dear friend Selena had gotten out of bed. Heavily, but with a comic dance, she soft shoed to the bathroom, singing, 'Those were the days, my friend...'"

"Later that evening Ann, Susan and I were enduring our five-hour train ride to home. After one hour of silence and one hour of coffee and the sandwiches Selena had given us she actually stood, leaned her big soft excavated body against the kitchen table to make those sandwiches. Ann said, 'Well, we'll never see *her* again.'"

These strong, tender, obnoxious, endearing women stretch beyond the precious "vulnerability" so popular in current fiction to become solid people, made of thought and *action*. While Paley's fiction is fuelled with social concern, her artistic momentum, unlike the work of some politically conscious peers, is not so much guilt as celebration. She concludes "Friends" by stating: "But I was right to invent for my friends and our children a report on these private deaths and the condition of our lifelong attachments."

In person and in fiction, Paley's accessibility is a complex art practiced with integrity and skill. Frequently critics complain that Paley should have written more than three books by now, that she should have spent more time at her desk creating fiction and less time on the streets agitating against American militarism. These people don't understand how her art and politics are mutually sustaining. Those who would curtail her activism for the sake of literature are looking for the golden egg in the wrong place. Indeed some of her stories emerge from her experiences organizing against conscription at the Greenwich Village Peace Center in the 1960s and against nuclear warfare with the Women's Pentagon Action in the 1980s. Occasionally a jail sentence will keep her from deadlines, but when life and career conflict, she chooses life. Ultimately her audience is the richer for it.

Grace Paley's politics affect the content, style, and process of her stories. As she questions and provokes with her open endings, readers become those active participants I mentioned earlier. Like Bertolt Brecht, she presents you with contradictions; she leaves you with issues and feelings buzzing in your head about your own social responsibilities.

Paley beautifully articulates her approach to storytelling in "A Conversation with My Father" in *Enormous Changes*.[1]

> "I would like you to write a simple story just once more," he says, "the kind de Maupassant wrote or Chekhov, the kind you used to write. Just recognizable people and then write down what happened to them next."

I say, "Yes, why not? That's possible." I want to please him, though I don't remember writing that way. I *would* to try to tell such a story, if he means the kind that begins, "There was a woman . . ." followed by plot, the absolute line between two points which I've always despised. Not for literary reasons, but because it takes all hope away. Everyone, real or imagined, deserves the open destiny of life.

NOTE

1. Please note that Paley uses quotation marks around dialogue in one book and not in the other. This is the reason for inconsistency in punctuation here.

Quiet Outlaws

Confessions of Madame Psyche is a novel of contradiction and mobility, classically Californian in character, theme, form, and setting. This richly polycultural journey is (as James Houston describes West Coast fiction in general) a "dream running well in advance of the reality."

Dorothy Bryant redefines "vision," testing the lines between perception and deception, celebrity and invisibility. Madame Psyche, who begins as a fake psychic exploiting people's troubles, becomes an ascetic medium for profound truth. The "confessions," which initially seem to be an admission of pretense, take on the traditional connotation of spiritual autobiography. The very form of the book is a disguise, for Madame Psyche's story is presented as a memoir found by her lost daughter while the book is actually a fiction found in the imagination of Dorothy Bryant.

Like the mythical Psyche, Bryant's curiosity is boundless. Like her own character, Madame Psyche, she is indifferent to celebrity. Bryant's steady, straightforward image may have inhibited her acquisition of a "serious" reputation. In the popular market quirky personality sells books and in the academic world scholars tend to find more satisfaction in psychoanalyzing fragile artists than in reviewing books. Bryant started as an outsider, a Western woman from a working-class immigrant home. She has resisted the current trend to vacuous, solipsistic fiction, creating instead dramatic narratives where complex characters engage with serious social issues. She writes clear, accessible prose which springs from a fascination with people and a practiced common sense. Bryant is so much at odds with mainstream publishing that she opened her own house, Ata Books, in 1978. Her versatile fictional repertoire includes stories of convicts (*Prisoners*), gay men (*A Day in San Francisco*), feminist mystery (*Killing Wonder*), Utopian philosophy (*The Kin of Ata Are Waiting for You*), as well as my favorites, *Miss Giardino, The Garden of Eros,* and *Ella Price's Journal*. Dorothy Bryant, like many of her characters, is a quiet outlaw traveling between classes and cultures.

Mei-li Murrow is born in San Francisco in 1896 to a poor Chinese woman and a

---

This essay originally appeared under the title "California Dreaming" in the *Women's Review of Books,* March 1987.

philandering alcoholic white man. Her crafty, white half-sister, Erika, notices the child's intuitive powers and linguistic facility. Erika gives up her job as a prostitute and begins to manage Mei-li's career as the medium Madame Psyche. What follows is a series of exploits which would be improbable if Bryant hadn't created such an intricate, appealing character. Travel to Europe, sudden marriage, loss of husband and child, retreat to a Utopian commune in Northern California, unexpected fortune—and misfortune, at the hands of Erika.

Mei-li's destiny is foreshadowed by the Chinese myth spun by her mother—"beautiful children were easily caught by jealous goddesses who would not let them return to their mama until they had performed awesome tasks"—and by the Greek myth taught by her schoolteacher:

> I read it over and over, loving Psyche most when she was disobedient—talking about Eros when he told her not to, sneaking a look at him when he warned her not to. Her abandonment by Eros disturbed me not at all because I was thrilled by the punishments of Aphrodite, which took Psyche to far places and strange adventures. . . . Miss Harrington explained that the god loved her for her curiosity, for her mind. (Pp. 17–18)

Mei-li sets off on what she eventually recognizes as her course, through unpredictable people and places. At first the journey is external, while Mei-li learns to survive as a poor, half-caste, unschooled female. After a spiritual awakening partway through the story, the movement becomes an inner one. The other characters are multidimensional people—from the conniving but charming Erika to the enthusiastic artist Stephanie to the passionate labor activist Helena to the pacifist hospital aide Buddy—but this is a *Bildungsroman,* and the other figures are most significant as steps toward Mei-li's enlightenment.

Mei-li is a protean personality, imperceptibly changing from psychic to communalist to farmer to mental patient. Her chameleon temperament protects her more than once. "The rumor spread that I had died in the fire. That is, the Filipino or Japanese boy, Lee, or the half-Russian Chinagirl May Lee, or that white woman in the Chinese pajamas—whatever mixture of identities the tellers of my death perceived." Throughout the story she maintains a wise innocence. She is modest, humorous, generous. The passion of her nature is cerebral, although she does have several sexual relationships. Her seeming egolessness, which allows her to adapt to each new task from Aphrodite or the water goddess, is actually a tough, flexible core.

Unlike some spiritual figures, Mei-li doesn't transcend worldly concerns, but engages deeply with social issues. Perhaps one of the most powerful aspects of Bryant's book is its polycultural authenticity. So often white novelists omit characters of color for fear of slipping on a dialect or out of some misplaced notion of political correctness. While it's important to honor the distinctiveness of literature by women of color, too much fiction by white feminists is completely Eurocentric. *Confessions of Madame Psyche* recalls the cosmopolitan casts of *The Kin of Ata Are Waiting for You* and other Bryant novels. It unfolds in the context of anti-Chinese riots and terrorist arson against Mexican-Americans and the racial segregation of Blacks in liberal San Francisco.

Bryant's use of labor history is likewise realistic and nonpolemical. The descriptions of agricultural work draw upon her own family's experience as prune pickers in the Santa Clara Valley. Mei-li works in the fields and in the cannery. During the 1931 canners' strike, she is caught between her Latina friends Helena, the activist who encourages her to protest, and Angelina, the individualist who tries to dissuade her.

> I could not move. I had no idea of not moving, no idea one way or the other until that moment when I simply could not move forward past the group of picketers. Angelina turned to look at me. In one glance, she understood more than I did. "Don't be a fool," she whispered. "There's no real union, and there are ten people looking for every job in there. The strikers have already lost—a few hours waving signs and they're out of a job, that's all. We can't afford that." She pulled at me again, but I could not move. I looked at her fresh young face. She was as white as her hairnet. I felt as frozen as if I were looking at the Medusa. (P. 250)

Mei-li's open attitude to lesbianism, pacifism, and other practices would have appalled her contemporaries. When she makes love with Stephanie, it is an extension of their friendship:

> We became lovers just as if we had always been. The comfort of our warming each other in bed became caresses of soothing pleasure. There was no "falling in love." We had always loved each other, had always been dear to one another. . . .
> My sexual relation to Stephanie was the last I had with anyone, and the best. (P. 189)

Mei-li's acceptance of pacifism during the "Good War" is equally natural: committed by her sister to Napa State Hospital, she develops an abiding friendship with Buddy, a conscientious objector working there.

At Napa Mei-li reclaims the meaning of asylum. First she is frightened by the hospital's cold brutality. She spares no details about the mental health profession in the 1940s and 1950s (including the presentation of the Nobel Prize for the advance of lobotomy). Ultimately she makes the asylum a refuge from the materialism of the outside world.

> Just before he left three months later, Buddy did me one last favor, misfiling my medical records with the "congenitally dysfunctional" so that my case would not come up in routine reviews for discharge. There has never been, to my knowledge, any thought of moving me from here. I have become familiar yet forgotten.... (P. 358)

As a native Californian, Bryant attends closely to the nuances of Western environment, which often elude visiting Easterners who snap, "There's no weather in California." She lovingly details the climates of San Francisco Bay, the Sequoia Eden of Santa Cruz, the fertile Santa Clara and Napa farmlands, charting the Northern California geography of change.

During her eighteen years in the asylum, Mei-li reflects on her surroundings.

> Of the many seasons of the California year, February is the most beautiful. Since June the hills have been brown and dry, and the winter rains have only turned them soggy, still dull in the weak sun of the short days. But in February fresh grass sprouts overnight, a bright, iridescent green suddenly flooding the landscape. Fruit trees bloom, the tule fog disappears, and the sun shines as brightly as in summer, without parching the land. (P. 348)

California is also a metaphor for extremity and synthesis. Mei-li lives on the rim of the continent as well as on the edge of her imagination. She is the meeting of East and West. She embodies those California characteristics of idiosyncrasy, idealism, and risk. Her first spiritual epiphany occurs on a Pacific beach, facing the Orient of her mother's past and the time zones of tomorrow.

The iconoclastic form of *Confessions of Madame Psyche* recalls May Sarton's *Magnificent Spinster* in the way it plays on the borders of biography and fiction. Mei-li's memoir has four separate parts: the written autobiography; photographs of family friends and homes; letters written to Buddy after he leaves the asylum; and brief editor's notes from Dorothy Bryant about how the "manuscript" reached her. It's all quite convincing, even the footnotes in which Bryant makes a cameo appearance.

This structure heightens the tension around visibility and perception. Mei-li's solitude is protected by the memoir format. No third-person voice intrudes to observe or to judge. Because the book is published "posthumously," Mei-li has no direct contact with editors or readers. The notion of omniscient narration is challenged by the fact that the manuscript is discovered by a daughter whom the narrator believes to be dead. In fact, although she appears only a few times, Joy is a major presence in the book. She is acknowledged in the introductory note, and we cannot read the memoir without imagining her discovering her mother through it.

The visual images remind Bryant fans of the imaginative graphics accompanying the text of *A Day in San Francisco*. Bryant's own friends collaborated on the novel by sharing old photos—further undermining the traditional concept of fiction writing as private practice. Using their ancient pictures adds another level of interpretation to the word *medium,* whose function in the novel is already equivocal.

Some readers will be amused by the format. Others will be annoyed when they turn back to the copyright page and settle on the words, "This is a work of fiction." But I found the form a wholly appropriate vehicle for its mysterious character.

Confessions of Madame Psyche reveals how appearances are deceptive: appearances of Mei-li, of her autobiography, of Dorothy Bryant. The 1906 earthquake creates a new San Francisco. War brings love. The Garden of Eden ignites into Hades. An inheritance materializes as penance. The restraints of Napa become a refuge. The confessions are subtle parables. Spiritualism turns to spirituality. "All the earlier endings were new beginnings. All Psyche's mistakes were doors opening. All her punishments were tests that transformed her and the gods as well."

Novelist Shen Rong and the Art of Literary Survival in China

"At middle age" is an apt description for China's contradictory literary scene at this historical moment. China is both a sophisticated and a developing nation. On one hand Chinese writing has broad appeal and ancient traditions. Today a population of one billion is hungry for books which must serve a vast range of literacy. On the other hand, as an economically developing country, China is burdened by a continual suspicion of the worth of art compared with subsistence necessities.

Writing has been suppressed at various stages since the Long March of 1934. For instance, during the Cultural Revolution (1966 to 1976), the Chinese Writers Association suspended activity. In 1978, the association, which functions as a cross between a literary guild and a government cultural agency, resumed work and now has twenty-nine branches across the country. Writers are enjoying this renaissance with a healthy degree of circumspection.

At Middle Age, the controversial novella by Shen Rong, is catching China's imagination. The book has sold over three million copies there and is available to Americans in the collection *Seven Contemporary Chinese Women Writers.* A movie based on the story is being shown in packed theaters as well as on television in China. Shen Rong's book hits tender nerves about the exploitation of middle-aged workers and, as an indictment of the Cultural Revolution, contributes to a growing "literature of the wounded."

The eighty-five-page novella describes the exhausting life of Dr. Lu Wenting, a forty-two-year-old oculist, overwhelmed by obligations to her patients and her family. Despite two decades in medicine, she is still only scratching out a living. The story begins as Lu cracks under the strain and suffers a severe heart attack.

Shen's writing moves with a swift, spare intensity. From her hospital bed, Lu reflects on her life—the early dedication to healing, idealistic hopes for marriage, a long friendship with her colleague Jiang. Her most dramatic recollections concern bitter experiences during the Cultural Revolution. Once, the Red Guard burst into the room where she was performing a delicate eye operation to halt surgery on a

---

This essay originally appeared in the *Christian Science Monitor,* 6 January 1984. Since then Shen has continued to publish fiction, including a new novella, *Scattered People.*

"bourgeois" official. "All that could be seen of her were her eyes and her bare arms above the rubber gloves.... Lu said tersely from behind her mask, 'Get out, please!' The rebels looked at each other and left."

Such steely resolve is Lu's strength as well as her ultimate defeat because she refuses to acknowledge mounting physical and emotional pressures. The hospital gives her more responsibility; family demands increase; her friend Jiang is "deserting" her for a new life in Canada. Middle age becomes unbearable.

The carefully compassionate novella leaves readers with a provocative, open end. "It had rained for a couple of days. A gust of wind sighed through the bare branches of the trees. The sunshine, extraordinarily bright after the rain, slanted in through the windows of the corridor. The cold wind blew in too. Slowly Fu, supporting his wife, headed for the sunlight and the wind." Lu recovers, but will her job improve? Will the family tension subside? The inconclusive conclusion, a popular technique in China, effectively focuses the audience on such questions in their own lives.

Lu's tale is emblematic of the experience of many middle-aged professionals in China—people who have endured the political and economic vicissitudes of the Long March, World War II, the Great Leap Forward, and the Cultural Revolution. As a generation, they have survived ideological assaults on the value of professional work and considerable personal setbacks in their careers. Despite years of labor, they still face shortages of housing and food. While maintaining a faith in China, their generation is often overlooked, situated as they are between their more visible elders who control the country and their noisier young compatriots who clamor about high unemployment among youth.

> Middle age, middle age. Everyone agrees that middle-aged cadres are the backbone of our country. The operations in a hospital depend on middle-aged surgeons; the most important research projects are thrust on middle-aged scientists and technicians; the hardest jobs in industry are given to middle-aged workers.... At work they shoulder a heavy load, at home they have all the housework. They have to support their parents and bring up their children. They play a key role not just because of their experience and ability, but because they put up with hardships and make great sacrifices.

At Middle Age had a particularly powerful impact on me because I met Shen Rong this summer while traveling in a twelve-woman delegation of American authors. At formal conferences with Chinese women writers in Beijing, Nanjing, Shanghai, and Guangzhou, we shared readings from our work and theoretical papers. By far the most rewarding exchanges occurred when writers invited us to their homes. Shen is especially memorable because we saw evidence of her new success everywhere and because she so clearly embodies her own themes of personal integrity and perseverance.

Shen attended three meetings in Beijing, where she appeared as an intense, chain-smoking, official host. We learned the basic details: At forty-eight she is a prominent novelist and screenwriter and is planning her second trip to North America. We really began to know her the evening she came to the opera. Her formality and nervousness vanished as we all became absorbed in the magnificent colors and acrobatics of "Mi Guiying Takes Command."

Afterward, she invited us to tea. Our bus driver was reluctant to extend his evening duty. However, when he discovered he would be meeting the author of *At Middle Age,* he was happy to escort us. In the small, book-lined room of her flat, Shen, still smoking furiously, emerged as a quick, candid woman with a history of persistence. When the conversation turned to education, the bus driver was delighted to learn that he had taken more middle school than Shen herself.

Shen left junior middle school to clerk in a bookstore. In 1952, she was transferred to the *Southwest Workers Daily* in Chongqing. Two years later her unit sent her to study Russian in college. Then health problems forced her away from her family in Beijing. As she was recuperating in a peasant home in Shanxi, she realized her deepest vocation was writing. By the mid-60s she was back in Beijing writing plays and in the 1970s she turned to fiction.

This evening she introduced us to two of her sons, a literary scholar and a factory worker, both of whom, she noted with relief, would be leaving home soon. Although her fifteen-year-old daughter will still be there, Shen looks forward to more time and space to write. Her husband works for the *People's Daily.*

As she served us tea and hard candies, my attention was distracted by the huge shortwave radio in the center of the tiny study. The radio haunts me like a wry metaphor, an appropriately awkward and earnest prop on this intercultural stage. Shen answered our questions with animation. Clearly she was relishing contact with American writers and was gratified by the acknowledgement her work was finally getting in China.

When we left, I wondered how many Western egos could have survived the wide fluctuations in official policy toward individual writers and toward the very meaning of literature. Shen has survived, indeed flourished, because of her seasoned optimism. Her success lies in the graceful yet determined ways her novella conveys the middle-aged complexities of China, Dr. Lu, and herself.

Marge Piercy and the Candor of Our Fictions

Fly Away Home, Marge Piercy's eighth novel, is a taut, rich, vibrant story. After thirty years of writing, Piercy is finally emerging as an important voice in American fiction. For years her reputation (and, to a certain extent, the work itself) was muzzled in the room where literary labels are made. Her acknowledgment came as a "feminist writer" or a "political writer" and, perhaps as a consequence of these tags, as a "young writer." One might wonder why Piercy's work is so often relegated to the shelf of "ideological fiction," whereas parochial fatalism is found under "literary fiction."

By the same token, one notices that Piercy is still thought of as young, while her near-contemporary, John Updike, seems to have attained respectable middle age.

In the hollows of American literary politics where a few New York institutions control the criticism, the prizes, and the money and pretend to define literature, original vitality like Marge Piercy's rarely breaks through the dull roar of strangled WASP yawns. Piercy has neither the personal pedigree nor the correct education. She is a raw, tough, wilful, magnificent novelist and poet.

Her most powerful contribution is her passion for work—for social activism, for the detail of labor, for delineating the American class system. Such enthusiasm is capsulized in the title poem of her book, "To Be of Use."

> I want to be with people who submerge
> in the task, who go into the fields to harvest
> and work in a row and pass the bags along,
> who stand in the line and haul in their places,
> who are not parlor generals and field deserters
> but move in a common rhythm
> when the food must come in or the fire be put out.

Piercy's relish for "moving things forward with massive patience" is manifested in her own productivity. In addition to the eight novels, she has published nine books of poetry, a play, and a collection of short prose.

This essay originally appeared as a page 3 essay in the *Christian Science Monitor,* 4 May 1984.

Piercy is at her best writing about class, particularly the seams in the lives of people caught between working-class pasts and middle-class presents. Herself a child of rough Detroit streets, Piercy now lives comfortably on Cape Cod. In *Fly Away Home,* the protagonist, Daria Porfirio Walker, grows up in a poor Italian family in East Boston. With her ambitious husband and two daughters, she treks from Back Bay to Brookline to Arlington to Cambridge apartments and then to their first house in Newton. Despite Daria's status as an acclaimed cookbook writer and the wife of an affluent developer, she never forgets she is a Porfirio. Ultimately she realizes she will always be treading in a cultural limbo, alienated in the bourgeoisie, yet unable to return home.

Fly Away Home is a novel of ideas about innocence and responsibility, about an individual's place in society and in the changing shape of family. The book opens on Daria's forty-third birthday as she surveys the blessings of her upward mobility and her stable home. Soon, however, she is confronted by corruption, arson, and death. From here on, readers are breathlessly caught up in Daria's devastating suspicion that she is dangerously implicated. Partly because Daria seems such an "ordinary person," with an average amount of hope and greed and kindness, you leave the book wondering about your own unconscious iniquities. In contrast to previous novels like *Vida* and *Braided Lives,* in which Piercy focuses on economically or politically marginal characters, here she presents the inhabitants of the American Model Home. This apparent normality makes Daria's dramatic discoveries about her private and public life all the more stunning.

Soon after her birthday, her mother dies, leaving a rift from which she anxiously reexamines her world. The closer she looks, the more uneasy she becomes. Is her husband, Ross, having an affair? Why is her older daughter, Robin, so cold? Daria is annoyed that her family doesn't take her writing seriously. She is hurt by their cracks about her plumpness. Her body, which is almost the same size as the one in which she was married, seems quite comfortable to her, but the family is an increasingly uncomfortable, even hostile, territory.

Fly Away Home is unusually lush for a city novel. Daria revels in the colors and textures and odors of her back garden. She lavishes sumptuous meals on her family: "she had planned a traditional English dinner of roast beef, Yorkshire pudding, of course the plum pudding for dessert. Too much consistency in English food would make anyone dull, so she steamed the brussels sprouts lightly to crunch between the teeth and served them with her own ginger sauce; the potatoes were lyonnaise and the dressing for the salad a light chive vinaigrette." Daria's cats are a continual source of sensual pleasure. As in past Piercy novels, sex is described in tender detail as a form of enjoyment as well as spiritual communication. Piercy is most seductive when describing sweet domesticity: "Her eyes fixed on the darting tongues of the fire — orange with flashes of green — she half drowsed like a cat before the hearth. This was the first Christmas without Nina to talk to. . . . Daria yawned, her eyes closing. If she could pass through that scrim of memory that seemed so flimsy back into another year, how could she resist?"

One day Daria wakes up and everything is missing — her family, her income, her belief system, her role in the world. Ross moves across the hall and then out of the house. She hunts through his papers, spies on him, and learns that he is involved with Gail Abbot-Wisby, a thinner, younger, richer woman. While she is watching Ross, a group of activists is watching her — tenants from East Boston who are protesting treacherous conditions in the Walkers' buildings.

Daria's dawning awareness of her own complicity in the destruction of her old neighborhood is the emotional and moral hinge of the novel. A hard-working American, she believes she has earned her way out of the slums years ago. An obedient wife, she has let her husband make all the investments, even those in her name. Confronting her, one of the protesters says that "You've made a big decision to be innocent. Totally innocent. What kind of luxury is that? No adult is as innocent as you make yourself out to be." So, in addition to investigating Ross's romance, she investigates conditions in the family's buildings. She finds that a series of fires has wrought a healthy income from insurance policies, and gradually she understands that Ross has been involved in setting those fires. "Innocent, that hulking sadist had called her, innocent as if that were an insult. Maybe at her age it was an insult. Was innocent the opposite of guilty or the opposite of wise?"

On the whole, the narrative weave is tight and complex. The few thin spots might have been caught with another draft or with closer editing. Some dialogue is stiff, particularly exchanges about the divorce, which could have been lifted from a pop psychology text: "She needed time to do her research and the role-playing put emotional distance between them."

Like her fiction, Piercy's poetry risks offending the tweed critics as well as some of her untraditional friends. The poems range from such agitprop as "For Shoshana-Pat Swinton" to the ritual of "The Lunar Cycle." She has won somewhat more recognition for her poetry than for her fiction, perhaps because poetry critics are not so keen on detached narrators in regulation dress. But the mutual influence of the genres is evident in the narrative cohesion of her poems and in the deft lyricism of much of her prose. Piercy playfully repeats images in the fabric of her stories. In *Fly Away Home* the fire weaves from the title to the arson to the cozy hearth to the desserts *flambé* to Daria's single name, Porfirio (derived from porphyry). Much of the poetry reflects the socially conscious themes of the fiction. As Piercy explains in her book of short prose, *Parti-Colored Blocks for a Quilt,* "The notion that literature has nothing to do in the world but be consumed in a vacuum is recent heresy. Go on, sit down with Aristophanes, with Euripides, with Catullus, with Horace, with Alexander Pope and Dryden, with Dickens and George Eliot, and Georges Sand and Tolstoi and explain to them that art has nothing to do with our morals, our politics, and our behavior."

What distinguishes Piercy from many other contemporary writers is not so much the heat of her convictions as her candor about how they surface in her work. American critics are doggedly provincial in their church-and-state separation of art and politics. In this year when we are rereading Orwell, we might return to his essay "Why I Write." "The opinion that art should have nothing to do with politics is, itself, a political attitude." Yet we tend to label people writing leftist or feminist material as "young artists," implying their work will mature when their politics disappears or grows more conservative. This is, of course, ignoring people like Pablo Neruda, Grace Paley, Ding Ling, and Tillie Olsen, who have continued as radical writers in their sixties, seventies, and eighties. But if in fact marinated cynicism is the climax of postmodern literature, themes of hopeful engagement will be easily dismissed.

Fly Away Home is Piercy's most accessible novel and, therefore, her most politically powerful one. Through characters from this Model Home, she shows how everyone — even archetype Americans — make daily choices of social consequence. It is the most organized and sustained of any of her novels. Here she has succeeded in reaching beyond her own milieu, to write with curiosity and respect about a woman very different from herself. She draws a variety of readers into deep and delicate questions about their own lives.

Piercy will continue to irritate and surprise and "move forward with massive patience." As she says in the introduction to *Circles on the Water: Selected Poems,* "I have readers who love my poems about the Cape, about zucchini, and lettuce and tomatoes, and simply skip or tune out the poems about an old working-class woman lying in a nursing home, or about nuclear power. Then I have readers who love the poems they call feminist or political, but ask me why I write about blue heron and oak trees. . . . I have to confess for me it is all one vision."

The Brilliant Career of Thea Astley

Sydney, Australia. The compact, graying woman with the bright blue eyes is one of the first passengers off the tardy morning train in Sydney's grim Central Station. Although we have never met, Thea Astley dashes straight toward me, apologizing a-mile-a-minute for her delayed train. "I knew you would be all right, though; Americans are smart. You would have checked the arrival board."

We take to each other and, almost immediately, she invites me to return home to her land on the Southeast coast. "Oh, I should have invited you straightaway, but I thought you would be like those American journos on TV—like Barbara Walters." Ten minutes later, we are sitting down to lunch in my flat, and the intense, sixty-three-year-old writer refuses to let me get a question in edgewise as she pumps me with queries about my own novels. Finally, when she pauses to light her first cigarette, I manage to turn things around. This interview with one of Australia's most heralded novelists is going to be more fun—and more difficult—than I reckoned.

First she tells me how much she enjoyed her stint as writer-in-residence at Memphis State University last spring. She will make her second bicentenary trip to the United States in November when she gives a reading with Thomas Keneally at the 92nd Street Y in New York. Five of her ten novels have been published in the United States: *It's Raining in Mango, The Acolyte, A Kindness Cup, The Slow Natives,* and *Beachmasters.*

Here she has won many literary honors, including the prestigious Miles Franklin Award (named after the author of *My Brilliant Career*). While she suffers somewhat in the marketplace because she is regarded as a serious literary author or "writers' writer," all Australian authors are profiting from the growing wave of cultural nationalism. During the last fourteen years, Australian books have progressed from 15 percent of national sales to 50 percent. She is delighted to tell me that her sixth novel, *A Kindness Cup,* about the massacre of Aboriginals by white settlers in central coastal Queensland, has been set on a state matriculation list.

"The Brilliant Career of Thea Astley" originally appeared in the *Los Angeles Times Book Review,* 7 August 1988. The review of *It's Raining in Mango* was first published in the *Los Angeles Times Book Review,* 22 November 1987. The review of *Reaching Tin River* originally appeared in the *Washington Post Book World,* 29 April 1990, © 1988, The Washington Post. Reprinted with permission.

Astley recently retired after thirteen years as Fellow in Australian Literature at Sydney's Macquarie University. Before that, she taught for twenty years in infant, primary, and high schools. Currently she is writing full-time at her six-acre bush retreat in West Cambewara. She and her husband, Jack, have been married forty years, she tells me with satisfaction. "I picked him up after a chamber music concert in Brisbane."

Astley's work reflects a marvelous balance between acerbic and charitable, irreverent and zealous, politically astute and mournfully romantic. She loves jazz and classical music. "I'd die to be able to play piano like Oscar Peterson or to sing good Lieder."

Her conversation is sardonically rough, and I imagine her as one of those sophisticated girls who used to sneak into the school bathroom to smoke. "No," she tells me. "I didn't start smoking until I was forty. I had to do something; I don't drink or use drugs." The contradictions between Astley's self-presentation as the raspy-voiced social critic and the lady artist reflect the profound contrast between the opulently crude Queensland of her first twenty-three years and the more proper ambiance of New South Wales, where she has spent most of her life.

Such tensions are eloquently expressed in *It's Raining in Mango,* my favorite of her books. The tightly written, anti-saga follows four generations of the Laffey family in the brutal, seductive world of Northeastern Australia. "Cornelius Laffey is based on my Irish grandfather," she tells me. "And Mango, where 'Hunting the Wild Pineapple' is also set, is actually Kuranda, a place inland from Cairns where Jack and I had a holiday house."

Australians refer to Queensland as "the deep north," comparing the region's literature to Southern U.S. writing, but Astley's work is more reminiscent of Somerset Maugham or Graham Greene. Beginning with her first novel, *Girl with a Monkey,* published in 1958, Astley has been preoccupied by steamy dramas in the Australian tropics and neighboring Pacific islands. She writes with the passionate anger and the longing of a long-term exile.

Another Astley theme joining her work to Greene's is her insider-outsider relationship with Roman Catholicism. Reared in strict Catholic schools, she is a vehement critic of the church's capitalism and an unabashed fan of the Latin Mass. Her brother is a Jesuit, but she, herself, has lapsed.

"I still pray, of course. Don't *you* pray?" she follows me into the kitchen as I make tea. "The church has provided a richness of metaphor for my writing. And the concept of sin is useful. You learn to examine your conscience when you are a baby, at seven. That allows you to see the ticks beneath the surface in other people.

"My ears are like radar dishes. I overhear something, and I feel I have to write it down." She admires the short story form but finds the novel more compatible personally. "In a story, the craftsmanship is fully exposed. A novel is like charity; it covers a multitude of faults." Her current project is another semihistorical novel, "about a woman connecting with something one hundred years in the past." She explains: "It came from hearing a radio announcer say he was about to play 'a no-frills version of the Rustle of Spring.'"

For Astley this is a particularly exciting time to be an Australian author. "The Australian writing scene is very vigorous now. A lot of that is due to the support of the Literature Board. It's been a terrific boost that we can get published in the United States. Writers like Patrick White bring a great energy to the culture." She says she also admires the novels of David Malouf, Rodney Hall, and Elizabeth Jolley. "But I don't review books. That's tricky in a country as small as this."

When Astley returns to New York this fall, it will be her fourth visit to the United States. Previously she has read at the Guggenheim Museum and the Chicago Public Library. Her early artistic influences included Hemingway, Steinbeck, and Nabokov. "I like books with stories in them. Do you like Calvino? I don't like Calvino or *Flaubert's Parrot*. I thought that was a wank." Her favorite American contemporaries include Raymond Carver, Tom Robbins, and Tess Gallagher.

Reflecting on distinctions between Australians and Americans, she says, "Americans are more polite. They use different slang. They have a different sense of humor. Ours is more understated and dry." She is clearly appalled by Americans' poor knowledge of her country's geography. "I knew where New Orleans was when I was thirteen!"

When the taxi arrives to take us back to the station, she climbs in next to the driver, in typical Aussie egalitarian fashion. They swap heat stories about Queensland and Bombay. At Central Station, she dawdles by the gate, pressing me again about my own writing and my impressions of Australia. "Are you sure you wouldn't like to get on the train and come down to the bush with me now? Jack would love to meet you. You could spend the night." I am at the point of giving in.

It's Raining in Mango

Hot. Sticky. Intense. *It's Raining in Mango* is about four generations of the Laffey family in the seductive, brutal world of Northeastern Australia. The intricate novel reads like a dream reunion where relatives swap stories with ancestors and descendants about disease, flood, racism, violence. They talk about how things never change.

Like the characters in Sartre's *Huis Clos,* the Laffeys discover there is no way out. Australia is the end of the earth. Yet they maintain an almost inexplicable will to continue on the edge of despair.

Thea Astley's powerful tenth novel follows a white Catholic family from the 1860s to the 1980s through immigration, settlement, desertion, suicide, and rebirth. Shards of family legend intersect at provocatively odd moments. It resembles an album in which photos that seem carelessly placed actually establish a revealing psychological order.

In the 1860s, Jessica Olive and Cornelius immigrate to Cooktown and their family becomes "Bedouins of the sticky leaf." Cornelius practices a roving form of journalism, enthusiastic about frontier possibility and outraged about the violent racism of other white settlers. Hardship tears the family to shreds. Fourteen-year-old Nadine has a baby, then runs away to join a brothel. Eventually Cornelius abandons Jessica Olive and their son George and Nadine's son Harry. Jessica Olive battles on, running the Port of Call Hotel and raising the two boys. Years later George buys property in the rain forest near Mango and has two children, Connie and Will. Both Connie and Will are transformed by World War II—Connie because of her brief marriage to an American serviceman, which produces a son, and Will because of a gay affair that haunts him until his suicide in 1983. The book opens with Connie's son Reever trying to preserve Mango from development bulldozers, although if there's one thing he should have learned from Laffey history it's that you can't preserve anything in Mango.

Astley's Australia is an arduous land that shapes a wilful people—circumscribing their daily lives and seeping into their bones. No satisfaction goes unabated. Even in her title, she dampens the lush pleasures of Mango. "Cut-off, Jessica Olive thought, peering critically about, sniffing at woodsmoke. But when were we anything but that, she mused, in this dangerously new country?"

The Laffeys hold on to each other for self-definition in the natural and social wilderness. Their relationships are engaging, addictive, repulsive, and tenacious—from the reckless hardiness of Cornelius's fatherhood to the incestuous attraction between Connie and Will. The story is told in bloodlines. Anti-epic in form, *It's Raining in Mango* is a tight 208 pages, compressing individual stories, as if squeezing out all the air or hope, as if all that mattered were where the line was leading. "'I am Jessica Olive,' he heard her say absent-mindedly over breakfast. 'I am Cornelius and Nadine and George.'

"'So am I,' Reever says as he flings muscle about the house. 'So am I.'"

Even outside the family, Astley's portraits are drawn with compassionate intensity. She introduces aborigines, adventurers, hippies, and prostitutes. Behind everyone lurks the shadow of the drifter: from Cornelius to the wild bushman who impregnates Nadine to the starving traveler who visits little Connie and Will, to Reever, projected five years into the future.

For Astley the Australian promise always falls short. If it is not Sartre's Hell, it is Purgatory. She juxtaposes Catholic images of temptation, sacrifice, and redemption. *It's Raining in Mango* reveals the hypocrisy of the Church (through the blustering Father Madigan) and the urgency of Faith (through Reever hanging from a tree to halt the bulldozers). This complex, intimate narrative might be compared to a secret rope, made of seemingly random bits and strongly knotted, woven by a prisoner to pass the time. The rope becomes, alternately, a rosary, a noose, and a lifeline.

Reaching Tin River

In Thea Astley's *Reaching Tin River* a young, white Australian searches for home, for a center, for security. She travels easily, but lands with difficulty. She is pulled by nostalgia for another era, by immigrant parents, by eerie, determinist dreams.

Reaching Tin River is the raw, frantic, first-person narrative of a Queensland woman named Belle, who treads a fine line between going crazy and going on. Belle's rambling notes, presented without chapter or section breaks, waver unsteadily between past and present.

Belle is tugged between the physical rigors of the New World and the psychic pressures of colonialism, in a classic Australian search for identity. She is plagued by recollections of practicing "Rustle of Spring" on a piano in a land untouched by European spring. A teacher and librarian in her late twenties, she is rootless, aimless, and practically invisible. "My own fairness is outrageous. *Almost albino,* Marie says unkindly when I annoy her. *Like a negative, aren't you, darling?*"

If Belle is a negative, her mother Bonnie is a 3-D technicolor movie—the war bride who becomes a jazz musician, moves to the United States long enough to get pregnant and be deserted by her husband, returns to the family farm in Australia, resumes her shaky music career, then retires to the countryside as an aging hippie. Belle moves between admiration for her mother's social independence and anger at her maternal indifference.

So Belle looks for her center in men. "There is a rider to Euclid's ninth proposition in Book III which states that the locus of the middle points of two parallel chords of a circle passes through the circle's center . . . I need a center in which I can merge. An alter-ego center. Isn't that what we all look for?" She fails to find her center in her self-involved husband. She fails, too, when on a brief trip to the United States she manages to meet her long lost father. She tries with various other men, including a former teacher who threatens her with a gun.

Finally she settles on a center from the past. In her work as an archivist, she stumbles upon references to a farmer-businessman, Gaden Lockyer, dead for over half a century. Belle later grows obsessed with Lockyer, leaving her job to assemble pieces of his story in a quest that takes her back to Drenchings, where Lockyer farmed and where Belle grew up.

One of the most inspired strokes in this gripping, imaginative novel is Belle finding herself mentioned in Lockyer's diaries. He describes a stranger walking across his farm. "I thought at first it was a man, she was outlandishly dressed. Trousers and shirt like a farm boy. But as I rode closer I could see her hair pulled back in a long fair tail, so fair it was almost white and her face delicate and singularly moulded." Later, his wife says she saw no such person. Lockyer's journals continue to reveal glimpses of the strange, pale woman. Even after he has retired to the resort of Tin River, she continues to haunt him: "She's back, that young woman, the girl I wrote about all those years ago."

Thea Astley's brass and marshmallow voice offers the perfect range for Belle's furious, courageous search and Astley offers no neat resolution. Does Gaden Lockyer exist because Belle discovers him in the archives? Does she exist because he imagines her? Does Belle need a center or a context?

The Political Development of a White
South African

This versatile collection of essays reflects the compassion and intelligence that make Nadine Gordimer one of the foremost writers of our time. *The Essential Gesture,* a fine companion to her seventeen books of fiction, is infused with historical conscience while attending closely to the emotional moment and physical detail of contemporary South Africa. She takes as her theme Roland Barthes's premise that for an author, one's work is the "essential gesture as a social being."

Gordimer writes as a "minority-within-the-white-minority," her anger, insight, and courage mounting as these twenty-three essays progress from 1959 to 1985. The introductory memoir about her early writing shows how her politics developed out of a moral imagination: "I was looking for what people meant but didn't say, not only about sex, but also about politics and their relationship with the black people among whom we lived as people in a forest among trees. . . . And the 'problems' of my country did not set me writing: on the contrary, it was learning to write that sent me falling, falling through the surface of 'the South African way of life.'"

The momentum throughout the book is Gordimer's political development as an artist. The section called "A Writer in South Africa" begins with an essay, "Where Do Whites Fit In?," which comes across today as somewhat naive and patronizing, but which accurately distills the liberal, multiracial optimism of 1959. Dated twenty years later, the last essay in the section shows Gordimer to have acquired considerable sophistication about Black separatism but still holding out hope for "the artist as prophet of the resolution of divided cultures."

Among the most striking pieces are profiles of Chief Albert J. Luthuli, the first South African to win the Nobel Prize for Peace (1960), and Bram Fischer, the Afrikaner Communist activist imprisoned for his support of Black liberation. Both essays proceed with precise elegance through a twentieth-century history of South Africa, and both are graced by the novelist's eye for subtleties of character and revealing incident.

Gordimer follows Luthuli from his ancestral home on the coast of Natal to

---

This essay was first published in the *Philadelphia Inquirer,* 27 November 1988.

his election as Zulu chief in 1936; his radicalization in government battles; his election as president of the African National Congress in 1952; and his banning and imprisonment. The concluding scene crystallizes the ironies of South African life in 1958:

> When he walked out of the Drill Hall, the sudden release of his freedom was fresh upon him, lightheaded, like a weakness, though the weight of the ordeal of trial to which his colleagues were committed oppressed him, and he even looked a little lonely. And such are the paradoxes of human behaviour that, as Luthuli crossed the street, two of the white police officers who had become familiar figures on duty in the Drill Hall all through the preparatory examination came around the corner and called out, forgetful, across the barrier of apartheid that seeks to legislate against all human contact between black and white and across the barrier of hate that the pass and baton have built between police and the black man in South Africa. "Well, hullo! You look fine! What are you doing around here? Can't you keep away from the old Drill Hall, after all?" And rather gingerly, Chief was amiable in reply.

Travels through Africa

Gordimer expands her consciousness as "A Writer in Africa" in the next section, traveling to Egypt, Zaire, Madagascar, Botswana, Ghana, and the Ivory Coast in search of commonalities and differences in the Pan-African experience. She puts her narrative skills to good use as she observes village life from a boat on the Congo River and as she muses on the philosophical debates taking place via slogan-bearing stickers on taxi dashboards in Accra. For North Americans and Europeans who sometimes narrowly construct South Africa as a satellite of their own guilt, as simply a branch plant of IBM or Barclay's Bank, this section is a useful reminder that South Africa is set—geographically and politically—on the African continent.

The final section of essays, "Living in the Interregnum," discourses on the excesses of government racism, the madness of white denial, and the powers of censorship. Gordimer recounts the official banning of her novel *Burger's Daughter* in 1979 and the subsequent international outcry that forced South African authorities to release the book. She characterizes the canceling of this ban as a diversionary government tactic:

> The release from ban of a few books by well-known white writers is not a major victory for the freedom to write, and . . . the action carries two sinister implications: first, those among us who are uncompromising opponents of

censorship with wide access to the media can be bought off by special treatment accorded to our books; second, the measure of hard-won solidarity that exists between black and white writers can be divided by "favouring" white writers with such special treatment, since no ban on any black writer's work has been challenged by the Directorate's own application to the Appeal Board.

The Voice Stands Out

While the fundamental spirit of this book is brave, humane, and sometimes revolutionary, one wishes that Gordimer had written with more acuity about the interconnections of oppression across class, race, sex, and cultural lines. Her exhortatory tone is tinged with a perplexingly elitist individualism, excessively conscious of the singularity of her own voice. The dismissal of women (even in the most recent essays) ranges from her reflexive use of the pronoun "he" to her reference to the black *man* and her choice of such words as *prophetess*. Although she frequently quotes and mentions male authors, she exhibits comparative unconsciousness of South African or foreign women writers.

Meanwhile, her comments about American literature (particularly about the ostensible lack of censorship here) reveal an ignorance about protest writing in this country as well as about numerous erosions in the First Amendment. One does not detract from the primacy of the liberation of Black South Africans (half of whom are women) to acknowledge threats elsewhere.

Minority of the Minority

While one hopes for even more extensive coverage of South Africa here, it is useful to acknowledge that some Americans let the urgency of apartheid distract or absolve them from also confronting racism at home. Similarly, it is wise to remember that Gordimer is a minority-within-the-white-minority, and while praising her considerable accomplishments, one might ask why American editors and readers pay so much more attention to her writing than that of any Black or Asian South African.

The Essential Gesture is enlightening reading for longtime admirers of Gordimer's fiction and an inspirational introduction for those about to embark on her short stories and novels. Gordimer's convictions about the inextricability of art and politics are heartening in an age of postmodern nihilism. *The Essential Gesture* is a passionate chronicle of a writer who has not always taken the right steps but who has had the wit, integrity, and honesty to get back on her feet and keep moving. As Gordimer says in her first essay, "The truth isn't always beauty, but the hunger for it is."

III. Reviews

I write reviews because I like to read books and I find that I read more carefully if I have a review assignment. As a critic, I feel obligated to reread and my evaluation often shifts on a second or third encounter with the book. I am assigned a variety of books but because I am a novelist I usually review fiction.

I like to review because I am a "social hermit," someone who feels best when she has been alone all day—with good books. But I am compelled to respond. I prefer reviewing to simply reading for the same reasons I prefer writing letters to keeping a journal. It seems more *useful* somehow.

This section of *Rumors from the Cauldron* includes reviews from a variety of media. As I said in "The Feminist Reviewer," the context of a review determines much of what I want/am allowed to say. A number of these reviews are of story collections because the short story form, a particular interest of mine, does not receive enough attention in the media. There are, of course, a few I want to rewrite. As Ursula LeGuin says in *Dancing at the Edge of the World,* "I have decided that the trouble with print is, it never changes its mind" (p. vii).

This is a simple introduction. Responding to literature with rigor and sensitivity does not have to be a convoluted exercise. There's a difference between complexity and obfuscation. It's important for people who work at universities and colleges to participate in popular consciousness about new works of art. Reading nonacademic reviews can introduce us to noncanonical texts. Writing nonacademic reviews gives us practice in plain speaking, a skill rarely fostered in the academy. Put simply, here are some of my ideas about book reviews.

I write reviews because they help me to read.

I write reviews because I want to share my pleasure in particular books or authors.

I write reviews to help good but marginalized authors become more visible.

I write reviews to argue aesthetic and political opinions.

I write reviews while I wait for the revolutionary forces to gather.

I write reviews because I want to keep my name in print since three to five years may pass between publication of my novels.

I write reviews to supplement my income (slightly).

I write reviews of women's books and of international fiction because this work is most provocative to my own.

I write reviews of women's books and international fiction because I want Americans to read more widely.

I don't write reviews to change an author's mind.

I don't write reviews to transform the world.

I don't write reviews with an illusion of seriously counterbalancing the unfair advantage of some authors who win enormous promotion budgets. Like any other critic in a capitalist society, my power against the blockbuster complex is minute.

I don't write reviews for tenure—"book review" is noted as seventeenth in my department's priority list of publications for tenure consideration, below "a brief scholarly note" and "an article in a local newspaper."

I don't write reviews to earn fame or fortune.

I don't write reviews of books I hate unless I am coerced because (1) there isn't enough editorial space for good fiction and (2) I don't want to read a horrible book the number of times necessary to do a fair review. This reminds me of correcting bad student papers—my idea of hell.

I don't write reviews to get back at people who have reviewed me negatively or to reward those who have reviewed me positively.

I don't read reviews of my work anymore because I think they will shift my focus from developing my art to building my career. Career building is a worthwhile task; however, the task is separate from that of refining one's skills as a fiction writer.

I don't read reviews of my work because I am weak willed and I would get caught in trading favors and/or barbs with other writers.

I don't read reviews of my work because as a reviewer myself, I know reviews are political—determined by how much advertising space one's publisher has/hasn't purchased in a journal, by the ideological preferences and personal friendship networks of review editors and critics.

I don't read reviews of my work because I believe in Virginia Woolf's model of the reviewer in the shop window. I consult critics personally *during the process* of writing a manuscript. My last novel had over twenty readings by colleagues before it was completed. I trust these responses to be more thorough and more provocative than the responses published within the necessarily circumscribed context of review sections. Let me repeat a suggestion by Woolf, quoted earlier in "The Feminist Reviewer":

Let the reviewers then abolish themselves, and resurrect themselves as doctors. The writer would then submit his work to the judge of his choice; an appointment would be made; an interview arranged. In strict privacy, and with some formality—the fee, however, would be enough to ensure that the interview did not degenerate into tea-table gossip—doctor and writer would meet; and for an hour they would consult the book in question. (*Reviewing*, p. 20)

The Joy Luck Club by Amy Tan and Seventeen Syllables and Other Stories by Hisaye Yamamoto

Amy Tan's *Joy Luck Club* and Hisaye Yamamoto's *Seventeen Syllables and Other Stories* are the work of first-generation (American-born) daughters of immigrant mothers. Tan, who was born in 1952 in Oakland, sets her impressive first novel in northern California. Yamamoto, born in Redondo Beach in 1921, concentrates on the southern California landscape in a collection of fine stories spanning her forty-year literary career.

For the first-generation daughter everything is supposed to be possible in the land of education and affluence and self-expression. She knows her mother wants her to be successful. Yet even as she acquires American privilege, because she speaks a different language or dialect, she is both obeying and betraying her mother. Legacies wash in and out of focus. Sometimes it takes a stranger to point out one's mother's accent, her accent in one's *own* words and attitudes. Time passes. Secrets are revealed: The daughter learns of two more sisters, three more uncles. She becomes conscious of unasked questions. The ache grows deeper. Can she return to a place she has never been? When I finished reading The *Joy Luck Club* and *Seventeen Syllables,* I found myself weeping about the chasm between my own immigrant mother and her lost ancestors and descendants.

The *Joy Luck Club* is a segmented novel eloquently blending the voices of four Chinese immigrants and their daughters. The mothers become friends, meeting regularly in what they call "the Joy Luck Club" to play mah-jongg, buy stocks, and gossip. The novel is narrated horizontally as well as vertically; friendships and rivalries develop among the daughters as well as among the mothers:

> Auntie Lin and my mother were both best friends and arch-enemies who spent a lifetime comparing their children. I was one month older than Waverly Jong, Auntie Lin's prized daughter. From the time we were babies, our mothers compared the creases in our belly-buttons, how shapely our earlobes were,

This review originally appeared under the title "The Daughters' Journeys" in the *Nation,* 24 April 1989.

how fast we healed when we scraped our knees, how thick and dark our hair was, how many shoes we wore out in one year, and later, how smart Waverly was at playing chess, how many trophies she had won last month, how many newspapers had printed her name, how many cities she had visited.

Tan's book is organized into four chapters—the first relating the separate lives of the mothers; the next two focusing on the daughters' stories; the last returning to the mothers. Tan is a deft, vivacious conductor, evoking spirited individuality as well as harmony.

The mothers bequeath dramas of loss, courage, and survival. An-mei Hsu watches her own mother, a concubine, commit suicide. Lindo Jong runs away from a suffocating marriage and emigrates to the United States under the pretext of being a theology student. Suyuan Woo escapes the Japanese invasion of Kwelin with two babies on her back. Ying-ying St. Clair is abandoned by a rich husband, goes to live with poor relatives for ten years, then meets a white American visiting China and settles with him in California.

The daughters' journeys—less epically proportioned—also reveal strength and grace. Each of these children of the 1950s has achieved some American success and each has remained close to her difficult mother. We meet Jing-mei Woo at the beginning of the novel, several months after her mother, Suyuan, has died. The three other members of the Joy Luck Club have decided to send Jing-mei to China to find her lost half-sisters. Rose Hsu Jordan reflects about the day her brother was drowned; she is coping with a divorce and consulting (foolishly, her mother thinks) a psychiatrist. Waverly Jong, under ambitious maternal management, becomes a chess champion and tax attorney. Lena St. Clair, an architect, is weathering a troubled marriage, living (against her mother's objections) in a refurbished barn.

Throughout The *Joy Luck Club,* Tan tests the distance between expectation and reality. Jing-mei Woo explains, "America was where all my mother's hopes lay. She had come here in 1949 after losing everything in China: her mother and father, her family home, her first husband, and two daughters, twin baby girls. But she never looked back with regret. There were so many ways for things to get better." But she goes on:

> In the years that followed, I failed her so many times, each time asserting my own will, my right to fall short of expectations. I didn't get straight A's. I didn't become class president. I didn't get into Stanford. I dropped out of college. . . . For unlike my mother, I did not believe I could be anything I wanted to be. I could only be me.

Each of these first-generation daughters is a guardian angel, helping her mother negotiate the baffling San Francisco culture. And the mothers remain loyal to their often-disappointing daughters. The women in each family are held together by pride, embarrassment, and longing. They are, indeed, the loves of one another's lives.

Tan has a remarkable ear for dialogue and dialect, representing the choppy English of the mothers and the sloppy California vernacular of the daughters with sensitive authenticity. These stories are intricately seamed with the provocative questions about language that emerge from bilingual and trilingual homes. In families where verbal exchanges can prove problematic, one sometimes turns to other kinds of oral communication: Tan's cooking scenes are drawn with subtle intensity. "My father hasn't eaten well since my mother died. So I am here, in the kitchen, to cook him dinner. I'm slicing tofu. I've decided to make him a spicy bean-curd dish. My mother used to tell me how hot things restore the spirit and health. But I'm making this mostly because I know my father loves the dish and I know how to cook it. I like the smell of it: ginger, scallions and a red chili sauce that tickles my nose the minute I open the jar."

The segmented structure of The *Joy Luck Club* encourages readers to think simultaneously in different directions. There are some flaws. Several characters, particularly Rose Hsu Jordan and Ying-ying St. Clair, could be more fully developed. Occasionally a device used for narrative effect—such as when Jing-mei Woo asks in the last chapter, at age thirty-six, what her Chinese name means—defies credibility. Generally, however, The *Joy Luck Club* is a stunningly auspicious debut. Tan is a gifted storyteller who reaches across cultures and generations: "Then you must teach my daughter this same lesson. How to lose your innocence but not your hope."

The title piece in Hisaye Yamamoto's *Seventeen Syllables and Other Stories* shows a girl observing her mother's literary ambitions:

> The first Rosie knew that her mother had taken to writing poems was one evening when she finished one and read it aloud for her daughter's approval. It was about cats, and Rosie pretended to understand it thoroughly and appreciate it no end, partly because she hesitated to disillusion her mother about the quantity and quality of Japanese she had learned. . . . See, Rosie, she said, it was a *haiku*, a poem in which she must pack all her meaning into seventeen syllables only, which were divided into three lines of five, seven, and five syllables.

Yamamoto's mothers and daughters, like Tan's, are memories and premonitions of one another. Rosie seems to be an all-American girl, flirting with the boy next door, complying obediently and impatiently with her parents' demands. Rosie's understanding of her family grows more complex than she might wish. Eventually her mother confesses that she left behind a lover and a still-born son in Japan. As an alternative to suicide she became a picture bride. Rosie does not want to know this story any more than she wants to know the content of her mother's poems: "Ume Hanazono, who came to life after the dinner dishes were done, was an earnest, muttering stranger who often neglected speaking when spoken to and stayed busy at the parlor table as late as midnight scribbling with pencil on scratch paper or carefully copying characters on good paper with her fat, pale green Parker."

Seventeen Syllables represents a range of work—memoir, short story, short-short story—written between 1948 and 1987. Many of these pieces were first published in the Japanese-American journal *Rafu Shimpo* as well as in *Partisan Review, Harper's Bazaar,* and the *Kenyon Review*. Yamamoto writes with distilled realism about ordinary people experiencing romance, racism, and family responsibilities. Throughout the book she balances on an optimistic, fey wit.

"Yoneko's Earthquake" is another coming-of-age story set in the southern California countryside. Yoneko and her family live on a farm with a hired Filipino worker, Marpo. Yoneko's father, injured during an earthquake, gets on his daughter's nerves as he recuperates at home. He tells her not to waste sugar by making fudge. He reproves her for painting her nails.

> Mrs. Hosoume immediately came to her defense, saying that in Japan, if she remembered correctly, young girls did the same thing. In fact she remembered having gone to elaborate lengths to tint her fingernails: she used to gather, she said, the petals of the red *tsubobana* or the purple *kogane* (which grows on the underside of stones), grind them well, mix them with some alum powder, then cook the mixture and leave it to stand overnight in an envelope of either persimmon or taro leaves.

The bond between Yoneko and her mother is discreet but strong. Both of them fall in love with Marpo and are deserted by him in different ways. The story ends, as does "Seventeen Syllables," with a revelation about a dead brother and a passionate admonition from mother to daughter.

A distinguishing characteristic of Yamamoto's work is her multicultural casting, and this is especially effective in such stories as "The Brown House," "Wilshire Bus," "The Eskimo Connection," and "Reading and Writing." *Seventeen Syllables* is a book not just about Japanese-Americans but also about Chicanos, Blacks, Filipinos, Eskimos, and whites of various classes. The collection reflects Yamamoto's rich variety of experiences growing up in California and speaking English as a second language, being interned in Arizona during World War II, reporting for the Black weekly *Los Angeles Tribune,* becoming active in Catholic Worker projects in the 1950s, and then raising a family with her husband, Anthony De Soto.

Seventeen Syllables was published by a press that may need a note of introduction. Kitchen Table: Women of Color Press, in Latham, New York, has published work from a range of Third World women since 1981. One of their recent titles is the long-anticipated second collection by Mitsuye Yamada, *Desert Run, Poems and Stories.* According to the informative introduction and detailed bibliography accompanying *Seventeen Syllables,* Hisaye Yamamoto has a considerable body of work awaiting publication in book form. Perhaps we can look forward to a second collection from her too.

In recent years Asian-American women's lives have grown more visible through fiction by Willyce Kim, Maxine Hong Kingston, Ruthanne Lum McCunn, Yoshiko Uchida, and others. This year [1989] Calyx Books in Corvallis, Oregon, has published a remarkable Asian-American women's anthology, *The Forbidden Stitch,* edited by Shirley Geok-lin Lim and Mayumi Tsutakawa, which celebrates the rich variety of emerging work. As Lim observes, "If we form a thread, the thread is a multi-colored, many-layered, complexly knotted stitch."

The Philosopher's Pupil by Iris Murdoch

In *The Philosopher's Pupil,* her twenty-first novel, Iris Murdoch reemerges as one of our most brilliant, prolific, daring, and curiously underrated contemporary novelists.

Murdoch's unabashed intellectualism is always provocative. Though I disagree with certain beliefs and wish her themes were less moral and more political, *The Philosopher's Pupil* is utterly compelling. In contrast to so much current fiction which forgoes plot for fragmented episodic insight, Murdoch's novel is rich with dramatic movement. She catches her characters in philosophical dilemmas, confronting them with the consequences of intention and action.

The Philosopher's Pupil describes an unpredictable summer in the English spa town of Ennistone. The town turns upside down when a local celebrity, the internationally acclaimed philosopher John Robert Rozanov, comes back for a visit. All the characters—as well as the readers—become the philosopher's pupils. Rozanov's power is created by popular projection and is exacerbated by his own obliviousness to other people's feelings. He has a particularly potent impact on the McCaffrey family. One McCaffrey falls in love with him; another tries to kill him. In the end, his appearance provides a catalyst for everyone to reconsider notions of family commitment, perversity, responsibility, and love.

The spa, where townspeople bathe and swim and soak, works as a variable metaphor for characters seeking forgiveness, a new life, and, in some cases, a return to the womb. The baths are the center of Ennistone activity—the scene of political debate, business transactions, courtship, and death.

Murdoch underlines the arbitrariness of social identity by reducing everyone to the commonality of bathing suits. She relishes paradoxical characters: the Jewish priest; the innocent prostitute; the powerful servant. At one point, a male homosexual dresses up as a woman and passionately embraces a lesbian. Murdoch tells readers that life is more complex than you imagine, and if you find this scene confusing, wait until you reach the next page.

The most fascinating character is the philosopher Rozanov, the grandson of a Marxist Russian immigrant. "John Robert Rozanov was tired of his mind. He was tired of his stong personality and his face and the effect he had upon people. He often thought about death. But something still remained which bound him to

---

This review was first published in the *Progressive* (Madison, Wisc.), December 1983.

the world. It was not philosophy." Rozanov is most intriguing in the distorted reflections he represents for people like the McCaffreys. The family is torn apart as members pursue their individual fantasies about him, desperate to know what actually "bound him to the world."

The uneasy answer is Hattie, Rozanov's demure granddaughter, fresh out of secondary school. Rozanov brings Hattie to Ennistone while he tries to sort out her future. It becomes excruciatingly clear that he has fallen in love with his granddaughter. To protect them both from his passions, Rozanov decides to match Hattie with young Tom McCaffrey. Partially because of the philosopher's arrogant single-mindedness, Tom becomes interested in Hattie. Their relationship—coming together, moving apart, and coming together again—provides much of the story's suspense.

If Hattie represents unconscious innocence, Tom's elder brother, George McCaffrey, personifies ineffectual evil. George, who studied under Rozanov, is mesmerized by Rozanov's rejection of him. He hooks himself into a tortuous chain, seeking approbation from, and vengeance upon, the philosopher. Although George wantonly destroys property and attempts two murders, he is doomed by Rozanov's judgment to limbo rather than hell.

Experienced as a philosophy don herself, Murdoch finds fiction more accommodating than scholarship to the intricacy of her ideas. Unlike the characters in much contemporary fiction, Murdoch's people are not predetermined by genetics or neurotic constructions. Rather, they proceed from free will where each move is an ethical choice, rendering their decisions all the more gripping.

Yet, after a few hundred pages, I longed for the intellectual complexity to be balanced by more emotional texture. Attempting to populate the novel with all manner and conviction of people—even those she does not understand—Murdoch opts for sarcastic cameos of such "types" as feminists, Eurocommunists, and Americans.

Murdoch occasionally resembles Rozanov in her omniscient pronouncements. Some judgments and conclusions seem ordained by the author rather than developed within the reader's experience of the story.

Philosophical fiction, by nature, poses a tension between narrative enclosure and ongoing discourse. Novels usually end; philosophical discussions usually continue. Therefore any fictional conclusion is bound to be dissatisfying. Next time, Murdoch might be more satisfied to rest on her articulate paradoxes.

The Lover of Horses by Tess Gallagher, Raven's Wing by Joyce Carol Oates, and And Venus Is Blue by Mary Hood

Across the country, the renaissance of the short story has introduced some fine new writing, such as Tess Gallagher's *The Lover of Horses*. However, the story industry has also produced a number of inbred, redundant collections, such as Mary Hood's *And Venus Is Blue* and Joyce Carol Oates's *Raven's Wing*.

I'm not advocating the resurrrection of Booth Tarkington or soliciting sentimental, uplifting fiction. But I do worry about a nihilistic postmodern art that aims narrowly at the parochial appreciation of other writers. And I grow cranky when these overly cerebral exercises are also boring. What we are seeing too often nowadays is a neglect of narrative movement in favor of self-conscious style. Storyline disappears completely. Metaphors are more closely observed than character development. Life is presented as stagnant or numbing, and the best that can be expected is an interesting day.

Mary Hood's punk exhibitionism, for example, in *And Venus Is Blue* wears thin after a few of her mean and desperate sagas. Hood's second volume of stories is a burlesque of tough-but-tender Sam Shepard men dancing with tedious, ineffectual Ann Beattie women.

The characters in *And Venus Is Blue* are named Floyd, Ida, Chip, Harve, Candy. They have revolving charge accounts at J.C. Penney; they always get someone else to buy the drinks; they are silent when their spouses beat them; they close the curtains and let their children wander the streets. Often they are too much like parodies to be credible, and when they are credible, they are uninteresting. At best, Hood's writing is sharp and pungent, but it skids into slick one-liners in stories like "After Moore," an overdrawn account of a cracking marriage:

Rhonda said, "The fortune-teller swore my next husband's name would start with a J."

"Will it?"

This review originally appeared under the title "Stories of Floyd, Ida, Chip, Harve, Ada and Esther" in *Newsday*, 9 November 1986.

"Yeah," Rhonda said. "Jerk."

Joyce Carol Oates's *Raven's Wing* offers various voices: a newlywed student, a young boxer, the timid woman teacher at a Jesuit college, a glib professional cheating on his wife. Most of her vulnerable characters are on the edge of despair or madness or danger. She is brilliant at exposing the raw side of these people, but after a while I have to ask, what is the point? Why are all these women and men suffering hatred, panic, and violence? Do they learn anything? Does the reader? Does anything happen or are these stories simply voyeuristic slices of vapid lives?

> She never prayed. Once or twice a day, usually while driving her car, she made a systematic effort to empty herself, so that God might fill her. If nothing happened she felt saddened but not upset. Hers was to be a life, she knew, in which nothing would frequently happen.

Oates is one of our strongest and most prolific contemporary writers. She is a voice to be reckoned with in *them,* her powerful novel about poverty in Detroit, and in *Son of Morning,* a breathtaking portrayal of religious and political corruption. She can call upon a wide range of experience from her working-class childhood to the faculty of Princeton, where she now teaches.

But *Raven's Wing,* though versatile and full of promise, is disappointing. The stories seem tossed off, first drafts of bad dreams. Reading this collection is like attending the symphony and hearing instead a series of virtuoso performances of unfinished pieces. So much is left unsaid, unthought, unfelt.

Tess Gallagher's *The Lover of Horses* is a welcome exception here. Gallagher writes complex stories about real people. She refines her tales through a sophisticated intelligence and a deep empathy. The stories are laced with warnings about miscommunication, but they have an underpinning of hopefulness. Gallagher's exceptional books of poetry, including *Willingly* and *Instructions to the Double,* reveal a dramatic narrative sense which she develops in this, her first collection of stories.

Gallagher's characters are open, searching, thoughtful people leading deceptively simple lives. An aging widow falls in love again with a childhood sweetheart; a young girl cherishes her first pair of glasses; a maverick photographer robs a bank. The tales are both mythic and realistic, recalling the fey humor of Muriel Spark and the street savvy of Grace Paley.

"Girls" vivdly recreates a reunion which transcends memory: "Ada had invited herself along on the four-hour drive to Corvallis with her daughter, Billie, for one reason: she intended to see if her girlhood friend, Esther Cox, was still living."

However, Esther has suffered a stroke and doesn't remember Ada at all. Gradually the two women find that they share enough—memories of the same people and a common compassion—to bridge the gap of forty-three years: "'I don't know who you are,' Esther said. 'But I like you. Why don't you stay the night?'"

Throughout the evening, Ada tries to jog Esther's memory; she rubs her old friend's feet; lies down beside her and talks; joins her in a meal of wieners and green beans, fixed the way she'd had them back home, with bacon drippings. In the morning, the new, old friends part tearfully.

The revival of short fiction makes me wonder again about the tension between story and story collection. Hood, Oates, and, to a lesser degree, Gallagher, suffer from the constraints of the short story collection.

Reading these pieces one after another is much like eating an antipasto too fast. Individual stories lose their flavor and one remembers only a general tang. How varied should "collected" stories be, anyway? Should the pieces have a consistent voice or an interconnected theme? Is the book an arena for the writer's decathlon performance, or should it be a cohesive experience for the reader? In evaluating the work, does one consider the stories separately or the book as a whole? Sometimes exquisite stories distract from each other, like butterflies in a cage.

The very form of a book leads the reader to expect depth and continuity. Perhaps short fiction is, after all, best published in the limelight of pamphlets and periodicals.

Common Ground edited by Marilyn Berge, Linda Field, Cynthia Flood, Penny Goldsmith, and Lark

If you trusted Canadian fiction you would have to believe that most of the women in the country with any real presence at all are over fifty, and a tough, sterile, suppressed and granite-jawed lot they are. They live their lives with intensity, but through gritted teeth, and they are often seen as malevolent, sinister or life-denying, either by themselves or by other characters in their books.

—Margaret Atwood, *Survival, A Thematic Guide to Canadian Literature*

Common Ground, a collection of twelve fine short stories by Canadian women, goes a long way to redressing Atwood's complaint. Here we meet women of varied ages and intensities and degrees of gritted teeth. The book is important as a reflection of contemporary Canada, as a link in the international women's movement, and as a statement about form in feminist art.

Americans are notoriously numb to life north of our border. American feminists are just as culpable as American capitalists of cultural imperialism. Deluded by the notion that The Women's Movement centers here, we often overlook ideological challenge and aesthetic stimulus from other countries. Our ignorance is compounded by a mediocrity complex which has caused Canadians to demean their culture in comparison to their powerful neighbors. So the 49th Parallel has never fulfilled its potential as the metaphorical back fence over which Canadian and American women exchanged stories.

Common Ground is a back fence which draws us together. The book considers Canadian issues and sensibilities within the commonalities of female experience. We encounter such "great northern themes" as alienation, victimization, survival, as well as notions about regionalism, frontier identity, branch plant mentality, the ethnic mosaic (as opposed to the American melting pot). The book is unified by a distinctly Canadian mood—a kind of reflective edge, drawn from close watching.

This review was first published in the *New Women's Times Feminist Review,* January–February 1982.

Two political movements have encouraged Canadian women to raise their voices—feminism and Canadian nationalism. During the late sixties and early seventies, consciousness grew about American dominance and the need for Canadian autonomy. During this period, I was one of many Americans who immigrated to Canada in protest of the war in Southeast Asia. Most of us were stunned by the extent of Americanization and then amazed by the vehemence of Canadian resentment. I didn't know that Americans owned more than half of Canada's manufacturing, mining, and petroleum industries, that publishing was virtually U.S. controlled, and that Americans held one-sixth of university professorships. Consequently I was unprepared for the "Canadianization" of the work force and for the nationalistic celebration of the authentic Canadian voice. Now, ten years later, even Americans have heard of writers like Margaret Atwood, Margaret Laurence, and Alice Munro. Feminist publishers like the Women's Press in Toronto and Press Gang in Vancouver continue to educate us. We still have a long way to go, especially in our understanding of Francophones and Canadian minorities, but books like *Common Ground* make a significant contribution.

This collection is a carefully constructed whole—representing styles ranging from social realism to journal entry to dramatic dialogue to flood of consciousness. We meet lesbians and heterosexual women, crones and children, daughters and mothers and sisters of various economic classes. Here, because of space limits, I'll focus on four stories, but each of the twelve pieces is moving and well crafted.

"Pink Lady" is a grim legacy of despair from a young woman named Sandy as she fades from life after taking an overdose of pills and alcohol. L. L. Field opens the story with Sandy in the bathtub, getting pink—her body floating in the hot water and her soul floating in quantities of wine. She tries to numb herself from her dreary job and her overbearing man. Alcohol is the most accessible and complete escape. We watch Sandy being raped, then subjected to other physical and psychological coercion by her "lover." The story is tough and honest, confronting issues of working-class women without sentimentality. We read, breathless, as Sandy wavers between resistance and surrender.

"Cadillac at Atonement Creek" is a finely drawn meeting of past and present—an American expatriate's encounter with nationality through a visit from her mother. Kathryn Woodward writes,

> That word, *Canadian*. It gives my mother trouble, something I noticed the few times we talked on the telephone. She finds it a difficult word to shape to her Southern accent, so that in her mouth the syllables become that much more alien. Probably she has found substitutes—*Those People, That Place, Up North*—but only for those times when she cannot avoid my new nationality.

Throughout the story, the narrator struggles to understand her mother while preserving her own integrity. Ultimately their connection is forged through their mutual love for the daughter of the next generation.

"Six Weeks" in the life of Anna Fletcher, a fifty-year-old farmer, usually pass with the weary routine of cold dawn milkings and dull evening card games. But this six weeks is a time when her husband of thirty years is laid up in hospital, a time when the hired man finds his way into her bed, a time when she faces feelings and hopes and disappointments and possibilities that she thought she had buried forever. Marlene Wildeman writes with precise grace about this taciturn woman. The simple, explicit language complements Anna's tentative circumspection and taut strength.

"Nobody's Women" by Anne Cameron is one of those tales which holds you on a tightrope between compassion and futility. The imagistic, fragmented piece chronicles the life of a nurse in her painful, exasperating work with psychiatric inmates. Cameron unflinchingly reveals the mutual victimization of patients and staff. She even packs some humor in her survival kit. The narrator, recovering from an assault, wakes up in the nurses' infirmary with a big bandage under her nose. "'I've seen some rare uses for sanitary pads, but jesus, to wear one on your face like the Lone Ranger...' Dale is grinning. 'Kid, you've worked here too long if you think that's where they go!'"

Reading *Common Ground* makes us consider the short story collection as an archetypal feminist literary form. The succinct completeness of each piece accommodates the patchwork of female existence as we move from reading to cleaning to reading to childcare to reading to typing to reading.... It's not surprising that two-thirds of these stories are told in the first person style. Like the sewing bee or the CR group or the back fence gossip session, this kind of book allows for quick bursts or for profound testimony. Such compressed intimacy highlights our similarities and differences. Ultimately the book becomes a chorus of women—writing in parts—about how we share this earth, this common ground.

Stepping Out: Short Stories on Friendship between Women edited by Ann Oosthuizen

Stepping Out is *live* fiction—fresh, engaging, alarming, written from the pulses of real women. Many feminists will see themselves revealed with striking familiarity in this British collection of stories. Such fiction reminds us that no matter how alienated we are in the larger world, the women's movement has provided a society, a scene, a culture, and sometimes even a community.

These stories are about women *stepping out* together—out of social stereotypes and into many different spheres. Personally, the book made me nostalgic for a country in which I used to live and for the literary milieu in which I first started to write fiction. But I do have two criticisms. The subtitle is misleading, for some of these pieces are not about friends. Perhaps this subtitle describes the editor's original intention more accurately than her outcome. My other criticism is that the collection is uneven, and several stories need more work and development. Generally, however, this is a gripping book—both in the originality of the styles and in the breadth of cross-cultural perspectives. In fact, it is the "common differences" among these authors and their subjects that make *Stepping Out* so provocative.

Stepping Out is an inspiring contrast to the current revival of mainstream short fiction in the United States. Magazines and newspapers are running more short stories, recalling an era when writers could actually earn a living from periodical sales. But so much of what passes as "serious" American fiction today is self-conscious nihilism. Ennui in Westport is a typical narrative journey. The most celebrated contemporary stories are suffocated in the narrow province of "sensibility." We get too many books in which nothing happens and people with time on their hands spend hours pondering their vacuous lives.

However, *Stepping Out* is filled with social connection *and* individual expression. Things happen in these funny, angry glimpses of everyday women's lives, four of which I want to discuss in some detail. I don't believe hierarchical rating is useful. But these four particularly caught my fancy.

The lively, realistic pace of "5½ Charlotte Mews" is clear from the opening.

This review first appeared in *Conditions,* Fall 1987.

"Base to Lizzy. Base to Lizzy. Over."

Middle of New Oxford Street. Damn the bloody radio. Impossible to stop now, have to edge to the kerb, just when she'd achieved the right-hand lane. (P. 1)

Lizzy rides a messenger bike around London twelve hours a day, eking out her living in the rain. The only thing that makes the job bearable is a friendship with Kit, an older woman dispatcher. One day Kit learns that Lizzy is a dyke. This ends her special favors to the messenger, to say nothing about her friendly nods and winks. The story is spun with tenderness and humor. You hold your breath as Lizzy tries to navigate through the London exhaust and her own exhaustion until . . . until Kit makes that special call. Suddenly there is new meaning to the phrase, "Over and *out*" (italics mine).

In "Falling," Barbara Burford tests the lines between Black and white, heterosexual and lesbian with grace, intelligence, and ultimately surprise. Alison, a white lesbian, is nervously awaiting the arrival of Joan, a Black woman who will be staying in her flat while she takes a dance therapy course. Alison and Joan have known each other through many years of feminist conferences, and they have not always been allies. Joan is, of course, just as nervous as Alison.

Burford draws both women with an intricate empathy as they slowly approach and avoid one another—Alison trips over her racist assumptions, as Joan offends Alison by referring to a male lover. Gradually the two women come together.

Joan was dancing. In a big empty room with no barres or mirrors. Dancing by herself, but not alone, for her gestures and movements clearly outlined for Alison the partner, invisible with whom she danced, or tried to dance. Again and again Joan would approach this other, trying to make her aware of her. Just the movement of her hand as she tenderly turned the invisible face towards her, only to have it turn heedlessly away, tightened Alison's throat, raised her off her heels, so that she felt herself beginning to flow forwards. (P. 47)

Everyone knows the Judy in Michelene Wandor's story, "Judy's Kiss." Wandor writes about the reunion of Judy's consciousness-raising group. Although Judy doesn't appear, she is the center of attention, as each woman recounts how Judy has managed to step into her own life, use her temporarily, and then disappear. Their stories are a capsule of the personal/political choices made by many contemporary feminists: childbearing, political activism, poetry writing, lesbianism, spiritual growth, female friendship.

Wandor leaves the reader with uncomfortable questions about who used whom.

How can someone be everywhere and nowhere? Ubiquitous and absent, at one and the same time.... A heroine? No, not at all. The very opposite? We feminists don't believe in villains. We don't believe in saints and therefore we don't believe in devils. Or do we? (P. 51)

"Since Agnes Left" by Jackie Kay begins as Beulah reflects on the past two years without her lover, Agnes. Her descriptions of these characters are vivid and engaging from the beginning.

> Deep and dark, [Beulah's] eyes looked as if once you went into them, you would never return. Her cheeks were black with an orange-red glow like the highlights in a fire. She had that fresh look of someone often outside in the tough winter air.
>
> Agnes was taller than Beulah and younger by seven years. She dressed with style and her face was often dramatically made up. Her hair was thick and straightened, her skin, lighter than Beulah's, a sort of cinnamon brown. She loved dancing and listening to music and her expressions conveyed her passion for life. (Pp. 90–92)

Beulah reexperiences the stunning blow of Agnes's farewell note, the possible reasons for the breakup, the bitterness, the emptiness. It's an exquisite piece, rendered with understanding, delicacy, and passion. Kay writes about their struggles in the outside world with economic pressures and discrimination as well as their own domestic drama about self-determination. Eventually "Since Agnes Left" is a healing testimony, ending on the perfect note.

> They listened to Sarah [Vaughan] sing in a voice that crossed the country of their imagination and traveled the pain of their pasts. She sang, *In this world of overrated pleasures, of underrated treasures, I'm glad there is you.* (P. 109)

Not all the stories are so satisfying. In particular, Honora Barlett's "Some Notes on Evolution" and Moy McCrory's "Strangers" need more development. "Some Notes" was more a philosophical statement than an engaging narrative. And "Strangers" struck me as the core of a novel rather than a natural short story.

The rest of the pieces range over a variety of cultures and styles. Ann Oosthuizen's "A Fine Romance" tells about the friendship between two publishers and their romance with words. Marsha Rowe's "Who's she—the cat's mother?" describes women who learn that growth doesn't come without destruction. "The Mother Right," by Andrea Freud Lowenstein, an American temporarily living in

England, reveals the struggles between two women for custody of a child. Told in alternating voices, it recalls her interesting experimentation with points of view in the novel *This Place* (1984). Jo Jones reminds us of the continuing presence of Joan of Arc in our lives through her stunning tribute, "Superbity." And Sara Maitland fantasizes a Chagall-like world in which women fly over London in her "Let us now praise unknown women and our mothers who begat us."

Stepping Out made me consider moving back to London. I miss the particular ways our British sisters integrate politics into character and setting as well as their tantalizing, worldly humor. Even if this collection doesn't make *you* book passage on the next transatlantic vessel, it will have you playing with new possibilities of *stepping out* in your own life.

In Custody by Anita Desai

In Custody, Anita Desai's fourth work of fiction, is a lush, subtle, graceful, and emotionally acute novel about contemporary India. What begins as a touching story about a beleaguered young man shifts into a disturbing investigation about the paralysis of the individual in the treacherous territories of art and class.

Deven, a talented but obscure college lecturer in Mipore, yearns for a life where he can teach more promising students, write his poetry, and meet other artists. He is defeated before his time by obligations and depressed that he must teach Hindi rather than his beloved Urdu. He returns each night to a meager home and a petulant wife. Escape beckons when Deven's old friend Murad, a magazine editor, invites him to interview the venerable Urdu poet Nur in Delhi.

The story is, by turns, complex, suspenseful, hilarious, and desperate. Unfortunately, Desai's compassion is at least equaled by her contempt, and the novel is edged with cynicism: Desai, the patrician, patronizes her poor Bartleby, and Desai, the celebrated novelist, condescends to the fledgling poet. *In Custody* dissolves into stereotypes of the artist as scoundrel and, insofar as Deven takes too long to perceive the corruption of literary commerce, into yet another portrayal of the Indian as child.

> Later, Deven could not understand how it had all come about—how he, the central character in the whole affair, the protagonist . . . how he, in the course of that evening, had relinquished his own authority and surrendered it to Siddiqui who now emerged the stronger while he, Deven, had been brought to his knees, abject and babbling in his helplessness. *How?*

Deven's first trip to Delhi is full of disappointment—the great poet treats him offhandedly, and his interview seems impossible. But Deven returns, determined to learn from his idol and to preserve Nur's words for posterity. He finds that the poet, long past his artistic prime, has been wallowing in alcohol, sex, and the company of unsavory groupies. Still, Deven persists. He manages to cut through hideously overgrown bureaucracy to win a leave from college as well as the loan of a tape recorder and a technician.

This review first appeared in the *Los Angeles Times Book Review,* 24 March 1985.

Eventually, the project extends so long that it endangers the issue of Murad's magazine and threatens Deven's job and marriage. He proceeds doggedly, only to find that the final tape—like his own mind—is cluttered with the cacophony of Nur's fans and street noises while relatively empty of literary luminescence. After Deven returns to Mipore, he receives letters from Nur, demanding money for his medical bills and insisting that Deven find his son a scholarship. Despite all the mishaps, Nur's poetry remains an inspiration and a momentum for Deven.

That friendship still existed even if there had been a muddle, a misunderstanding. He had imagined he was taking Nur's poetry into safe custody, and not realized that if he was to be custodian of Nur's genius, then Nur would become his custodian and place him in custody too. This alliance could be considered an unendurable burden—or else a shining honor. Both demanded an equal strength.

In Custody would be a deeper novel if Desai had exercised more sympathy and less clever sarcasm. The women, in particular, emerge as sullen creatures with "tongues like whips." Deven's wife is a petulant, messy character who "hisses" and "snaps." Desai is at her best testing artistic idealism against the constraints of bureaucracy and poverty. She writes with tight, bitter elegance, tinged with a delicious shade of irony, even when her cynicism overshadows Deven's integrity and the power of his vision.

Rape: The Power of Consciousness
by Susan Griffin

All women know the routine. Be sure to leave the office or the factory or the library before dark; keep to the best-lit streets; check the back seat of the car before getting in. After unlocking the front door, look in the closets and under the bed and through all the rooms. Then latch the door securely.

We have learned to see out of the corners of our eyes, have practiced karate chops and judo flops, have stockpiled cans of mace. Yet even those of us who successfully avoid personal assault are confined by the culture of rape.

Most of us have forgotten how to move without fear. Susan Griffin tells us that the best defense against rape is the power of consciousness. First we must understand that rape is misogynist terrorism. Then we must reclaim our right to live safely and wholly in the world.

Griffin's book consists of three essays: "Politics," the groundbreaking indictment of rapist society that appeared in *Ramparts* in 1971; "A History," an overview of violence against women and the feminist response; and "Consciousness," a more philosophical consideration of patriarchy, feminism, and a vision of a society without rape. The essays are supplemented by an extensive listing of rape crisis centers in North America as well as a collage of comments about rape from feminists around the world.

"Rape is a form of mass terrorism," writes Griffin in the first piece, "for the victims of rape are chosen indiscriminately, but the propagandists for male supremacy broadcast that it is women who cause rape by being unchaste or in the wrong place at the wrong time—in essence, by behaving as though they were free." Here she discusses the pervasiveness of rape, the sexist treatment of victims by the police and the courts; the fear and guilt that keep women from reporting rape and the effectiveness of rape as a form of social control. When this essay first appeared, it provoked both grass roots campaigns as well as further written analysis, such as Susan Brownmiller's *Against Our Will*.

During the last eight years the violence against women has become more

This review was first published in *In These Times*, 5–11 December 1979. Reprinted with permission of *In These Times*.

visible. We are experiencing a backlash against feminism with the trashing of abortion clinics and women's presses. We are also beginning to hear stories of women defending themselves: Joann Little, Yvonne Wanrow, Dessie Woods, and Inez Garcia. In 1976, an International Tribunal of Crimes against Women was held in Brussels. In North America alone we have hundreds of rape crisis centers.

In "A History" Griffin pauses to criticize the Left's longstanding insensitivity to issues of violence against women. However her remarks about socialism and Marx are too brief and offhand. She would do well to consider the serious work of many feminist socialists who are moving the Left to a different consciousness.

The final essay asks how our society is shaped by patriarchy and served by rape. Rape is more than a physical attack. It is a denial of our autonomy, a blind pulled down on our vision of the world.

> We are frightened all of our lives by the incipience of this violence. The rapist may be a stranger, or a man we thought we knew. The act of rape for women is of its very nature never predictable, never *chosen*, never a fight one has wagered on, always a surprise attack, and for no reason. In the moment of rape a woman becomes anonymous. . . . Absorbed by his violence, her soul and the history of her soul are lost.

Some feminist socialists will consider themselves too earthbound for Griffin's talk of soul and spirit. But her discussion of Greek mythology, for instance, provides historical metaphors about the treatment of women. No doubt some will close this book at the first mention of Iphigenia, Clytemnestra, or Persephone. One of the great tragedies of feminism is that the internal splits—such as that between "political" feminists and "spiritual" feminists—often occupy us more than our fight against sexism. But we will not be free of rape until we go deep into our history and psychology, root out the misogyny, and begin to conceive of a new humanity.

Some will say Griffin is outrageous and hysterical. But she's used to that. They said the same thing about her *Ramparts* essay, now considered one of the pioneering analyses of rape. She isn't disowning that essay. Here she extends it.

Zami: A New Spelling of My Name
by Audre Lorde

Vision. Visibility. Sight. Hindsight. Insight. Second Sight. This is the metaphorical spectrum of Audre Lorde's bright new prose work *Zami*.

Zami is a Carriacou name for women who work together as friends and lovers. This "biomythography"—which blends past and present with dreams—describes the varied women who shaped Audre Lorde's life. As the daughter of West Indian immigrants, she traces passionate umbilical ties back to Carriacou, the island of her mother's birth. Lorde felt her way along the streets of New York to become a noted poet and English professor at Hunter College. Her story is a marvelous excursion into the imagination of hope.

Unlike many early literary memoirs or conventional *Kunstlerromans*, *Zami* does not fetishize the isolated artist as individual seeker. Rather Lorde describes the lives of many other women to highlight and underline her own experience. She is explicit about the racism and homophobia she suffered. This social consciousness adds heart and power to an autobiography which moves with the subtle drama of good fiction.

Sight—being seen, being able to see—is the line of suspense on which the story is drawn. As a child, Lorde was almost blind. Finally she got her glasses, which separated her from the other kids. As the youngest daughter of exhausted parents, she was often overlooked. As the Black student of white nuns, she was easily discriminated against. Her mother "protected" her from racial prejudice by trying to ignore it, by insisting, for instance, that the white people who spat on young Audre did so at random, by accident. Other people denied her color, like the man who, after serving her breakfast for seven years, expressed amazement that she had won a Negro scholarship. Also, as a lesbian, she met many people who knew and did not want to know her identity. Often Lorde felt that part of her was hidden to everyone else in the world. Ultimately what made her fully visible— and *Zami* proves she is now a flaming presence—was her own uncanny sight and her powerful gift to communicate what she saw.

At home, my mother said, "Remember to be sisters in the presence of strangers." She meant white people, like the woman who tried to make me

This review was first published in the *American Book Review* 5, no. 6 (October 1983).

get up and give her my seat on the Number 4 bus, and who smelled like cleaning fluid. At St. Catherine's, they said, "Be sisters in the presence of strangers," and they meant non-catholics. In high school, the girls said, "Be sisters in the presence of strangers," and they meant men. My friends said, "Be sisters in the presence of strangers," and they meant squares.

But in high school, my real sisters were strangers; my teachers were racists; and my friends were that color I was never supposed to trust.

Zami takes readers from Lorde's childhood to her twenties. We see the poet discovering her own intelligence, finding the voice to write, hacking at grubby jobs to make her way through school, going to Connecticut to work as an X-ray technician (a poignant section for those who have read *The Cancer Journals* and know that she would later have a mastectomy), spending time in Mexico, observing McCarthyism and the early Civil Rights movement, dancing and drinking in the gay-girl bars in the 1950s. The momentum is so intense that it's hard to believe at the end of the book that we've only traveled the first half of Lorde's life.

Always this is more than one woman's story. It is a eulogy and benediction for the women who helped Lorde to see and to grow visible: her taciturn mother; her two sisters; her first playmate, Toni; her teenage friend Gennie who commits suicide; her first woman lover Ginger; the pickled and pungent expatriate Eudora; her Communist roommate Rhea; her tender-mad partner Muriel; and, finally, Afrekete, who shines her light on what it means to be a loving, proud, Black lesbian.

Lorde's language is graceful and sensuous. Her honesty is uncompromising without being rigid. Boldy, she describes a physical attraction for her mother, concluding the book with the line, "There [in Carriacou] it is said that the desire to lie with other women is a drive from the mother's blood." The scenes between Lorde and her lovers are gorgeous. *Zami*'s vitality heightens all the senses, but particularly the sense of smell—the aromas of sex, food, flowers, and New York City itself.

The narrative is fairly straightforward chronologically, but illumined by momentary flashbacks and flashforwards. Lorde creates her own "Manual of Style" to redress traditional visibility, using capital letters for *Black, Colored, Negro,* and lowercase for *white, american, catholic.*

The epilogue is a spirited coda, drawing together the women who have enlightened her. "Their names, selves, faces feed me like corn before labor. I live each of them as a piece of me, and I choose these words with the same grave concern with which I choose to push speech into poetry, the mattering core, the forward vision of all our lives."

Going Too Far by Robin Morgan

Going Too Far is a feminist missal—with a calendar of the women's movement over the last decade, a communion of saints, and a liturgy appropriate for witches' covens, CR groups, or political rallies.

Robin Morgan's eloquent documentary is a welcome stemming of the tide of fundamentalism running in the United States today. In the wake of the Supreme Court's limits on reproductive rights, the Hyde Amendment, the Dade County (Florida) vote, and the pending cuts in HEW affirmative action funds, *Going Too Far* reminds us that we have at least come some of the way. However sexist this society may be now, it used to be worse. Morgan testifies to the personal and political changes that have been wrought by the women's movement, how feminists are continuing to go "too far."

Unlike *Sisterhood Is Powerful,* the classic 1970 primer where she anthologized many women's work, *Going Too Far* is pure Morgan, a highly subjective collection of speeches, poetry, essays, and articles.

Her first chapter is "Letters from a Marriage." Morgan has been married for fifteen years, to poet Kenneth Pitchford. They both are frank about their relationship and their bisexuality, without apology to sexual separatists. Their marriage is all the more engaging because it was tested and toughened during the sixties.

These letters begin in 1965 with the quixotic will of a young bride, "And I will love him enough and more. And that will make everything possible." In 1966, she is criticizing herself for late laundry, unsewn buttons, dowdy dress, unadventurous cooking, and infrequent vaginal orgasms. During later years, she writes about their struggles with gender roles and with literary competition. Her urge to record is so strong that she writes two of these letters during the birth of her son. While Kenneth times the contractions, she types, interrupted every few paragraphs by labor pains. At such moments, her self-scrutiny is more obsession than documentary. Usually, however, her intimacy serves her theme—the personal is political—with profound tenderness. "The Women's Movement, ironically, would present at once the most serious threat to our relationship (as it then stood) and the most hopeful possibility *for* our relationship (as it would change)."

This review originally appeared in the *San Francisco Review of Books* in November 1977. Since then, Robin Morgan has published *Sisterhood is Global* (1984) and, as the editor of the new *Ms.* magazine, has introduced significant international content to the journal.

"The Emergence of Women's Liberation" chapter takes us back to the first protests against the Miss America Pageant and to the WITCHES' (Women's International Terrorist Conspiracy from Hell) attacks on Wall Street and the New York Bridal Fair. The naive blunders of the early movement are recorded unabridged—the rhetoric and the abrasiveness, the way feminists threatened women and the way they wasted energy trying to recruit the male Left. Morgan ends this section with that marvelous piece, "Barbarous Rituals," which she included anonymously in *Sisterhood Is Powerful.* It's worth a rerun.

> Woman Is:—Kicking strongly in your mother's womb, upon which she is told, "It must be a boy if it's so active!"...dying of shame because your mother makes you wear a "training bra" but there's nothing to train,... finally screwing and your groin and buttocks and thighs ache like hell and you're all wet and maybe bloody and it wasn't like a Hollywood movie at all but jesus at least you're not a virgin any more but is this what it's all about?—and meanwhile he's asking, "Did you come?"...coming home from work and starting *in* to work: unpack the groceries, fix supper, wash up the dishes, rinse out some laundry, etc. etc....learning to hate other women who are: younger, freer, unmarried, without children, in jobs, in school, in careers—whatever. Hating yourself for hating them....getting older, getting lonelier, getting ready to die—and knowing it wouldn't have had to be this way, after all.

Those early essays stand out because of the passion with which she feels the events and the clarity with which she describes them. More than that, they impress the reader with her prescience and courage. All of them were written before 1970.

The last three chapters go beyond raising and rousing consciousness to consider three particular developments—struggle with the Left, radical feminism, and feminist metaphysics. Morgan shows us where some women—those who haven't dropped out along the way for a token academic or executive position—are taking the movement. She says feminism now means the constituting of alternatives to patriarchy—politically, aesthetically, and spiritually.

"Good-Bye to All That"—the infamous article from the women's takeover of *Rat,* a New York underground newspaper—is a searingly articulate indictment by name and atrocity against "The good guys who think they know what 'Women's Lib' as they so chummily call it, is all about—and who then proceed to degrade and destroy women by almost everything they say and do.... The token 'pussy power' or 'clit militancy' articles. The snide descriptions of women staffers on the masthead. The little jokes, the personal ads, the smile, the snarl. No more, brothers.

No more well-meaning ignorance, no more co-optation, no more assuming that this thing we're all fighting is the same. . . ."

Here and in the subsequent political pieces, Morgan refuses to acknowledge that many strong women have foraged into Marx and have emerged with their feminism intact. Granted, feminists in the late sixties and early seventies needed a divorce from both the New and Old Lefts, to develop their own analysis and autonomy. But Morgan regards contemporary feminist-socialists as confused lackeys. Many of her attacks on the Left continue to be valid: "Two evils pre-date capitalism and have been clearly able to survive and postdate socialism: sexism and racism." But to deny that feminism and socialism can coexist is to ignore the struggles of women in Mozambique, Tanzania, Cuba, Vietnam as well as in this country. Sometimes Morgan sweeps too much away with her stiff witch's broom.

The chapter on "Radical Feminism" contains germinal (not "seminal"— Morgan appreciates the politics of language) essays on pornography and women's studies. In the article "International Feminism," she rails against the censorship of *New Portuguese Letters* by the Three Marias. This is the only piece where Morgan breaks through the isolationism endemic to American feminism. When she does make extranational references, they are often embarrassing. For instance, she reports a visit to "Saskatchewan, Canada." Does she mean Saskatoon? Her knowledge of Pankhurst country is minimal. Why does she confine Ann Oakley and Juliet Mitchell to one footnote? Why does she ignore Sheila Rowbotham? What about the feminists in France, Italy, and Scandinavia? What about the fundamental contributions being made by women in developing countries? Morgan is not alone in her Yankee provincialism, but someone who rhapsodizes about feminism reshaping the world should cross a few borders, personally.

The brilliance of this fourth chapter, and perhaps the best article in the book, is "Lesbianism and Feminism: Synonyms or Contradictions." Morgan draws heterosexual women and lesbians together from political strategy, from their common herstory and from their instinctive sisterhood. She shows how the split only serves men, "although the Man will probably want to get me for hating men before he gets me for loving women." She laments the self-destructiveness in the splintering among lesbians, lesbian feminists, dykes, dyke-feminists, dyke-separatists, "old" dykes, butch dykes, bar dykes, and killer dykes. Morgan draws women together, not as a female conciliator, but as a feminist militant:

> And if a woman isn't there when the crunch comes—and it is coming—
> then I for one won't give a damn whether she is at home in bed with a
> woman, a man or her own wise fingers. . . . We have enough trouble on our
> hands. Isn't it way past time that we stopped *settling* for blaming each other,

stopped blaming heterosexual women and middleclass women and married women and straight women and lesbian women and white women and *any* woman for the structure of sexism, racism, classism and ageism, that no woman is to blame for because none of us had the power to create those structures.

The final chapter shows us the direction of current women's psychology, metaphysics, and aesthetics. It is the most exploratory part of the book. She writes about paranoia as a female survival tool, about feminist art, and about gynocentric philosophy, which, she thinks, is providing an ethical framework for the new society. The reader can go from Morgan to Mary Daly, Adrienne Rich, and Susan Griffin for more extended study.

Going Too Far is subtitled "The Personal Chronicle of a Feminist." Although we would hardly abridge her feminist politics, we might ask her to edit her ego. She declines the mantle of everywoman, but describes herself as some sort of superwoman, comparing her work to Susan B. Anthony's crusade. Perhaps this is just part of that syndrome among American radicals to create figureheads and to drop names, especially their own. Morgan seems to live some parts of her life so she can document them. However, most of *Going Too Far* is the best kind of testimony—vision born of courage, expressed in distilled, graceful language. It is a volume of inspiration and cheer. Morgan gives us a compass for the road ahead, a road on which we can never go too far.

The afterword, "Going," is a frenzied celebratory hericane, a whirling dance of all the witches and housewives and lovers and artists and mothers Morgan has ever been: "*Breathe me in,* I am the smoke of your own flesh, the bracelet of bright flame about the ankle. . . . Breathe me in. We are dancing in the still-warm ashes of our burnt-away selves, *endlessly birthing.* Insurrection. *Resurrection.* Come along now, *you too,* don't you think it's time we started?"

Seven Contemporary Chinese Women Writers edited by Gladys Yang

We were right, as children, to imagine that we reached China by digging. If we dug deep through the earth, we might begin to appreciate the vastness of the journey. For grown-ups, the most likely form of digging is reading. Indeed, this is a wise way to prepare for China, learning through its own voices before we begin to ask—and answer—too many Western questions.

The stories in *Seven Contemporary Chinese Women Writers* (Panda Books) describe the lives of women in China, the impact of the Cultural Revolution, the power of art to transcend individualism, and the use of fiction to engage readers in social decisions. This summer I met six of these writers when I went to China in a twelve-woman delegation of American authors, sponsored by the Chinese Writers Association.

The difference between my readings of *Seven Contemporary Chinese Women Writers* before I left and after I returned is the most accurate measure of the distance I traveled. At first, this collection disappointed me. The stories seemed stiff, with the emphasis on action and choice at the expense of emotional texture. Some authors' messages blared out, denying the audience a sense of discovery.

But after returning from China, rereading the stories was like coming upon another book. I perceived new intricacies; I better understood the psychological nuances and I came to appreciate that, because the center of their struggle is so collective, these particular themes have profound personal authenticity.

While the protagonists are strong, complex women, the lack of feminist consciousness in these pieces will distress many American readers. Gladys Yang says in her introduction, "But there is no women's liberation movement in China, partly because women's position is infinitely better than before, partly because they see their problems in the general social context and are working for modernization to lighten their burdens." Although Yang's point about the special trials faced by women in a developing country is significant, it does not address the discrimination they encounter daily. Such experience could be more thoroughly explored in this volume.

This review was first published under the title "China" in *In These Times*, 23 November–6 December 1983. Reprinted with permission of *In These Times*.

As we were traveling, one of my greatest frustrations was the duplicity between the official rhetoric of equality and the reckless disregard of sexism. Everywhere we went, we were reminded that women hold up half the sky. They must have been very busy up there in the stars because only a few of our literary meetings were chaired by a woman. Of the 2,000 national members of the Chinese Writers Association, 140 are women. At a gathering in Guangzhou, a man greeted us warmly, recalling Gorky's sentiment about women being important because they are the mothers of poets and writers! In public, the Chinese women themselves were moderate about feminism. Several expressed amusement that we would travel in an all-female group. Yet as we became better acquainted, they were more candid about their restrictions and their anger.

Thus, while readers can't expect scintillating feminist analysis from these stories, they can learn a lot about the lives of Chinese women.

Ru Zhijuan's story, "The Path Through the Grassland," is a vivid study of the life of an oil worker as she faces the tensions between friendship and romantic love. The piece is set against the confusion of a people shakily emerging from the Cultural Revolution.

The contradictions are sharp—between individual desire and collective necessity, between the integrity of means versus end, between friendship and marriage. No catharsis is offered. At the conclusion, the oil worker remains in a quandary, stimulating readers to consider such choices in their own lives.

Ru is an impressive woman, straightforward and tough. At our meeting in Shanghai, she spoke of the importance of writing about women's issues, such as female infanticide. When one American delegate said she considered that part of her own liberation was that she could now write in a male voice, Ru took a long draw on her cigarette and said, "I, myself, would be the last one to write about men."

A soldier during World War II, she is now working on a novel about "the War Against Japanese Aggression"—from a woman's point of view. This autumn, she and her daughter Wang Anyi will be traveling around the United States and participating in the visiting writers program at the University of Iowa.

"The Flight of the Wild Geese" by Huang Zong-ying portrays the precarious route taken by intellectuals who have managed to survive World War II, the Long March, the Great Leap Forward, and the Cultural Revolution. At first, this piece of narrative journalism seems to be about the career of a woman scientist, Qin Guanshu, who works with herbs in the countryside. Qin had to abandon her beloved research on poplars, which was dubbed "a revisionist subject, because it has nothing to do with production." However, the story soon becomes a portrait of the author, writing a portrait of Qin. Huang becomes overwrought about whether to depict her subject as a hero (Qin has worked hard with the peasants to develop herbs) or a hopeless individualist (Qin has a reputation for irascibility and likes to do things her own way). The portrait of the portrait represents the strain between private feeling and public action endemic among Chinese professionals today.

> Qin's heart ached to see that many good species of Chinese poplars had been dug up. She often strolled among the small foreign poplar trees. Though a strong-willed woman, she thought of suicide several times. The specimens she had collected over the years had been taken away; her notebooks had disappeared. Furious, she had sold her books, which she had bought with the money she had saved, as waste paper, or simply burned them as kindling to light her stove.

The reporter's nagging ambivalence about the value and veracity of her journalism reflects the disorientation Qin experienced on the shifting ground of the Cultural Revolution.

We met Zong Pu at a conference of the Chinese Writers Association where her work was also described as "concerned with the emotions and feelings of intellectuals." Although the Association provides full salaries to a few writers, Zong, like most artists in China or the United States, supports herself with an outside job. She works at the Foreign Literature Research Institute of the Academy of Social Scientists.

As in other stories in the collection, Pu's "Melody in Dreams" explores the emotional life between two women—in this case between Murong Yeujun, a cellist in her fifties, and Liang Xia, her nineteen-year-old apprentice, who is the daughter of a close friend destroyed in the Cultural Revolution. "Aunt Yeujun" risks being labeled a counterrevolutionary for harboring the young woman, but she does it anyway, out of loyalty to her friend. The bond between the cautious, idealistic Aunt Yeujun and her fiery, cynical protege is especially touching.

> "How many years have you been playing the cello?" Yeujun looked at her cello. "You love music, don't you?"
> "No I don't..."
> "Why bother learning to play the cello if you don't like it?"
> "To make a living of course," Liang Xia giggled.

If she had heard such a reply 10 years ago, Yuejun would have been insulted. Now nothing astonished her.

The women give each other courage to continue and finally Liang becomes active in opposing the Gang of Four. This story, like others in the collection, leaves an open end. Will young Liang return? Will she be destroyed like her parents? But the piece concludes with a curiously didactic note: "The dream of the people will be fulfilled. The reactionaries will be smashed. Historically this is inevitable." This rhetorical crescendo so contrasts with the natural vitality of the plot, I wonder if the story somehow has been abridged.

The longest and strongest contribution to the book is the novella, *At Middle Age*, by Shen Rong. Shen is a sophisticated, successful novelist and playwright who has made one trip to America and is eagerly studying English in preparation for her next visit. Her novella sold three million copies and has been made into a popular movie. I saw the film in a crowded Beijing theater and then again on TV in Shanghai.

At Middle Age courageously examines the troubles of middle-aged professional women in today's China. While Chinese youth often face severe unemployment and disaffection, the middle-aged generation continues to be paid poorly for demanding jobs and sees little progress in their individual lives. *At Middle Age* opens as Dr. Lu Wenting, a forty-two-year-old eye surgeon, has cracked under the pressures. We meet her in a hospital bed where she is fighting back to life after a sudden heart attack.

Shen skillfully traces Dr. Lu's early dedication to medicine, her trials during the Cultural Revolution when the Red Guard burst into her operating room in the middle of delicate surgery, the demands of her young children, the loss of a close friend. The story swings back and forth between Dr. Lu's bed and the stresses that landed her there. *At Middle Age* closes with tempered optimism and—as always—an open end: "Leaning on her husband's shoulder, Lu walked slowly toward the gate. . . ."

Shen Rong exudes the same kind of steady endurance that saved her hero. She began her career as a music editor and Russian translator, but a blood condition brought fainting spells and left her an invalid for ten years. She turned to writing as a form of therapy, which she could work at between bouts of sickness. Now she is a popular and critical success. One late evening in Beijing, she invited four of us to tea in her fifth floor walk-up flat. She spoke with relief about the prospect of her two sons leaving home this year, giving her more space and time for writing. A shy, but determined woman, she was clearly finding middle age to be *her* prime.

Zhang Jie joined us at a meeting in Beijing. She is a quiet woman of forty-six. Her high-necked silk blouse posed an elegant contrast to the Maoist drabness of her colleagues and expressed the country's new liberalized code. Like many of the women we met, she spoke against the necessity of a separate feminist movement in China. "I don't think this exists politically or economically, but ideologically. We need to educate people who have prejudices against women. Meanwhile, women must do their own work arduously and diligently. Our commitments are the same as those of men."

Zhang's "Love Must Not Be Forgotten" is about a thirty-year-old woman recalling the tragedy of her mother's unfulfilled love from an old romance. Sometimes the narrator spurns her mother's sentimentality; at other moments she admires it. By the end of the story, the protagonist calls for the freedom to remain single, quite a radical demand for a Chinese woman. Although she is writing about a love affair, she, like most of her contemporaries, avoids any explicit sexual description.

Attitudes toward sexuality were among the biggest distinctions between the Chinese and American writers. At a discussion with the editorial board of *Chinese Literature* magazine, the editor, Yang Xianyi, told us that it was easy to publish in China, as long as you were not writing about "unhealthy topics." He did not elucidate, but later we learned there is censorship of many sexual details. When Western work is translated, the sexual passages are often toned down or omitted. In Beijing, a translator told me that it would be hard to publish Grace Paley's stories because she has written so much about divorce. In Guangzhou, we were informed that some of Joyce Carol Oates's work had been selected for translation because it was not sexually explicit and because it addressed the problems of intellectuals.

If graphic heterosexuality is taboo, homosexuality is extraterrestrial. When one Chinese woman learned that some of us were lesbians, she was astonished. She spent a long time asking intense questions. This seemed like a useful exchange until—on one of the last days of the trip—she came up to me and declared, "There are no lesbians in China. Do you think homosexuality is—like alcoholism and drug addiction—a corruption of capitalism?"

Wang Anyi's "Life in a Small Courtyard" is a splendidly flourishing finale to this album of Chinese life. The crowded conditions and personal dilemmas faced by the inhabitants of the courtyard reflect the paradoxes raised by the previous authors. This story traces the frustration of Songsong, a young dancer, weary of her transient life and eager to settle down and have a child. As Songsong investigates the complicated lives of her neighbors, she comes to appreciate her husband's loyalty and the stimulation she finds in her art. The piece seems representative of Shanghai in its optimism, color, noise, and cultural diversity.

This cosmopolitan quality is a tradition of Shanghai writers, Wang Anyi told me one day as we walked along the Bund, an old European financial district by the harbor. As much as Beijing reminded me of Moscow in its dour beige regimentation, Shanghai reminded me of a Southern European city. Laundry flapped on lines above the sidewalks where people squatted, washing clothes in bright porcelain bowls. Wang said that the definition of a local aesthetic was a topic of eager debate among Shanghai writers.

She was predictably happy with her lot as an artist. When she returns from a four-month trip to the United States with her mother, she will receive a full-time salary from the Chinese Writers Association to continue her fiction. She says the biggest trouble she experiences as a young writer is that she has known so little personal trouble that she doesn't have sufficient depth of experience from which to write well. She was being either modest or politically correct—probably both.

Before I went to China, I found the book's moral and political trend rather flat-footed. Now I understand that the fiction's comparative lack of emotional introspection simply reflects one of the borders between our two cultures. In comparison to Americans, the Chinese stew less in their personal psyches. Meanwhile, scrutiny of social conscience holds more fascination for readers there. Moreover, Mao's injunction to "go deep into the masses" is not just jargon. It expresses a classic Chinese appreciation for social context as well as a socialist commitment.

After talking with people about their tortuous experiences between 1966 and 1976, I realize more fully why five of these pieces hinge on the Cultural Revolution. The book is part of a national sigh of relief and bitterness.

Likewise, some of the book's shortcomings—such as class bias—become more visible after viewing a larger picture of the society. Why does a book that purports to represent contemporary China concentrate on the lives of professionals (or people aspiring to be professionals)—musicians, scientists, doctors, teachers, dancers, writers? Throughout the trip, I was frustrated by the disdain many "intellectuals" expressed for the "peasants." Perhaps part of my difficulty lay in the translators' choice of words—intellectuals and peasants—which conjured visions of pre-revolutionary France. So often, I was told that the problems of infanticide and birth control rested with people in the "countryside."

Of course, it is foolish to assume the Revolution could have wiped out thousands of years of feudal divisions. And the rift of privilege was exacerbated during the Cultural Revolution when "intellectuals" were persecuted not only for their own positions but also for the positions of their parents. Finally, I have to acknowledge that the extraordinary class bias of this collection is all too similar to the gaps in contemporary collections by Western women.

Doubtless a rhetorical style seen in this collection—such as the exhortatory messages concluding the stories by Zong Pu and Zhang Jie—is the legacy of a period when art was gauged by utilitarian value. Gladys Yang explains in her introduction:

> The ultra-left line in literature in the past encouraged writing according to set formulas, and the 10 years of turmoil deprived young would-be writers of a good education and the access to classical Chinese and foreign literature needed to raise the quality of their work. This is evident from the immaturity, lack of sophistication and verbosity of certain stories. But the last few years have been a period of experimentation in finding fresher forms and styles, and women writers are paying attention to this. However, their works are above all significant because of their subject matter and the honest picture they present of life in China today.

Visiting China is, for most Westerners, an act of imagination. Taking this journey is like reading a good book in that the depth of experience hits us afterward and continues to reverberate in our lives. Only since I have been home, reread their words, and reconsidered my encounters have I begun to understand and appreciate *Chinese Women Writers*. I am eager to return.

Ding Ling's Fiction
by Yi-Tsi Mei Feuerwerker,
Selected Stories of Xiao Hong
translated by Howard Goldblatt, and
*Born of the Same Roots: Stories of Modern
Chinese Women* edited by
Vivian Ling Hsu

Ding Ling is a small, round, intense woman of seventy-nine. She has led a tumultuous life as a writer and political activist in China. Her story is almost too demanding for one person; indeed, the stormy interplay of national history and personal integrity could well create a composite drama about the lives of many contemporary Chinese writers.

She was born in 1904 in Hunan and raised by her widowed mother, a fiercely independent woman. While studying in Peking, Ding Ling fell in love with another writer, Hu Yepin. In 1931, three months after the birth of their son, Hu was executed for Communist sympathies. His martyrdom intensified her commitment to the Left. Two years later Ding Ling was kidnapped by the Kuomintang. Rumors of her death circulated. Her fame grew through "posthumous" publication of stories, memoirs, and eulogies. After three years, she managed to escape. Setting out for the Communist party's headquarters, she disguised herself as a soldier, traveling on foot and horseback.

Mao welcomed her as a hero. During the years at Yanan, they clashed over the function of literature and the role of women. Still, at the founding of the People's Republic, Ding Ling was honored as a prominent writer. In 1951, she won the prestigious Stalin Prize for her only novel, *The Sun Shines on the Sanggan River*. By the mid-1950s, she was targeted in a campaign against veteran revolutionary writers. In 1958, she was exiled to the Great Northern Wilderness to do labor reform for twelve years.

This review was first published under the title "China Imagined" in the *Women's Review of Books*, January 1984.

Her troubles escalated in 1966 with the advent of the Cultural Revolution. She was sent to a small, thatched hut and then locked in a cowshed for six months. In 1970, she was put into solitary confinement in Peking for the next five years. Only when she was released did she learn that her husband, Chen Ming, had been placed in the adjacent cell the entire time. Now that the Cultural Revolution has been condemned, Ding Ling has reemerged as a matriarch in Chinese fiction. Despite—and because of—all this, she continues to write.

When I think about Chinese women writers, I am struck by their endurance and courage in the face of many changes in their country's attitude toward writing and toward women. As a novelist committed to an international women's movement, I am especially excited by what Chinese fiction shows about balancing political consciousness with artistic excellence; about describing the individual in a social context; and about portraying race, class, and gender in a nonrhetorical, liberatory way.

Ding Ling's Fiction is a study of ideology and narrative, spanning the twentieth century. *Selected Stories of Xiao Hong* offers fine short fiction from the 1930s and 1940s. *Born of the Same Roots* is a broad anthology of fiction about modern Chinese women from the People's Republic and overseas.

Yi-Tsi Mei Feuerwerker, like many people inside and outside China in the 1970s, presumed Ding Ling was dead. The month she was finishing *Ding Ling's Fiction*, Ding Ling was officially resurrected and rehabilitated by the Chinese Communist party. Feuerwerker set aside the text and went to China for six months to meet with her subject. Although *Ding Ling's Fiction* is primarily literary criticism, the book vividly explores China's recent past.

Feuerwerker examines how changes in Ding Ling's convictions and circumstances led to profound transformation in her subject matter and style. She developed, particularly in relation to her readers. Communism encouraged her to reach for a broader audience ("go deep into the masses") and to abandon bourgeois notions of catharsis. Instead of providing answers, her stories raise contradictions which continue to resonate in readers' minds. Such open-ended fiction engages people in the construction of the narrative, thus providing the spirit to engage in the construction of society.

Ding Ling's progression from confessional subjectivism to investigative advocacy is demonstrated by her changing choice of protagonists, from writers and other professionals in the early pieces to peasants in the more recent material. Her most famous story, "The Diary of Miss Sophie" (1928), gained her a reputation as an emotionally outspoken representative of the radical May Fourth Movement. Sophie is a twenty-year-old woman living away from her parents in Peking. She suffers from a severe case of tuberculosis as well as from a masochistic infatuation with a Westernized man. The piece became notorious as an exploration of sexuality and depression.

Growing consciousness of women's social role surfaced in the 1940 story, "When I Was in Xia Village." A young woman who works as a prostitute, spying on the Japanese, returns to her village riddled with venereal disease. Ding Ling describes the neighbors' reaction—ranging from condemnation to commendation—to expose the trials of a woman caught between shifting standards. Her later novel, The Sun Shines on the Sanggan River, celebrates the land reform movement as a model for personal change and political liberation. In sharp contrast to the internal momentum of "Miss Sophie," Sanggan River validates individuals through their external contributions to society. Unlike the early fiction, the novel ends with a utopian vision, signaling possibilities for human progress.

Sanggan River was banned in 1958 and for the next twenty years Ding Ling's work was banished from the Chinese literary scene. Her problems stemmed from her assertion that fiction is separate from (although influenced by) history, and from her focus on women. Stories with female protagonists were singled out for criticism, then the author herself was identified with these characters and charged with sexual obsession and manipulation. Today Ding Ling is once more extolled by Chinese officials as a model writer. On the verge of her eightieth birthday, she is busy writing a 500,000-word sequel to The Sun Shines on the Sanggan River.

The weaknesses in Feuerwerker's study are largely endemic to the impossible task of distilling Ding Ling's life as well as translating and paraphrasing her work. At times the material is too compressed. Some statements lack thorough support, perhaps because a longer explanation would disturb Feuerwerker's complex weave. While she presents intriguing details about Ding Ling's early life, we have no clear idea of her relationships after the 1930s. Finally, she pays minimal attention to Ding Ling's renowned feminism. I was distracted, but therefore not surprised, by her reliance on men critics and the use of the generic male pronoun (the writer, he!).

The qualities of this book far outdistance the problems. This is a compassionate, exciting study, an excellent introduction to Ding Ling's work and a highly provocative discussion of ideology and narrative for writers from any culture. The competitive edge one often feels from critics toward their subjects is happily absent here. She admires Ding Ling without idolizing her. And Feuerwerker's articulation of Chinese aesthetics within the context of Western sensibilities turns the book into a stimulating framework for the study of other Chinese authors.

Seven years younger than Ding Ling, Xiao Hong was born in 1911 and died in 1942. Her life covered vast territory. Born in China's Northeast corner, Heilongiang province, she led a lonely, distressed childhood. She went to high school in

Harbin, ran away from her landlord family, and settled with the writer Xiao Jun. They escaped the Japanese takeover of Manchuria in 1933. Later, she moved to the Interior with another writer, Duanmu Hongliang. In 1940, they fled to Hong Kong, where she died in 1942, a month after the city was captured by the Japanese.

Despite the brevity of her life, Xiao completed four novels. For six of her nine writing years, she wrote shorter fiction. The pieces in this newly published *Selected Stories of Xaio Hong* describe women confronting and often being defeated by feudal traditions. Xiao considers such themes as the belligerence of male power and the brittleness of pride which sustains and destroys by turns. Six of the nine stories have female protagonists.

"The Bridge" is about a wet-nurse, Huang Liangzi, who is caught between tending to the master's son and caring for her own boy. The bridge which spans the deep ditch between their neighborhoods at times symbolizes reunification, at other times confirms distance between the classes and cultures. The bridge is her daily route of desertion as she leaves her own family to nurse the master's child. When the boys grow older, they play together and Huang imagines the bridge disappearing. But the children begin fighting and she punishes her own son sternly, refusing to let him cross the bridge again. The story ends with the boy's death, in the deep ditch. "Peace came to the head of the bridge on the day of the last rainfall of the year. From that time on Little Liangzi was no more."

Some of Xiao Hong's concerns—the tortuous choice between work and love; the conflict between individual success and family unity; the impossibility of cross-class movement; the survival of the richest—foreshadow the revolution.

Rigid strictures controlling sex and class are also reflected in "Hands." A young dyer, Wang Yaming, enters school in hopes of learning enough to take back and teach her younger siblings. But her hands—stained blue-black from years of dying clothes—set her apart. The prejudices of teachers and students exacerbate her slowness at lessons and her awkwardness at social events. Eventually she is forced to leave the school and abandon hopes of a different life.

Reading these sad stories after following Ding Ling's exhilarating survival is like being left in a storm, the blind of night suddenly pulled down without any hope of morning. How would Xiao Hong have written at age sixty or seventy or eighty? What changes would have been wrought by historical events? Her early death at thirty strands readers in a heavily troubled stillness.

(*Selected Stories* was translated into clear and lively English by Howard Gold-blatt, who also translated her novels, *Tales of Hulan River* and, with Ellen Yeung, *The Field of Life and Death,* published by Indiana University Press in 1979. He has written an extensive study of her work, *Hsiao Hung* [Xiao Hong], published by Twayne in 1976.)

Born of the Same Roots, a collection of stories about Chinese women living in different parts of the world, is more exciting in promise than content. While the subtitle is "Stories of Modern Chinese Women," only six of the eighteen contributors are female.

The six authors—Xiao Hong, Pin Hsin, Ling Shu-Hua, Ts'ao Ming, Yu Li-hua, and Chen Jo-hsi—write with originality, heart, and grace. Pin Hsin's "West Wind" describes a professional woman who, meeting her former lover on a journey, becomes haunted about whether she was right to choose her career over romantic love. Ling Shu-hua's story, "Little Liu," recalls the poignancy of Xiao Hong's "Hands" as the young women in a school shun and taunt one of their classmates. Yu Li-Hua's piece is the most Western in subject and style. "Nightfall" describes a daughter torn between feuding parents. She sympathizes with her mother, who has been humiliated by her husband's sexcapades, but also with her father, who has been shut out by his wife's coldness.

The translations are natural and idiomatic. The few women's stories included here are themselves excellent pieces of fiction. Yet I finished this collection feeling that it was published not from authentic enthusiasm for the lives of Chinese women, but rather from a commercial enthusiasm for the growing market in women's books. Such false advertising is regrettable when we need more women's voices translated. (A good alternative is the collection *Seven Contemporary Chinese Women Writers,* recently published by Panda Books.)

The underrepresentation of women in this anthology indicates, at best, an indifference to the astonishing trials and accomplishments of female writers in modern China. Chinese women face problems getting published, making their work visible, and earning the respect and wages accorded to male colleagues. Of the 2,000 members in the national Chinese Writers Association, only 140 are women. Therefore, one might argue that Hsu's ratio of one-third is not so bad—if it were not for several factors.

First, she calls this book a book of "stories of Modern Chinese women," not a book of "stories by Modern Chinese Writers" or of "stories by Chinese men about Chinese women." Common sense as well as feminist scholarship would alert her to the value of adding more women's voices to the tales of women's lives.

Second, she had an enormous pool of women's stories from which to choose. Her explanation, "The selection is based not primarily on the sex of the authors, but on the quality and representative nature of the works," dismisses many fine writers, including Ding Ling. If 140 women have squeezed into the national Chinese Writers Association, we can safely surmise there are more women in the less prestigious branch levels of the CWA and even more who have not yet been considered for membership.

Third, it's curious that Hsu selects expatriate women to represent the newest voices in her collection of "the experience of women in twentieth-century China." While it's valuable to include the rich stories of "overseas Chinese," Hsu's lopsided representation leaves the impression that the future of Chinese women is outside China. Three of the six women contributors live in the West. In her introduction to Chen Jo-hsi, Hsu writes, "Like most of her contemporaries, Chen Jo-hsi came to study in the United States after graduation. She attended Mount Holyoke College and Johns Hopkins University...." To say the least, Chen Jo-hsi's mobility is decidedly *unlike* that of most contemporary Chinese women.

The literature from China today can be daunting, thrilling, paradoxical. Despite a rhetoric of equality, ancient attitudes linger; the traditions that bound women's feet still constrict their imaginations and inhibit their political movement. In this turbulent context the very writing of good fiction is an act of courage.

What Feuerwerker says of Ding Ling might be applied to many Chinese writers. They "intensify our awareness of the contradictions, ambiguities and precariousness of literature as it tries to survive in a radically changing world." At a time when American fiction faces a crisis of imagination and depth, I look abroad for motivation to continue writing. Modern Chinese storytellers are impressive in their willingness to risk a moral vision; their cross-class scope; their commitment to involving the reader in the process of the text, as well as their literary quality. Such writing gives me momentum to carry on my own work in relatively privileged circumstances, and faith in the value of making art during troubled times.

At Paradise Gate by Jane Smiley and *Time Together* by Marian Seldes

At Paradise Gate and *Time Together* are novels about families and death and the deathlessness of families. Their authors consider the afterlife of survivors who, in their grief, encounter both sides of mortality—their relatives' deaths and their own continuing lives. Both writers indicate that death is more than the loss of a life; it is an exposure of human fallibility and an acknowledgment of inextricable kinship.

Jane Smiley watches the women in a middle-class Iowa family while Marian Seldes describes the daughters in a wealthy Manhattan home. Both suggest the mutability of family and remind us of its powerful hold. We witness genetic mirrors, primal imprints, and failed strokes of communication.

As *At Paradise Gate* opens, Ike Robison's three grown daughters sit downstairs waiting for him to die. Helen, Claire, and Susanna claim they came to help their mother, Anna, and to cheer Daddy to recuperation. But their nervous intensity, like the heavy stillness before an earthquake, is an unmistakable omen. The daughters sit steadfast, in a predeterministic, Protestant sort of wake. Their somberness is interrupted by Ike's granddaughter Christine. Bright, flush-faced Christine presents the family with a further problem—her pregnancy and forthcoming divorce. Jane Smiley strikes delicately all the chords between the women's stolid endurance of Ike's illness and their frenzied attempts to preserve Christine's young family.

So Helen, Claire, and Susanna wait in the familiar living room, which is cushioned with unstruck blows, insulated with unsaid words, electrified with decades of family tension. They are decent daughters, available for all the chores, emergencies, and rituals of life and death. Reading *At Paradise Gate* is like being confined to an endless Sunday afternoon, anchored at home by too much dinner and too many memories. The women recall their old rivalries, which are not so old after all. They discuss their shared traits and acknowledge that even their differences are the result of their reactions to one other.

Anna, their mother, is the most vital character. Unburdened by sentiment, she is angry that her husband is abandoning her and that her daughters remain so

This review was first published under the title "Domestic Novels" in the *New York Times Book Review*, 22 November 1981. Copyright © 1981 by The New York Times Company. Reprinted by permission.

dependent; although they are in their forties and fifties, they are still raiding her fridge. Her marriage has been hard—uprooting, violent, cold—but she has grown used to Ike. Who will share the spring lettuce? Anna's tart honesty and acute consciousness hold the book together when the story line dwindles.

> Stepping into and out of the bathtub had become disagreeably suspenseful, in spite of the white rubber daisies stuck to the bathtub for traction. Nothing worked right. Her legs were heavy as she raised them one by one, her knees ached slightly, as if bones abraded each other. One-legged, she always felt precarious and stuck. Fear of falling combined with fear of being unable to move.

At Paradise Gate is not so much about Ike's death as about Anna's life—a retrospective on her difficult past and a resolution of her remaining years. Death's imminence changes the dimensions of time. For Anna, one closely observed day has the complexity of ten remembered years. As she confronts her finiteness, she achieves a quiet certainty about her right to what's left of her world.

In *Time Together* Marian Seldes considers a mother's death from the perspectives of her two estranged daughters. Nana, the dour Riverside Drive chatelaine, controls Leonora and Martha with a brutal imperiousness, and she watches them run away from her materialism as soon as they can. Nana is more shadow than parent. Both Leonora and Martha have long awaited Nana's death, expecting to be set free to distinguish between family obsessions and their own individual passions. However, when Nana finally does depart (characteristically unperturbed, sitting in her chair listening to a radio serial), they face mortality rather than freedom. In losing their mother, they have also lost the possibility for reconciliation.

As young women, Leonora and Martha escape their posh purgatory and court Nana's disapproval. Leonora marries a Jew and has a baby, Nell, who is slow-witted. Despite, and because of, Leonora's desperate attempts to milk love from her husband, she winds up alone. She lives in awe of her adventurous sister, a successful decorator with a married lover in London. Martha works hard to find and create beauty for other people's homes, but ultimately she knows neither her rooms nor her lover belongs to her.

Both daughters fail to transcend the legacy of Nana's loneliness, although they have tried valiantly. In describing their different conflicts with love and work, the author carefully represents the dilemmas of many women who came to maturity during the Second World War. At the end, it is to the granddaughter, young Nell, that they look for hope.

Unfortunately, this slow child with the perfectly sweet temperament is not portrayed as genuinely as the other characters. She seems maudlin at times, precious at others. And the author glosses over Nell's marriage to her "stepfather," thereby dismissing the implications of incest, in an otherwise bravely realistic novel.

Marian Seldes's prose moves from graceful metaphor to the natural awkwardness of authentic dialogue. Her characters, rather than her plot, compel us. We are touched by the determination of Leonora and Martha to be different from their mother and by their love for each other and, finally, for themselves.

Jane Smiley and Marian Seldes both view the next generation with an almost evolutionary optimism. Is it hubris or instinct that draws us forward? Despite the dead, despite the treacherous disappointments of the living, families survive. Perhaps because they provide a continuity for compassion, a place for one more fragile attempt at love.

The Stories of Muriel Spark

Reading all of an author's stories is rather like sitting in her parlor amid mementos from different periods of her life. Muriel Spark's parlor is an eccentric clutter of ghosts, dragons, unsettled expatriates, mad pilgrims, and flying saucers of the finest china.

Critics often study a novel for autobiographical traces, but a complete collection such as *The Stories of Muriel Spark* makes a truer mirror of artistic development. Here is work spanning years, reflecting political, geographical, and aesthetic influences.

Muriel Spark's stories reveal that unique blend of reserved Scottish rationality and passionate Catholic irrationality which inspired seventeen novels, including *The Prime of Miss Jean Brodie* and *The Mandelbaum Gate*. Born in Edinburgh in 1918, Spark converted to Catholicism in 1954 after editing the letters of Cardinal Newman. In these two contradictory cultures, she finds common ground: a preoccupation with conscience and an obsession with human error. Thus Spark emerges as a highly judgmental satirist with a flair for supernatural resolutions.

Her Scottishness is felt in a general succinctness; a wry humor as well as in Celtic names of characters like Jennie, Johnnie Geddes, and Selwyn Macgregor. My favorite Scottish story is "The Executor," set in the Pentland Hills. Susan Kyle becomes literary executor for her famous uncle's estate. Susan sells the entire archive, save for one unfinished novel about an Edinburgh witch about to be executed. (Puns resound throughout Spark's fiction.) Cannily, Susan decides to finish writing the novel herself. However, Uncle's tenacious ghost intervenes, threatening the executor. "I stood in the hall by the telephone, shaking. 'Oh God, everlasting and almighty,' I prayed, 'make me strong, and guide and lead me as to how Mrs. Thatcher would conduct herself in circumstances of this nature.'"

A number of these stories are set in Southern Africa, where Spark worked, married, and had a son between 1936 and 1944. Stories like "The Curtain Blown by the Breeze," "Bang-bang You're Dead," and "The Portobello Road" use Africa as a primitive metaphorical backdrop against which expatriates work out their "civilized" issues of ambition and success. The protagonists are generally unsympathetic whites lost in their privileged narcissism.

This review was first published under the title "Muriel Spark: A Writer's Parlor of the Mind" in the *San Jose Mercury News*, 29 September 1985.

A striking exception is "The Go Away Bird," a brilliant fifty-page narrative about Daphne, orphaned at an early age, who grows up on her uncle's farm in "The Colony." Never comfortable as a colonial, Daphne yearns for the England she hasn't seen. When she finally struggles her way "home," the experience is a disaster. She returns to Africa, thoroughly dissociated, and dies the victim of a private war between her English uncle and his Dutch tobacco manager. "The Go Away Bird" is the name of an African bird as well as a symbol of Daphne's fortune.

Spark also journeys extraterrestrially with her apparitions, witches, and moon men. Like an architect who promises a simple house and leaves us standing in a surrealist sculpture, Spark often turns conventional stories upside down. She begins "The Dragon" straightforwardly, describing a couturier who is so popular that she needs a dragon of a secretary to keep her clients at bay. "Now one day I observed that she was breathing fire." After that, the couturier runs away with the secretary's boyfriend. "The Dragon ran up the road after us a little way, snorting and breathing green fire from her mouth—perhaps it was copper sulphate or copper chloride basis; I have heard that you can get a green flame from skillfully blowing green Chartreuse on to a lighted candle."

Other tales are set in the England to which Spark returned during World War II. Here she came into her own as an artist, and several pieces are about writers in London. The most successful of these, "Another Pair of Hands," combines her fascination with critics and her affinity with ghosts.

Yet other stories ironically describe British expatriates in Europe, where Spark has lived for many years now.

Savored slowly over a long period, there is much to enjoy in *The Stories of Muriel Spark*. Her observations are acute and irreverent, as in "The Fortune Teller": "Moreover he was dressed in beige, and I might say that every visitor to Baden Baden wears beige, both men and women." Her details are seductively indulgent, as in "The Dragon": "I had that deep blue silk-velvet, not quite midnight blue, but something like midnight with a glisten of royal blue which I would line with identical colored silk, for an evening occasion, with the quarter-centimeter wide lace hand-sewn on all the seams."

These stories are playful and compelling, urbane and fey. And for most of us, they are the only chance we'll ever have to visit Muriel Spark's parlor.

Dessa Rose by Sherley Anne Williams

Dessa Rose is a striking story about a woman escaping slavery in Alabama in the 1840s. Sherley Anne Williams, already a highly praised poet, playwright, and critic, has written a powerful, elegant novel, rooted in a profound appreciation of Black community.

Dessa Rose watches as one layer of her life after another is stripped away: Her brother is sold, her lover is murdered, she beaten and branded. Although young and pregnant, she is chained together with other slaves and herded to auction. One night, during a slave revolt in which a white man is killed, Dessa runs. The "Devil Woman" is caught and told she will be executed after she delivers her baby, the master's rightful property.

Williams eloquently conveys the rage, loneliness, and strength of Dessa as she awaits her child's birth and her own death. She maintains her dignity even during humiliating interviews with the priggish Adam Nehemiah, who is compiling an advice book for slaveholders. Ultimately, with the help of other slaves, Dessa escapes to the safe house of Ruth, a white woman, who runs a rickety plantation with the aid of fugitive Blacks.

Dessa and Ruth are based on two historical figures who never met. By introducing them, Williams has created a fiction that is both deeply true and brilliantly imagined. The novel's themes of friendship, loyalty, and knowledge are familiar subjects in Williams's poetry and her superb play, *Letters from a New England Negro*.

Dessa reflects, "You know I'm ashamed to say I didn't know this where cold weather come from, the north. That I'd never seed no real meaning in birds going south till Harker pointed it out to me. This is what I hold against slavery. May come a time when I *forgive*—cause I don't think I'm set up to *forget*—the beatings, the selling, the killings, but I don't think I ever forgive the ignorance they kept us in."

Williams deftly turns the tables on lies of the antebellum South. She tells how Nathan, a Black man, was forced into sex by his white mistress. And in one of her best dramatic scenes, Williams shows the fair Ruth suckling Dessa's beautiful Black baby.

This review originally appeared under the title "A Deeply Felt Story of an Escaped Slave" in *Newsday*, 9 September 1986.

Although the novel is written from various alternating points of view, the most absorbing voice is that of Dessa. Her language is graceful and intricate. She is wonderfully evocative in the sensual descriptions of having her hair braided, holding her baby, making love.

> "Dess?" Voice quiet as the night, "Dessa, you know I know how they whipped you." His head was right by my leg and he turned and lifted my dress, kissed my thigh. Where his lips touched was like fire on fire and I trembled. "It ain't impaired you none at all," he said and kissed my leg again. "It only increase your value." His face was wet; he buried his head in my lap.

Dessa and Ruth develop a grudging, then affectionate friendship. They both fall in love with Black men. Together with the men, they embark on an audacious moneymaking scheme. Ruth (with Dessa acting as her maid) takes the fugitives around the countryside, selling them to hapless slaveholders. The slaves escape, meet Ruth and Dessa in the next town, and repeat the process again. Dessa hopes to earn enough money to go West and live "free." Their adventure, by turns harrowing and hilarious, is told with great suspense.

There's a lot going on here, and *Dessa Rose* should be a longer book. The characterization and story line feel compressed by a tendency toward summary rather than action. For instance, Dessa's fondness for Ruth is stated, but not developed. It's not hard to see why Ruth would be attracted to the courageous, bright, charismatic Dessa. But what is there to admire in the naive, star-crossed white woman? Dessa lets Ruth into her heart when Ruth is sexually attacked by a white man because she is touched by their mutual vulnerability. While Dessa professes friendship, what she expresses is sympathy. Perhaps the imbalance of reflection versus action is a natural liability in writing historical fiction, by its nature drawn from hindsight.

It's unusual nowadays to finish a novel wanting more. In today's desert of chicly self-conscious fiction, *Dessa Rose* is nothing short of inspirational. Williams brings us into a vibrant world which, although distant in time, raises urgent contemporary questions about racism, struggle, courage, and the definition of freedom.

Lantern Slides by Edna O'Brien

Edna O'Brien transforms the lives of Irish women into a liturgy of premonition, doom, and enigmatic redemption. The twelve musical, fey stories in her latest collection, *Lantern Slides,* are usually sad. They are meant to be read slowly, as one would savor an elegantly presented dinner accompanied by perhaps one glass of wine too many—then a brandy for the road. *Lantern Slides* is a sensuous recasting of the Last Supper with late-twentieth-century Irish maidens and matrons.

They are girls in training to reproduce and iron and sweep the sacristy and die with the name of Christ on their lips. They are spinsters driven mad by invisibility. They are alcoholic mothers navigating the rocky voyage between self-pity and retribution. Images recur—the sea, nocturnal mist, fine wine, crumpled sheets, altar flowers, mean little parlors. Village life is suffocating and Dublin isn't much better. Indeed, O'Brien, who has lived in London for years, is more consumed by Irish pettiness than many writers who have remained in the country. Is her bitterness the cause of her exile or an unconscious link with home?

In two of the most poignant of these stories, middle-aged women retreat to the beach and find themselves haunted by past and present demands. Nelly, in "Another Time," repairs to a small seaside hotel to be alone, only to encounter unwelcome attention from the lascivious guest in the next room, the bumbling proprietors, a stranger who recognizes her from her long-ago career in TV, and an awkward girlhood acquaintance. Each exchange is provocative and painful in its incompleteness. Like many O'Brien women, Nelly faces the dilemma of balancing between what she wants to forget and what she needs to remember.

"The Storm" shows Eileen, her son, Mark, and his self-absorbed girlfriend, Penny, enduring a similarly problematic holiday. O'Brien is spot-on as she describes Eileen's irritable jealousy of the insensitive young woman: "She is irked that a girl of twenty can be so self-assured, irked at the languid painstaking way Penny applies her suntan oil." Eventually Eileen's suppressed resentments erupt in voluble fury, stunning all three of them. The next day, the couple head out on their own, a vicious storm ensues, and Eileen is sure they have been killed while sailing. She faces her vanity, her fears, and her regrets, and when the couple return unharmed she has decided that she prefers life to truth.

This review originally appeared in the *Philadelphia Inquirer,* 3 June 1990.

The earnest, innocent lasses in "A Demon," "Dramas," and "A Little Holiday" are among O'Brien's strongest characters. "Dramas" unfolds a rich friendship between a village schoolgirl and the eccentric new shopkeeper, Barry, who becomes popular with the local women because of his fine goods and fancy conversation. He talks about directing an amateur theatrical and intrigues his customers by imagining them as Cordelia or Rosalind. But in the end, he provides this audience with drama of a different sort—a drunken romp with two city men in which his sexuality and his campiness are fully exposed to unsympathetic villagers and unamused police. The young narrator, a devoted acolyte, recalls her dismay as "from the corner of my eye I saw him get into the big black van and saw it drive away with all the solemnity of a hearse."

The title story is a tour de force, recognizing and reconciling the cloistered lives of middle-class Dubliners as they gather at a swank birthday party for Betty, a plucky "woman of a certain age." In the big hall as the party begins to liven up, the fireplace mirrors the atmosphere—"a bit lugubrious, like a grotto, but this impression was forgotten as the flames spread and swagged into brazen orange banners." Betty's guests range from the romantic Mr. Conroy and his nostalgic friend Miss Lawless to the sybaritic Dr. Fitz and the warring Mr. and Mrs. Vaughan. As in other O'Brien tales, the central character becomes peripheral, and peripheral characters take center stage.

The flirtatious, bawdy conversation in "Lantern Slides" is punctuated by more reflective moments.

> All this time, Eileen Vaughan kept looking around the table wondering if at any moment someone would throw a word to her. None of them liked her, she knew that. Hard, hard was what they thought she was. Yet the day her world fell apart, the day she lost her last ounce of faith in her husband, what had she done. . . . She had prayed with all her heart and soul for a seizure to finish her off, but she just grew thinner and thinner, and tighter and tighter, like a bottle brush.

For all O'Brien's sacramental melancholy, she exudes a worldly passion for the moment. She seduces readers with her direct, piercing gaze and pleases with the rhythms of her storytelling diction. Most of these tales are set in a territory between human brutality and inexplicable salvation. O'Brien takes it all in—the small-mindedness, gossip, superstition, death of the spirit, and destruction of the body. Her characters dance on the edge of the grave, yet, perhaps because despair is for Catholics the only unpardonable sin, O'Brien often tosses them a mysterious line of absolution and hope.

Leader of the Band, The Heart of the Country, and Polaris and Other Stories by Fay Weldon

Fay Weldon sashays onto a page, flaunting her imagination against the structures of society and of fiction. The British novelist engages readers in hard questions about sexual politics, genocide, medical abuse, moral despair, and the disorder of the universe. This can be a heady mixture, particularly for American audiences lulled by the profitable tradewinds of literary solipsism.

Weldon's novels, *Leader of the Band* and *The Heart of the Country,* and her collection, *Polaris and Other Stories,* are strongly social fiction, enriched by historical consciousness, political acuity, and a luminous sense of humor. All three books are preoccupied with the consequences of marital infidelity and the ravages of gynecological trespassing. Weldon tends to moralize a bit, but she does so with zippy alarm rather than sober admonition. She confronts the deepest desperation and exits deftly on the side of optimism.

At first I don't like Starlady Sandra Harris Sorenson, the glib protagonist and narrator of *Leader of the Band.* Sandra, accomplished astronomer and discoverer of the planet Athena, has her own late night television show. Beautiful, brilliant, successful—what is there to like in this fast-talking, needy, middle-aged woman? Then Weldon traces a crack in her polychrome armor. And another. Soon Sandra has my complete sympathies as she gives up her astronomy and her conventional lawyer husband to travel across France making love to Jack, leader of a ragtag musical group called the Citronella Jumpers.

> The van was the best the Band could afford. For the Band was no wealthier than the sum of its members. How could it be? Its sound was New Orleans Revival with a touch of folk: it was out of fashion and therefore out of pocket: it was glad enough often enough to play and sing for its supper and no more. (P. 4)

The review of *The Heart of the Country* originally appeared under the title "Living through Politics" in the *Women's Review of Books,* July 1989; the reviews of *Leader of the Band* and *Polaris and Other Stories* originally appeared in the *Nation,* July 1989.

Sandra's adventure at the French folk festival and in her lusty affair with Mad Jack, the forty-four-year-old trumpet player, is a picaresque metaphor for her deeper movement of self-discovery about a past as authentic as it is incredible. Her father was a Nazi officer who raped her teenage gypsy mother in the interests of genetic experimentation.

> Obviously the younger the women who bore the babies the better: and the fairer the donor, and the darker the receptor, the easier to trace various traits through the generations. So very dark girl children—especially the gypsies, who tended to be pretty—were fed estrogen from fresh placentas removed from mothers at various stages of fetal development and brought to maturity early. Then impregnated—the techniques of fancy fertilization not yet having been developed—in the natural way, by the blondest and best. . . . Girls as young as nine had babies: it was also interesting to find out what effect the immaturity of the mother had on the fetus, so many were removed for study. My mother was really lucky, and was all of fifteen when I was born, at the very end of the war." (P. 109)

Leader of the Band jumps back and forth between the folk frolic and Sandra's excruciating autobiography. The Citronella Jumpers and their groupies camp in a flea-ridden Hotel de Ville, drinking late into the night. The band plays on. Sometimes on key. People are having a jolly if slightly uncomfortable time. Jack may be "long, blond and thin, with bright darting brown eyes" (p. 10), but it grows clearer he is a present tense diversion allowing Sandra to settle accounts with family ghosts.

She reflects on her mother's ultimate madness, her father's brutality, and her grandmother's prissy, steadying love. Perhaps because of her father's fascination with genetic blending, Sandra is obsessed with reproductive detail, describing her menstruation, abortions, cervical exams, and determination not to pass on her genes.

> I am a guilty person: I have to punish myself. My mother is mad; my brother is dead because my suppressed rage killed him: my father was shot because my birth was used as evidence against him. My anger is all powerful; could blot out the world. So it is never expressed. I am cool, rational, and for ever guilty. (P. 65)

But enough of the hard stuff. Back to time present. Too soon the Folklorique reverie is disrupted by the arrival of Jack's wife and Sandra's husband and TV producer from London. Que faire? Have another glass of plonk while we're sorting it out. Ghosts are troublesome enough; when live relatives materialize, Sandra finds it hard to cope. The narrative ends with a surprise which at first appears too neat and then is transmuted into a courageous act of faith.

Cosmologist or novelist, Sandra is always determined to locate the borders between fate and human culpability and to discover some order in the universe.

> I daresay it is absurd to seek so patiently and earnestly after truth, when self-delusion is so much more comfortable. Truth in any case is no constant thing; it changes from day to day. Even the two and two we used to trust to make four can no longer be relied upon to do so. By *assuming* two and two make four we can get to the moon and pay for the Band; for all practical purposes two and two still make four; but the fact is that they merely approximate four. The fact of adding destabilises the wretched numbers. Try to make two approach four by ever-increasing fractions and you'll never, ever get there. (P. 94)

In *Leader of the Band,* form and style and character are idiosyncratic. The breathless main narrative is followed by three stories, written by Sandra about her women friends. Starlady Sandra is at once eccentric and archetypal—an individual caught in the sway of domestic and international politics, attending to the good and evil "bred" into her bones. Sandra is not a neutral character. You love or hate her. I did both, not a bad literary experience given that reading contemporary fiction has become an increasingly detached spectator sport.

While there is much to admire in Weldon's depth, humor, inventiveness, and intelligence, *Leader of the Band* is just a bit too rushed. Although description is neither the strength nor the point of her agitprop theater, it wouldn't hurt to pause now and then to taste and smell the world around Sandra. Another draft might have erased problems of overstatement and repetitiveness.

In the end, I am overwhelmed by the profound generosity of spirit in Sandra and Weldon. After confronting mass murder, madness, child neglect, sexual attack, both novelist and novelist's novelist throw up their hands, declaring you might as well live. There isn't much Dorothy Parker irony here; for Weldon making choices is the essence of living and a firm belief in life is the source of writing.

The Heart of the Country is set in rural West Somerset, as much a metaphor for Thatcherite England as it is an actual place.

Fay Weldon's high irony leaves readers reeling. Just when we think nothing more can happen, just when we're gaining breath between gasps and laughs, something worse does occur. *The Heart of the Country* is a picaresque novel in which the protagonists, being village mums, don't go anywhere, but have more than their share of adventures, thank you very much.

The story opens on an average day in a middle-class home as Natalie Harris is preparing a dinner party for her husband and two other local couples. Until now, Natalie's biggest challenge has been how to keep the chicken entrée from drying out. During the day, she discovers another snag in the forthcoming soirée:

> Harry Harris ran off leaving his wife living in a dream bungalow mortgaged up to the hilt and beyond, no money in the bank and school fees owing. He left her with no job, unqualified and untrained, and with no experience other than as a businessman's wife and mother of two extremely self-centered children, aged eleven and twelve. (P. 7)

At first Natalie takes this in her stride, which is to say she denies what is happening. She manages to make it through the dinner party, pretending Harry has been delayed at work. But the next day dawns with a series of impossible realities. She has to remove the kids from private school, get rid of her housekeeper, put the bungalow on the market, surrender the car, and sell her soul to the Department of Health and Social Security. Shortly she moves her family into the crowded flat of her formerly despised neighbor, the ragged welfare mother Sonia.

Who is the protagonist—Natalie, treacherously sliding down the socioeconomic scale, or Sonia, already stuck at the bottom? (Sonia, the narrator, is relating this story from a mental hospital where she is serving time for arson and murder—but we are ahead of ourselves here.) Sonia, an insistent, sometimes intrusive, and always engaging raconteur, unveils her own life as she describes Natalie's. Another middle-class woman dumped into poverty by her husband, she proves more savvy than Natalie. She is a member of the Claimants' Union and is managing to raise her three daughters by herself. After taking in Natalie's family, she shows her how to negotiate with the DHSS and helps her back on her feet. In the process she falls in love with her, but manages to keep her feelings properly discreet so that they do damage only to herself.

Sonia and Natalie are a study in sympathetic contrasts. As clueless as Natalie is at the outcome, she is a survivor who winds up being taken care of by yet another man. Sonia, with her clear, radical analysis, is judged mad by society. In the end, she too survives, but forgoes the safety of heterosexual coupling to continue shaking up the world and risking a return to the padded clinker. Weldon presents both these options as reasonable and unreasonable and most of all as authentic.

Weldon's broad humor is seamed into the character's allusive names—beginning with Harry Harris, owner of the Harrix firm, who runs off with his secretary,

Marian Hopfoot. Natalie has an affair with Arthur, the antique dealer, who is married to Jane. After Arthur, she turns to Angus, the realtor, whose wife is named Jean. The men with the interchangeable spouses also have interchangeable positions in Tory consumerism—one sells houses while the other sells the things that go into the houses. We also meet the failed yuppie couple, Sal and Val, and the romantic bohemian Flora, who blossoms in her life at the town dump with her ever-faithful boyfriend, Bernard, woman's best friend.

One fine Weldonian stroke is the integration of statistics to support sardonic moments. Near the beginning of her story, Sonia alludes to a scene—which we later experience more fully as the climax of the book—where the local women ride on a commercial parade float.

> Who else but men would dress their wives and mistresses, those they torment, abuse and exploit, in the clothes of the fifties, hand them feather dusters, oblige them to smile and parade the streets of Somerset on a ninety-foot float consisting of pretty little estate houses with lace curtains? In a world where something like 40 percent of women are out at work (and 45 percent of men), 25 percent of mothers are on social security, 40 percent (and rising) are over 60 years of age, how can men still cling to the consoling myth of the loving female in the dream house? Husband out to work, two children at school, mother at home looking after them—that's the rarity these days, not the norm, just 23 percent of the total of households. (P. 53)

Weldon applies her seasoned skepticism even-handedly. None of her characters is politically correct or morally righteous. She is not saying that only males "cheat" on their partners, rather that because heterosexual men control the surroundings in which we all have sex, sleep, and eat, they usually wind up on safe ground. The narrative tensions build inexorably on a series of internal metaphors. Flagrant adultery within the sanctified homes of West Somerset is paralleled by mindless adulteration of the earth by entrepreneurs like Angus and Arthur, whose investment in British agriculture requires injecting carcinogenic additives into the soil.

The climax in this heartless country is a brilliant montage representing Thatcherite free enterprise. Angus and Arthur have commissioned a carnival float to parade their civic contributions. However, they leave construction of the mobile monument to local women, who create grotesque caricatures of the greedy businessmen. As the float passes through the village advertising Tory avarice, the crowds fall apart laughing at the effigies of Angus and Arthur. Then, in a stroke of Monty Python-esque headiness which Sonia hopes will be the crowning moment, she sets the float afire. Everyone escapes except Flora, who dies in the blaze. Weldon could have rescued Flora, but that would have resulted in a morality play in which the innocent are saved and the culpable damned, and she is less interested in didactic resolution than in Brechtian provocation.

Weldon's dialogue and sense of theatrical moment are impressive (she has written six stage dramas as well as thirteen previous books of fiction). What stays with me most, however, is the complex development of Sonia's character. As we proceed deeper into *The Heart of the Country,* Sonia gets saner and readers grow wiser. Sonia obviously enjoys telling her story, although parts of it are almost unbearably painful. She is sharp, economical, wry, and conscious of the place of feminist instincts in fiction and in real life.

> Not for Sonia, Flora's triumphant puff of smoke, her exaltation; not for Sonia, Natalie's glorious debasement; no, for Sonia comes a proposal of marriage from a good man, who knows her every failing. She can't accept, of course. Happy endings are not so easy. No. She must get on with changing the world, rescuing the country. There is no time left for frivolity. (P. 201)

Polaris and Other Stories amplifies feminist themes from *Leader of the Band* and *The Heart of The Country,* particularly in issues of family politics, female friendship, and gynecological assault. These twelve stories range from parable to bittersweet interlude to farce.

The title story, originally published in 1978, traces the first months of marriage for Meg and Timmy. When Timmy is called to his clandestine duties aboard the Polaris nuclear submarine, he abandons Meg in a small house on the harsh West Scotland coast to the company of a troublesome dog, unfriendly farmers, and an overfriendly Navy colleague. Although "Polaris" is in many senses the drama of Meg's solitude, it is even more interestingly an exploration of male bonding in the secret culture of Polaris. I am left with the image of Polaris as a lonely spermatozoon frantically seeking warmth in Arctic waters. Weldon often reveals stunning fluency with foreign worlds; this time her intimacy with military detail raises intriguing questions about the permeability of British naval security.

"And Then Turn Out the Light" is a tightly drawn parable about medical sexual harassment, following Tandy's life from the day her hymen was broken by her pediatrician through the abuse from her college doctor and her abortionist, to her unnecessary hysterectomy at the age of forty-seven. After many years of trying to become a doctor, herself, she gives up. "She became a grandmother and was glad it was a boy. 'They have a better life than girls,' she said, admiring the contained and tidy infant penis" (p. 117).

In startling contrast, "The Bottom Line and the Sharp End" is a tender reminiscense about a thirty-year relationship between a hard-working, straightlaced hairdresser and her mercurial, often down-at-the-heels client, a singer named Avril. "Helen thought the time for miracles was almost past. Both Avril's pennies and Avril's hair were getting thin. But she merely said, 'I'll do my best,' and ran her practised fingers through Avril's wiry curls without flinching" (p. 118). Despite and because of her fragile follicles, Avril insists on a thorough bleaching, which causes her hair to fall out. Avril emerges not only philosophical, but victorious as a bald nightclub performer in Mayfair.

My favorite story is the last one, "Redundant! or the Wife's Revenge," set in yet another hospital. Alan is having a facelift to improve his career prospects. Esther, his wife of twenty-four years, has just run off with a young man named Freddo. In the subplot, we meet Alan's daughter Hermes, who was having an affair with a woman named Val, and Alan's surgeon, Dr. Khan, who is sleeping with his nurse, Pony, and Mrs. Professor Khan, who is going abroad to practice medicine. But the subplots have a way of glancing into one another and ultimately "Redundant!" rivals the best Iris Murdoch bed-swapping as the deck gets shuffled, then tossed in the air to land in the most amazing variety of sweaty hands.

Polaris and Other Stories concludes with a classic Weldon moral, "The more we know, the older we get. The body withers away, in the harsh light of wisdom" (p. 237). It is fitting to leave our seasoned author here—smart, brave, yet wistful in middle age, continuing to write her provocative books with a courage born of wit.

Works Consulted

Amiran, Minda Rae. "What Women's Literature?" *College English* 39, no. 6 (February 1978): 653–61.

Anzaldúa, Gloria. "To Live in the Borderlands Means You." In *Borderlands/La Frontera*. San Francisco: Spinsters/Aunt Lute, 1987.

Bagdikian, Ben H. *The Media Monopoly*. Boston: Beacon Press, 1983.

Chevigny, Bell Gale. "Daughters Writing: Toward a Theory of Women's Biography." *Feminist Studies* 9, no. 1 (Spring 1983): 79–102.

Cliff, Michelle. "The Resonance of Interruption." *Chrysalis* 8 (Summer 1979): 29–37.

Cook, Blanche Wiesen. "Incomplete Lives?" *Women's Review of Books* 3 (1985): 5.

Coser, Lewis A., Charles Kadushin, and Walter W. Power. *Books: The Culture and Commerce of Publishing*. New York: Basic, 1982.

Cott, Nancy. *The Grounding of Modern Feminism*. New Haven: Yale University Press, 1987.

Daly, Mary. *Gyn/Ecology: The Metaethics of Radical Feminism*. Boston: Beacon, 1978.

Donovan, Josephine. "Feminism and Aesthetics." *Critical Inquiry* 3, no. 3 (Spring 1977): 605–8.

Fairbairns, Zoë, Sara Maitland, Valerie Miner, Michelle Roberts, and Michelene Wandor. *More Tales I Tell My Mother: Feminist Short Stories*. London: Journeyman, 1987.

———. *Tales I Tell My Mother: A Collection of Feminist Short Stories*. London: Journeyman, 1978.

Fraser, Kathleen. "On Being a West Coast Woman Poet." *Women's Studies* 5 (1977): 153–60.

Gordimer, Nadine. *The Essential Gesture*. New York: Knopf, 1988.

Gornick, Vivian. "Toward a Definition of the Feminist Sensibility." *Village Voice*, 31 May 1973, pp. 21–25.

Juhasz, Suzanne. "The Critic as Feminist." *Women's Studies* 5 (1977): 113–27.

Kolodny, Annette. "Some Notes on Defining 'Feminist Literary Criticism.'" *Critical Inquiry* 2, no. 1 (Autumn 1975): 75–92.

———. "The Feminist as Literary Critic." *Critical Inquiry* 2, no. 4 (Summer 1976): 821–32.

Kostash, Myrna, Melinda McCracken, Valerie Miner, Erna Paris, and Heather Robertson. Introduction to *Her Own Woman: Profiles of Ten Canadian Women.* Toronto: Macmillan of Canada, 1975.

Le Guin, Ursula K. *Dancing at the Edge of the World.* New York: Grove Press, 1989.

————. Letter. *Women's Review of Books,* September 1988, 4.

Levertov, Denise. "On the Edge of Darkness: What Is Political Poetry?" In *Light Up the Cave,* pp. 115–29. New York: New Directions, 1981.

Lorde, Audre. *Coda,* November/December 1983, 8–9.

Miner, Valerie. *All Good Women.* Freedom, Calif.: Crossing Press, 1987.

————. *Blood Sisters: An Examination of Conscience.* New York: St. Martin's, 1982.

————. *Movement: A Novel in Stories.* Trumansburg, N.Y.: Crossing Press, 1982.

————. *Murder in the English Department.* New York: St. Martin's, 1983.

————. *Trespassing and Other Stories.* Freedom, Calif.: Crossing Press, 1989.

————. *Winter's Edge.* Trumansburg, N.Y.: Crossing Press, 1985.

Miner, Valerie, and Helen E. Longino, eds. *Competition: A Feminist Taboo?* New York: Feminist, 1987.

Minnich, Elizabeth Kamarck. "Friendship between Women: The Act of Feminist Biography." *Feminist Studies* 11, no. 2 (Summer 1985): 287–305.

Olsen, Tillie. *Silences.* New York: Delta/Seymour Lawrence, 1978.

Perron, Wendy. "Susan Sontag on Writing, Art, Feminism, Life and Death." *Soho Arts,* 1 December 1977.

The Personal Narratives Group. "Truths." In *Interpreting Women's Lives.* Bloomington: Indiana University Press, 1990.

Petrement, Simone. *Simone Weil.* New York: Pantheon, 1976.

Pratt, Annis. "The New Feminist Criticism." *College English* 32, no. 8 (May 1971): 872–78.

Rich, Adrienne. *On Lies, Secrets and Silence.* New York: W.W. Norton, 1979.

Robinson, Lillian S. "Dwelling in Decencies: Radical Criticism and the Feminist Perspective." *College English* 32, no. 8 (May 1971): 879–89.

Sappho. *Sappho: A New Translation.* Ed. Mary Barnard. Berkeley: University of California Press, 1958.

Sarton, May. *As We Are Now.* New York: Norton, 1973.

————. *At Seventy.* New York: Norton, 1984.

————. *I Knew a Phoenix.* New York: Norton, 1959.

————. *Journal of a Solitude.* New York: Norton, 1973.

————. *The Magnificent Spinster.* New York: Norton, 1985.

————. *Mrs. Stevens Hears the Mermaids Singing.* New York: Norton, 1965.

Saum, Karen. "The Art of Poetry XXXII, May Sarton." *Paris Review* 25 (1983): 80–117.

Stanton, Elizabeth Cady. Address at the International Council of Women, 1888. In *The History of Woman Suffrage*, 4:133–34. New York: Source Book Press, 1970.

Stein, Gertrude. *The Making of Americans*. In *Selected Writings of Gertrude Stein*, ed. Carl Van Vechten. New York: Vintage, 1972.

University of California Lesbian and Gay Intercampus Network. "Report to the Regents of the University of California," 16 June 1983. Appendix A.

Vicinus, Martha. *Independent Women: Work and Community for Single Women, 1850–1920*. Chicago: University of Chicago Press, 1985.

Woolf, Virginia. *Reviewing*. London: Hogarth Press, 1939.

———. *Three Guineas*. New York: Harcourt Brace, 1938.